ANCIENT LAND,
ANCIENT SKY

ANCIENT LAND, ANCIENT SKY

Following Canada's Native
Canoe Routes

PETER MCFARLANE

WAYNE HAIMILA

Alfred A. Knopf Canada

PUBLISHED BY ALFRED A. KNOPF CANADA

Canadian Cataloguing in Publication Data

McFarlane, Peter, 1954–
Ancient land, ancient sky

ISBN 0-676-97147-4

1. Canada — Description and travel.   2. Indian trails — Canada.
3. Indian reservations — Canada.   4. Air travel — Canada.
5. McFarlane, Peter, 1954–   — Journeys — Canada.
6. Haimila, Wayne, 1949–   — Journeys — Canada.
7. Indians of North America — First contact
with Europeans — Canada.
I. Title.

FC75.M332 1999   917.104'648   C98-932407-9
F1017.M332 1999

Text Design: Gordon Robertson

Printed and bound in the United States of America

1 3 5 7 9 10 8 6 4 2

In memory of Robert Moses Manuel
1947-1998

CONTENTS

ACKNOWLEDGMENTS

We'd like to thank Gena Gorrell for her work in getting the manuscript into shape; Denise Bukowski, for arranging publication; Diane Martin for bringing the manuscript through its final stages; Olive Patricia Dickason for the historical review; Elias Letelier-Ruz for his work on the maps; and Canada Council for their support. We would also like to thank the people who provided interviews and information for the book, or who offered valuable suggestions, including Ralph Abramson, Gerald Taiaiake Alfred, Albert Angus, Donald Chatsis, Russell Diabo, Blaine Favel, Lucy Favel, Mary James, Terry James, John Jefferies, Manny Jules, Vera Kasokeo, Linda Leith, Arthur Manuel, Bob Manuel, Betsy McFarlane, Brenda McGregor, Savanna McGregor, Ovide Mercredi, Roland Pangowish, Bernard St. Onge, Léo St. Onge, Greg Sarazin, Konrad Sioui, Millie Spence, Richard Tootoosis, Harold Two-Heart, Gloria Vollant, Robert Whiteduck, Dana Williams, Terrance Dana Haimila and the grandmothers.

ANCIENT LAND, ANCIENT SKY

CHAPTER ONE

Terra Primum Visa

N EWFOUNDLAND's Great Northern Peninsula began as a thin pencil-line on the horizon. As we flew over the Strait of Belle Isle, which was dotted with ice floes carried south on the Labrador Current, the peninsula slowly broadened into a tundra plain. Beside me in the cockpit, Wayne Haimila studied the charts spread out on his lap, then scanned the bleakness below.

From three thousand feet, the peninsula is a barren land of deeply creviced slabs of grey rock, speckled with shallow brown ponds of trapped rainwater. The neighbouring Mi'kmaq called the island Wee-soc-kadao, or "leftovers." They believed that the Creator had formed it after he had made the rest of North America, by unceremoniously dumping the remaining jagged rocks, runt trees and boglands into the North Atlantic.

Our destination was St. Anthony's airport, on the edge of the barrens, where the flatlands begin to buckle into a steep ridge that buttresses the eastern shore against the sea. It was this shore that, five hundred years earlier, John Cabot had christened *terra primum visa*, the land first seen. The cliffs that marked the end of Cabot's historic ocean crossing would mark the beginning of our journey across the continent.

Wayne pointed south, to the black thread looping around and between the dark pools. It was Highway 430, he said. We could follow it to the airfield. As we approached St. Anthony's, I noticed smoke coming from a dump fire at the edge of the plain. It was slanted on a narrow angle, indicating a strong breeze below. I radioed the flight service station at the airport and the controller told us that the wind was fifteen-gusting-twenty knots and the runway in use was two-niner. We swung low over Hare Bay and lined up for a straight-in approach. The Cessna bounced a couple of times in the gusty wind, then settled dutifully, if not gracefully, onto the tarmac. We had arrived at the beginning.

The idea for our cross-country trip had been planted a year earlier, in a conversation Wayne and I had while we were working on a newspaper article about a native–RCMP standoff in the B.C. interior, where Wayne was living and working for the Neskonlith Indian band. I was in Montreal and he was feeding me information from B.C. One of our late-night calls ventured onto the subject of the upcoming five-hundredth-anniversary celebrations of John Cabot's landfall in the New World. As someone who traced his own ancestry in the Americas back twenty thousand years or more, he said, he always took offence at the idea of the New World — it was as if nothing had been there before. "Cabot thought he was in China," Wayne said. "He was looking for silks. He was just another lost sailor."

A few days later, the fax rang late at night and a curled-up sheet rolled across the floor. I unfolded it and found a hand-drawn map of Canada. There were no cities or provinces marked; instead the land was broken up into territories of various sizes with largely unfamiliar and unpronounceable names: Wabanaki, Nitassinan, Kanienke, Tenakìwin, Danaiiwaad, Ojibweg, Eeyou Astchee, Kanaiskshako, Ktwaxa and Secwepemcul'ecw. . . . Across the top Wayne had written, "The Old Countries."

When I called him back, he said, "This is what Europeans came to," he said. "Ancient civilizations with thousands of years of history."

It was then that the plan for our trip began to take shape. Beginning on the eastern shore of the Great Northern Peninsula, where Cabot and later Jacques Cartier had landed, we would follow the route taken by Europeans in their long procession to the Pacific — a journey that took three centuries to complete. Along the way, we would try to give a sense of those arrivals, of the moment when the first Europeans rounded the bend in the river, walked into the village clearing or struggled through the mountain pass — from the point of view of the people who had been living in these homelands for thousands of years.

Flying the route in my old Cessna had been part of the plan from the beginning. Flight would allow us to visit out-of-the-way communities in the great roadless regions of the country, like the four-hundred-mile stretch along the coast of the Gulf of St. Lawrence; but it would give us more than that. Crossing the country in a small plane restores its integrity — returns its vastness. From a mile up, even most southern Canadian cities and towns are revealed for what they are: clearings in the forest linked by trails through the wilderness.

Wayne and I spent the winter plotting our route. In the spring, he called to say that Brenda, the woman he had been seeing for the past two years, was pregnant. The child was due in early October. I suggested we put off the trip for another year, but he said no, he wanted to go. At forty-six he had been working in the Indian movement almost all his adult life. "Canadians still have no sense of the old countries," he said. "It's a story someone should tell."

Wayne arrived in Montreal in the first week of July for the flight up to the Great Northern Peninsula. The thousand-mile flight, which should have taken us a day and a half, stretched into four days as wave after wave of storm cells, towering thunder heads and driving rain forced us to pick our way up the river and the Gulf coast in short hops. The weather was created by hurricane Bertha, which had hit the Carolinas the day before we left with enough force to cause more than a dozen deaths, then moved up into New

England as a tropical storm, and into the Gulf of St. Lawrence as a string of violent summer storms.

We spent most of this time under leaden skies, drinking coffee in pilots' lounges — or more often pilots' shacks — at small airstrips along the route, waiting for a break in the weather that would allow us to make another short hop up the coast. Such delays are a fact of life when you're flying a small plane. Rain, fog or simply high winds can ground you for hours, even days. In the sea of air, a Cessna 172 is more a canoe than a freighter.

Our longest layover was a full day spent at the Natashquan airport, while the rains pounded the airfield for eleven hours straight. The only other person in the small terminal was a hefty Innu (Montagnais Indian) lineman who was slowly working his way through a book of *mots croisés* (crosswords).

While we were waiting, Wayne spoke about his work at the Neskonlith reserve for Chief Arthur Manuel. I had met both Wayne and Arthur at the same time, in the early 1980s. Both of them were working in Ottawa for national Indian organizations and they had turned up one evening at my flat on Chambord Street in east-end Montreal. They had been brought by a mutual friend, Dana Williams, a Potawatomi artist. Dana was wearing his usual paint-splattered jeans, but Wayne and Arthur, who'd just blown into town after a meeting with the Deputy Minister of Indian Affairs, were wearing suits. "This is Wayne and this is Arthur," Dana said with a hint of pride. "They're Indian lawyers."

At the time, I was working for a CBC Radio native-affairs program, and that first evening we spent several hours talking about Indian politics. After a good deal of banter, fuelled by a bottle of Scotch, the impression I was left with was that they were guys on a mission. Arthur said at one point that their job "was to take back their countries." Wayne smiled and added, "Then maybe we'll set up white reserves."

Over the next several years, we got together every few months. When Wayne and Arthur were in town, they would either stop by

Chambord Street or we would meet at a St. Laurent Street bar. We lost touch for a time in the late 1980s. I was working on a book on Central America and Arthur had headed back to Neskonlith, where he eventually became band chief and then head of the Shuswap Nation Tribal Council. Wayne followed him out west several years later to work for the tribal council and band. My work took me to B.C. on a regular basis, and Wayne and I went on to collaborate on a couple of writing projects, like the story of the Gustafsen Lake standoff we were working on that night when the old-countries map came through my fax.

During the long Natashquan layover, Wayne spoke about his work as band manager. The land-claim research was interesting, he said, but most of the files he was working on were fairly routine. The band was looking into the possibility of developing a gravel deposit on the reserve. There were highway billboard leases that had to be renewed, and there were endless meetings with a funding agency over retiring an irrigation loan. The band was also in the process of hiring more social-development workers and re-training some of the staff. A small housing project had just gotten under way, and they were drawing up a new bylaw to keep the kids from target-practising with their .22s near the village. Shooting was still a touchy subject around Secwepemcul'ecw because it had been mainly Secwepemc men involved in the shootouts at Gustafsen Lake.

I asked him why he stuck with it. He had come out of the 1970s with a law degree; he could have gone into private practice and ended up as a partner in a Vancouver or Ottawa law firm, instead of slaving away long hours for Indian communities for relatively little pay. He hesitated a moment before answering. "Probably," he said, "because of my granny."

Wayne traced his ancestors on his mother's and grandmother's side to Cree living in the Alberta/Saskatchewan border area on the northern plain, and to Red River Métis. His grandmother still spoke Cree, as well as English and some French, and in his mind she was a kind of Mother Courage who, like many native women of her generation, had raised her nine children alone. She had worked on neighbouring farms, tending horses, cows and chickens, while she farmed her own small garden plot and raised bees. Sometime in the dusty 1930s she was forced to retreat. She loaded her children and ailing father onto a horse-drawn wagon and hauled them across the northern plains to seek relief in Edmonton.

When he was growing up, he and his mother lived with his grandmother, but home remained somewhere way out there on the prairie. In his childhood imagination, he dreamed that someday his grandmother would harness the horses to the wagon and take them all back to their prairie homeland.

He never knew his father, who had drowned in the Skeena River, in the territory of his Tsimshian people, when Wayne was a teenager. When he graduated from high school, he knocked around for a few years, travelling to Mexico and working at a food co-op, before going to university in Victoria. With the help of a native scholarship, he attended the University of British Columbia law school. He went to work for Arthur's father, George Manuel, immediately after graduation because, he said, the elder Manuel was offering a ride on another kind of wagon — one driven by political struggle — that had the same destination as his granny's cart: the homeland. At the time, George Manuel was putting together what he called his Indian Peoples' Movement in British Columbia and serving as the president of the World Council of Indigenous Peoples. In 1980, Manuel led a cross-country protest that succeeded in having aboriginal rights included in the Canadian constitution. But the "Old Man," as his followers affectionately called him, had a serious heart attack later that year and ill health forced him to withdraw from the struggle. Wayne then went to Ottawa for several years to work for the Assembly of First Nations. Now he was back in B.C., working with Arthur, and their mission was the same one they had described at my Montreal flat in the early 1980s: to get their countries back.

I asked Wayne what Brenda, now well into the second half of her pregnancy, thought about his leaving for the summer. Brenda was also an exile of sorts. She was an Algonquin from Maniwaki, in northern Quebec, now working in Kelowna for the Westbank Okanagan band. Over the summer he would call her almost every night. At times I couldn't help overhearing some of the conversation, and it was evident, from the tenderness in his voice, that he regretted leaving her alone. "She's going to keep working until the beginning of September," he replied, "and she told me she was looking forward to spending time with Savanna," her eleven-year-old daughter.

The Cessna was parked on the ramp, as the tarmac around a terminal is called, just outside the window. With its high wings and splayed fixed landing gear, it always looked awkward. Alone in the pounding rain, it appeared almost forlorn. Wayne noted the call sign printed on the side: C-GUDD. "Charlie Gudd," he said, using the radio phonetic for C. "It looks like a Gudd."

There was no longer any chance of getting in the air that day, so we called a taxi to take us into the village. The Innu lineman nodded as we left. "*À demain*," he said. We'd heard that it wasn't unusual for small planes to be stuck in Natashquan for days on end.

But the storm broke during the night. In the morning the sky was dark blue with only a few feathery scud clouds, and we were in the air before the sun cleared the horizon. As we flew east, Wayne told me that when he'd been getting ready to leave the band office, Arthur Manuel, now the Neskonlith Band Chief, had stopped by and asked him, jokingly, to find out how Cabot had pulled off such a feat — coming out of nowhere to someone else's country, staying less than an hour on shore and walking away with legal title to the island and the whole continent in his pocket.

CHAPTER TWO

Arrivals and Departures

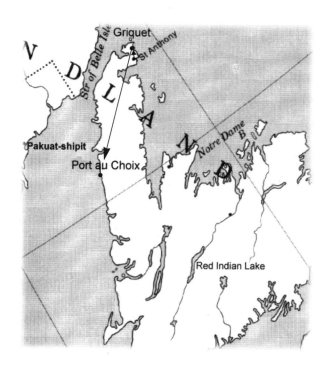

O N OUR TRAVELS across the country we would be meeting with descendants of the original citizens of the old countries we visited. Except in Newfoundland. In Weesoc-kadao, land of extinctions, all that remain are the bones. But the bones offer their own kind of testimony, pushing back to the surface to tell us about an earlier world and, at times, to demand an accounting.

When we arrived at the tourist cabins near Griquet, we were reminded that Newfoundland was obsessed with another looming extinction. Three years before, the government had closed the commercial cod fishery. A year before, the food fishery had also been shut down. A poster on the side wall of the rental office showed a harbour full of fishing boats, below which were the words: *In Cod We Trusted.*

After supper, we went over our maps and notes. During the previous months we had put together a bulky file on the stops along our route; it included explorers' accounts of first meetings and the locations and descriptions of native towns and villages. We were just a few miles up the road from Griquet Harbour, where, according to naval historian Samuel Morison, Cabot had made his historic landfall five centuries earlier. We would visit the site later, but that first morning we would be driving to a much older site on the west coast of the peninsula, where the ancients had lived and died four thousand years ago.

The two-hour drive from Griquet to Port au Choix took us back across the barren lands we'd overflown the day before. From ground level, the sense of desolation was even more pronounced. We passed over miles and miles of windswept plain broken only by odd clusters of stunted trees beside brackish ponds. When we reached the peninsula's western shore, we headed south through a series of tiny fishing villages, little more than collections of wood-frame houses huddled around twisted piers, with sombre names like Deadman's Cove, Lonesome Cove, Nameless Cove. As we continued south the terrain gradually softened, as did the names. By the time we reached Port au Choix the harshness had given way to rolling green hills.

The archaeological site, with a cairn and small interpretation centre marking the field where skeletons had been discovered, was on the edge of town. Millie Spence, the site curator, met us at the door. The small centre was crowded with glass cases full of prehistoric debris: bits of flint shaped into arrow and harpoon heads, bone scrapers, needles and a few miniature carvings, including a smooth stone replica of a killer whale and a wooden comb with a finely carved image of a duck on the haft.

As she led us through the exhibits, Millie spoke with affection, even a hint of motherly possessiveness, about the original inhabitants of Port au Choix, whose remains had been uncovered by a local contractor in 1967, when Millie was still a young girl. He was digging the foundation for a movie theatre, she said, when he suddenly struck bone. Then he uncovered an entire skeleton and, alarmed, called the police.

After examining the skeleton and checking out missing persons reports, the RCMP constable wondered if the bones might have something to do with Dorset Eskimo artifacts found along nearby Pointe Riche a decade earlier. He called in an archaeologist from St. John's, who judged the skeleton to be four thousand years old and continued to dig. Over the next nine years, 117 bodies were exhumed from this ancient seaside cemetery, with a wealth of grave goods that linked these people not to the Dorset Eskimos but to an even older and more mysterious Indian civilization. He called them the Maritime Archaics.

The Maritime Archaics can be traced back some nine thousand years, to the first people who moved into New Brunswick and up the north shore of the St. Lawrence River behind the retreating glaciers. Around five thousand years ago, when the ice was leaving Newfoundland, they migrated onto the island. They were distinguished by a taste for the grand scale. In parts of their territory they lived in longhouses over a hundred yards in length — the size of city blocks — with a dozen hearths for a dozen extended families. They spoke an early Algonkian language, one that gave rise to Innu in the north, Mi'kmaq in the south and Beothuk on the island. Most of their food came from the sea; they were among the most advanced hunters of sea mammals in the world. Seven thousand years ago, they developed the toggling harpoon head, an apparatus that worked its way farther into the flesh of the prey the more it struggled to free itself. That technology wouldn't appear anywhere else in the world for two thousand years.

The array of other tools unearthed in the Port au Choix graves shows that the people also hunted caribou in the interior, speared salmon in the rivers and trapped fur-bearing animals in the winter. The delicate needles and awls suggest that they wore some kind of decorative clothing. Archaeologists have concluded that they were generalists, living in the harsh lands at the edge of the glaciers and surviving by tapping every available resource. Their culture — rich and varied, drawing on both land and sea — survived for seven millennia.

Walking through the exhibit room, looking over the bits of shaped bone and fluted chert, Wayne said he almost had the impression that these ancients were little people, like Irish faeries. It wasn't until we saw a life-sized photo on the back wall that they took on a human scale. The photo showed two skeletons, an adult and an infant, still in the ground but with the soil brushed off.

The adult, who Millie said was a woman, was huddled around the infant. Later Wayne described it as a kind of ancient *pietà*, mother and child frozen in time for forty centuries.

"They had religion," Millie said. "You can tell by the way they took care of their dead." The graves were elaborate by any standard. Along with the wealth of grave goods — everyday articles as well as finely crafted works of art — the bodies had been anointed with red ochre from head to toe, a practice that was still common among the Beothuk four thousand years later.

We headed outside, to the land where the woman and child walked when they had flesh on their bones. Today it is a large, weedy field, bounded to the left by a white clapboard church and to the right by a group of modest new houses.

Millie explained how the seashore had been set back by the continuing post-glacial lifting, and said that at the time of the burials the spot where we were standing would have been shoreline. The alkaline content from the seashells had preserved the skeletons. She spoke with an archaeologist's enthusiasm about Ramah chert, a type of flint from northern Labrador found throughout Maritime Archaic mainland territory. "So they had trade," she said. In fact, at some four-thousand-year-old Maritime Archaic sites archaeologists had found copper in easy-to-transport rolled beads, from the north shore of Lake Superior, almost two thousand miles away.

While we chatted with Millie, we encountered the point where native and non-native histories diverge. To this day most Newfoundlanders deny any connection between the Beothuk and the ancients. The official account has the Maritime Archaics migrating onto the island, staying for three millennia, then being replaced by Dorset Eskimos, who remained for a thousand years before they too disappeared. According to this account, the Beothuk appeared out of nowhere to people the island in the wake of the Dorsets, and remained for a thousand years before conveniently joining the Maritime Archaics and Dorsets in oblivion to make room for Newfoundlanders.

The Innu (Montagnais Indians) of neighbouring Nitassinan, the Mi'kmaq of Wabanaki and an increasing number of archaeologists, including a few now working at the Archeology Unit of Memorial University in St. John's, tell a different story. Both the Innu and Mi'kmaq call the ancients not Maritime Archaics but ancestors. The Beothuk were cousins, the third nation descended from the grandfather people. When we mentioned this theory to Millie, her kindly smile dimmed. "There's no evidence for that," she said, denying any connection between the Beothuks and the ancients who had lain beneath our feet.

As might be expected, the Beothuk are a touchy subject in Newfoundland. Early Newfoundlanders are accused by most historians of hunting them to extinction in the eighteenth and early nineteenth centuries. In fact, as late as 1789 it was legal to kill Indians in Newfoundland. Today the Newfoundlanders' uneasy memory of the Beothuk is often expressed in bizarre local theories, including one from a book published just before our visit suggesting that the Beothuk were actually half-breeds, a people created by a mingling of Indian ancestors and Norse who visited the island around A.D. 1000. The conclusion was that the Beothuk, who were thus half-European themselves, had no more claim on the island than the Newfoundlanders who replaced them.

Other local theories presented the Beothuk as anomalies, claiming that their language was like none other known to man and that they followed an Egyptian-like religion of sun and moon worship. They were portrayed as too exotic to survive contact with the larger world — like hothouse flowers that wilt and die in the cool draft from an open window.

Their demise, Millie said, was caused by their own shyness as they fled their seaside villages to avoid contact with the arriving

Europeans. She referred to them as "the recent Indians" and explained that as settlers moved along the coast, the Beothuk retreated to the interior and were cut off from their vital maritime resources. She admitted that there had been conflicts between the Beothuk and the settlers, but dismissed them as skirmishes.

On our way out of the village, we made a final stop at the Sea Echo motel; we'd heard that an archaeologist from St. John's was working on a nearby site that he had identified as a thousand-year-old Beothuk camp. When we went into the adjacent restaurant to ask if anyone knew where the site was, an elderly woman was brought out of the kitchen as the resident expert on all things old. She said that people from St. John's had been digging behind the shed the year before, but that she didn't know if they were "looking for the Beothuks or the other kind."

On the strip of weedy ground between the shed and a gas station, we found a rectangular three-by-six-foot patch where the sod had been broken. There were no markers and no evidence that anyone planned to return to complete the work. In Port au Choix, it seemed, bones of "the other kind" could be safely displayed, but Beothuk bones were left discreetly in the ground — or, as Wayne put it, rattling in the closet.

The next morning we visited Griquet, where Cabot was said to have made his landfall. The village at the end of the harbour seemed deserted, with fishing boats pulled up along the narrow strip of beach. As we passed along the muddy road near the shore, only a barking dog suggested that this was a place where people still lived.

We turned up a path between two houses. The land rose steeply until the trail disappeared into a band of brambles that ringed the cliffs overlooking the sea. When we pushed through them to the summit, we found a plateau of mosses, tiny but colourful alpine flowers and twisted tucamores.

The harbour mouth to the left was formed by dramatic hundred-yard-high pillars of rock with several hundred yards of open water in between. Wayne pointed to six or seven humpbacks feeding in the surf, their arched backs glinting in the sun as they came up for air. They were moving south towards St. Lunaire Bay, where a trapped late-season iceberg was slowly melting in the July sun. We had been told that in spring polar bears rode the pack ice from Greenland on the Labrador Current, occasionally turning up, hungry and confused, in the villages along the coast.

A thousand years ago, the same current had brought the Norse to this country. They had landed and settled for two years on the tip of the peninsula — at L'Anse aux Meadows, five miles to the north of us — before the Beothuk, according to the Norse Sagas, drove them off in a trade dispute. In 1978, the Canadian government erected an elaborate multimillion-dollar interpretation centre at L'Anse aux Meadows, and constructed a full-scale reproduction of the Norse sod-hut village to celebrate the first brief passage of whites on North American territory.

At Griquet there are no markers. But according to Samuel Morison, this is where John Cabot's fifty-ton *navicula*, the *Matthew*, landed five hundred years after the Norse retreated. Morison, a seasoned sailor and former U.S. admiral, traced Cabot's journey from Bristol to his last known way point at Dursey Head in Ireland. Then he factored in Cabot's time en route, and the latitude-sailing navigation of the period, to calculate that the land Cabot sighted at five a.m. on June 24, 1497, was not Bonavista to the south, where the official five-hundredth-anniversary celebrations were to take place, but the cliffs at Cape Bauld, five miles to the north of us. When Cabot turned the *Matthew* south, looking for a harbour, he would likely have missed the first good anchorage, Quirpon, because its narrow off-centre entrance is difficult to spot from the north. Griquet comes after that, and its rock-pillared opening would have offered him a storybook entrance to the New World.

Although John Cabot — or rather, Giovanni Caboto — is credited with making what is now called the "intellectual discovery" of North America, his own background remains something of a mystery. A Genoese who seems to have worked out of various Italian seaports, he suddenly appeared in Spain in the mid-1490s, where he was apparently inspired by tales of New World wonders told by Christopher Columbus. Cabot moved on to London and convinced Henry VII to finance his voyages in search of a northern route to Cathay, asking in return a percentage of any wealth gained in the new lands.

As it turned out, the riches Cabot found came first in the form of offshore *estoqfis*, or codfish, which the Beothuk called *bobboosoret*. Cabot later reported to Henry VII that the fish were so numerous as he approached land that they slowed the progress of his ship. Catching them was simply a matter of lowering a basket over the side and drawing it up full to the brim.

On the evening of June 23, while the crew were still marvelling at the teeming ocean, the first signs of land began to appear. The crew caught "the odour of fir trees" in the salt air. As they continued sailing westward, they spotted "growing things floating out over the sea, low-hanging clouds, gannets, guillemots and other non-pelagic birds flying and screaming." Anchors were readied and a watch was set through the night for whatever land the dawn might reveal.

They would have entered Griquet at high tide, anchoring close to the south shore, near the flat section of land at the head of the bay where the cluster of wooden houses now stands.

"He did not go ashore save at one place of terra firma," a Cabot contemporary tells us, "which is close to where they made the first landfall, in which place they went ashore with a crucifix and raised banners bearing the arms of the Holy Father and the arms of the King of England."

The landing party probably consisted of a half-dozen or so men, because the *Matthew* had a crew of only eighteen and Cabot left a contingent of marines on board with crossbows to give cover fire if trouble arose on shore. Raggedly dressed and foul-smelling from weeks aboard ship, and with banners, crucifix and the solemn *terra primum visa* prayers, the Europeans would have made a strange spectacle on the deserted beach — especially when, after only a few minutes, the Genoese captain and the small party of Bristolmen suddenly wheeled around, scrambled into the long-boat and rowed back to the safety of the ship.

They had been startled by the sight of a root-twine fish net and "a spot where someone had made a fire, and . . . a stick of elbow length perforated at both ends and painted with brasil [red]."

"From these signs," the chronicler also said, "the land is judged to be inhabited." As Cabot "found himself to be with few men he dared not enter the land beyond a cross-bow shot, and he took on fresh water and returned to his ship."

If the Beothuk fishing party was nearby — as Cabot obviously feared — they likely mistook the approaching ship for a floating island and, like the Mi'kmaq to the south, the bearded sailors on the riggings for bears climbing the island's trees. But by the time Cabot and the Bristolmen were on the beach, it would have been clear that they were men — though possibly, because of the beards, *ash-mud-yim*, or devil-men. Watching from what were then well-treed slopes at the end of the bay, the Beothuk fishermen could hardly imagine that the brief procession below, with crucifix and banners and medieval invocations of Pope and King, would be the first of many European land-claim rituals on North American soil. And even though Cabot believed, as he strode along the stony beach, that he had reached the northern reaches of Cathay, the first lines in the history of the New World had been written.

Cabot returned to Newfoundland the following year, with five ships to fill up with cod. Somewhere off the coast four of the five, including Cabot's own, were sunk in a North Atlantic gale, but the fifth limped into a Beothuk harbour. While repairs were being made, a Beothuk fishing party approached. When the ship left, three Beothuk were on board, destined to become the first native North Americans to discover Europe.

In 1502, a chronicler at Henry VII's Westminster Palace recorded seeing two of the Beothuk. He described them as being "apparelled after the manner of Englishmen." He said they "speak a language no man could understand" but admitted that at Westminster "I heard none of them utter a word."

The campaign against the Beothuk began in 1501, when Gaspar Corte Real, a Portuguese privateer, sailed to Newfoundland with three ships. Corte Real joined Cabot on the sea bottom off the Newfoundland coast when the lead ship of his convoy sank, but the other two vessels returned to Lisbon with a cargo of fifty-seven Beothuk to be offered for sale at the slave market.

"Their manners and gestures," the captors reported, perhaps by way of advertisement, were the "most gentle, they laugh considerably and manifest the greatest pleasure. . . . The women have small breasts and most beautiful bodies and rather pleasant faces."

The Beothuk were also said to have a strong sense of modesty, something obviously lacking in Gaspar; before his ship went down, he named the Beothuk homeland Tierra de Cortereal. The name survived on European maps for decades, until it was replaced by Baccalaos — Basque for Codfish Land.

In the decades after Corte Real there was sporadic trade between the Beothuk and the European fishermen, but when the Beothuk began availing themselves of fishing equipment and supplies left on shore over the winter, relations soured. There were pitched battles between the local people and the fishermen, and numerous incidents when overwintering caretakers went on Beothuk-hunting expeditions. By the eighteenth century, both the French and the British had put bounties on Beothuk heads. Throughout this period, neither side seemed to know exactly what to do about the other, beyond identifying the other side as a threat and trying to drive it off. Beothuk fishing and hunting parties were ambushed, Beothuk villages were attacked, and in turn European overwinterers were slaughtered, their heads severed and carried off as trophies. By one account, a Beothuk war party killed sixteen Frenchmen, then donned their clothes and walked into a large French fishing station, where they killed twenty-one more. "Soe, in two dayes having barbarously maymed thirty-seven," a British observer wrote, "they returned home, as is their manner, in great triumph, with the heads of the slayne Frenchmen."

Between battles there were attempts at reconciliation. A trader and settler by the name of John Guy was approached by a group of Beothuks offering symbols of peace — a white wolf's skin and an arrow with the arrowhead snapped off. The two sides spent several days trading and celebrating a new-found alliance, with John Guy promising to return in the spring with more European goods to exchange for Beothuk furs.

But the following year another ship reached the harbour first. The Beothuks gathered on shore to welcome John Guy back. The captain, believing he was under attack, fired the ship's cannon and the Beothuks fled. The conflict reached its zenith with the 1801 massacre at Hant's Harbour. Some accounts describe up to four hundred Beothuk men, women and children being trapped on the point by European fishermen, with the Beothuk either shot or drowned in the surf while trying to escape. Very little was seen of the Beothuk afterwards. In 1824 a young Beothuk woman, Shawnadithit, was captured in the interior and put to work as a domestic. She died of tuberculosis in 1829, and the Beothuk are now listed as extinct.

It was quiet on the cliff. The only sound was the wind, which blew with enough force to bend the small evergreens and shake the tiny alpine flowers. We headed down the trail, which wound past one of the frame houses. A grey-haired fisherman in blue coveralls was on his knees in his garden, weeding what looked like a small potato patch. He straightened as we approached. "Looking for something?" he asked. Wayne told him that we'd heard that Griquet was where John Cabot had landed. The fisherman said he'd heard that too. Then, with a nod in the direction of the beached fishing boats, he added, "The way things are going around here, it would have been better if he never came."

A thick blanket of cloud began moving over the peninsula that afternoon, and by evening a light rain was falling. We turned on the radio for the weather report but instead found ourselves listening to a broadcast of the opening ceremonies of the 1996 Atlanta Olympic Games. Before the announcer had finished giving the roll call of the nations as they marched into the stadium, the radio went silent and the lights went out. The woman at the tourist office had warned us that a government-mandated power outage had been planned for the night, and had given us candles. "I'm looking forward to getting out of here," Wayne said when the candles were lit. "I know Newfoundlanders are the salt of the earth and I don't believe in any sort of mark of Cain. But I can't help thinking of Newfoundland as a crime scene."

On the island, the Beothuk had left no descendants, and the whites, no witnesses. In the end the Europeans had gotten what they wanted: all of the fish. The land had been emptied of its original people, the sea had been emptied of cod. *Terra nullius, mare nullius.*

Leaving Newfoundland took us two days. First the storms came from the southwest, roaring across the Gulf of St. Lawrence with gale-force winds. Then they shifted around to the north, bringing an icy rain and temperatures just above freezing, even though it was mid-July. Staff at the flight service station said it was already the wettest summer in memory. To the west of us, at our destination on Quebec's lower north shore, people were having an even worse summer, with the heaviest rains in ten thousand years — since the time the glaciers retreated and the ancients moved onto the land.

On the second evening we heard news of floods in the lands above Sept-Îles and Tadoussac, of walls of water bursting over and around hydroelectric dams, turning the streets of Jonquière, Chicoutimi and La Baie into boiling rapids and sweeping dozens of houses from the Saguenay flood plain towards the St. Lawrence River. At some point during the night, the highway that snakes along the north shore of the St. Lawrence was cut in seven places, washing out broad sections of pavement and swallowing automobiles in black holes of water and mud.

While waiting for the weather to clear, we found a motel near the airport. It looked like an old converted bunkhouse, and the room smelled like a mix of insecticide and mildew. It had two small beds, peeling paint on the walls, a worn brown carpet and, on the dresser, one of the largest cans of Raid I'd ever seen.

We spent a dismal two days going over our charts and notes and, every few hours, heading to the seedy bar up the road to call the airport for weather reports. Wayne, who had taken on the navigation tasks, plotted and, out of boredom, replotted our course. We would begin by looping around Quirpon, where Cartier had sought shelter in May 1534 to escape the pack ice. From there we would follow his route from his journal entries as he passed around the Strait of Belle Isle and along the north shore of the Gulf towards the Great River. We were heading to the land that Cartier had mistakenly called Canada, where the descendants of the people he'd met were still waiting to get their countries back.

When we arrived at the St. Anthony airport on that third morning, the mist was burning off the plains, with only a few patches clinging to low-lying areas. We stopped by the flight service station and the weather briefer assured us that we would have clear flying until just east of Sept-Îles, where the ceilings would lower to about two thousand feet. "You can also expect military traffic around Sept-Îles," he added. "The highway's cut and they're flying in rescue equipment." Thousands were homeless, and the region's road access to the rest of the world had been cut off. It was like the land itself was in rebellion.

CHAPTER THREE

Into the Heartland

T HERE IS A MOMENT just before takeoff, after you've taxied to position on the tarmac and you face thousands of
feet of runway — with the hash marks merging into infin-
ity in front of you — when you experience a quiet exuberance.
Other pilots I've spoken to agree that this is one of the moments,
after flight planning, walk-arounds and engine run-ups, when you
feel the beauty and wonder of flight — and the moment comes in
the form of pure anticipation.

Wayne, who was already developing the mental habits of piloting, glanced at the windsock and said a light crosswind was blowing from the right. I adjusted the controls and pushed in the throttle.
The Cessna accelerated along the centre-line, blurring the scrub-
land as it whipped by the window. When the airspeed indicator
showed sixty knots, I pulled back lightly on the controls and the
nose wheel lifted from the tarmac, followed by the main gear. After
levelling off for a moment to pick up speed, I pulled back again
with more force; the runway disappeared beneath the nose as we
climbed steeply into the sky. At 1100 feet we began a climbing turn
back towards the east to overfly the stretch of coast where the
Norse had landed in 1002, where Cabot had landed in 1497 and
where Jacques Cartier had pulled in during his 1534 voyage.

At three thousand feet we had a view of the peninsula as a sheltering arm thrust into the sea, catching icebergs, stranded polar bears and wayward ships swept southward on the Labrador Current. We took our bearings from the iceberg trapped in St. Lunaire Bay. Griquet was the next inlet. Five miles beyond it lay the horseshoe-shaped Quirpon Harbour. While Cartier was anchored there in May 1534 he had a brief meeting with a group of Beothuk fishermen. "They paint themselves with certain roan colours," he wrote. "Their boats are made of the bark of birch trees, from which they fish and take great store of seals." He described the people as "wild and unruly."

We banked back towards the west. As we crossed over the peninsula, we could see the Strait of Belle Isle, which, until Cartier sailed through it that summer, was thought to be a bay, and called Bay of Castles because of the steep rock cliffs along the Quebec/Labrador shore. We took our heading at Blanc-Sablon, the sandy point of land where the waters of the Strait and the Gulf meet. The shores of Nitassinan, land of the Innu (Montagnais Indians), loomed off to the right. As we flew west along the jagged, rocky coast towards the St. Lawrence, we would be following the route Cartier took on his second voyage, in the summer of 1535. It wasn't until then — more than three decades after the Europeans began fishing Newfoundland and Gulf waters — that the Great River that led into the heart of the continent was finally discovered. Like almost all of the European discoveries after Cabot, it was only made possible with the help of the people of the land — in this case, by a pair of reluctant guides, the sons of the Stadaconan leader Donnacona. As it turned out, this meeting of worlds provided a kind of curtain-raiser for the centuries that followed, as the old countries slowly revealed themselves to those who were drawn to its shores by dreams of its wealth.

Jacques Cartier was born in Saint-Malo in 1491, so he was one of Columbus's children, part of the first generation of Europeans to know that in sailing west you did not eventually fall off the earth into the abyss. Instead, there lay a giant new land, still shapeless, mysterious, tantalizing. Stories circulated throughout Europe of cities of gold in the southern regions, and European adventurers imagined that the north must also have its riches.

Cartier's most important discovery was not riches, but one of the interior countries led by a headman called Donnacona. In his journals, Cartier refers to their country as "Canada" and Donnacona as the "Lord of Canada." Cartier's Canada stretched along the St. Lawrence from Grosse-Île and Portneuf and contained half a dozen related Iroquoian communities, surrounded by cornfields interspersed with bean, melon and tobacco crops. The main town was called Stadacona.

The first meeting between Cartier and the people of Stadacona took place in the summer of 1534, at the Stadaconans' summer fishing grounds on the Gaspé Peninsula, a land they called Honguedo. The canoe journey from Stadacona usually took two weeks, but that summer Donnacona had taken a roundabout route, clinging to the north shore along the coast of Nitassinan to avoid, for as long as possible, touching on the coast of Wabanaki, Land of the Dawn.

The detour was a response to the devastating losses the Stadaconans had suffered the year before, when a fishing party of two hundred had been ambushed at night by the Mi'kmaq on one of the Bic Islands, just off the Wabanaki coast. The war party had set upon them in their sleep, and by dawn virtually the whole fishing party had been slaughtered, with only a few survivors returning to tell the tale.

When Donnacona's people arrived in Honguedo in early July 1534, the women went into the surrounding forest to cut wood for the drying racks while the men headed out to fish and set crab and lobster traps from their ballasted bark canoes. There was the usual festive summer atmosphere until mid-July, when the winds shifted from the west to the northeast and brought a ten-day storm. It was on the fifth day that Donnacona was called to the headland by one of the sentries to see the sight they had, until that point, only imagined: European ships sailing into their bay.

Donnacona's people had been hearing stories of the strangers' presence along the coast for years — and a few of their fine metal knives, axes and kettles had turned up at the Tadoussac trade fair. When they had asked the Innu traders where these things came from, they had been told that they were from the Iron Men plying the coasts. But the stories of these creatures had always seemed fanciful, like faery tales.

When Jacques Cartier and his three-ship convoy had sought shelter in Quirpon Harbour in May, his mission had been not fish but — as his patent from François I put it — the discovery of *"certaines ysles ou l'on dit qu'il se doibt trouver grand quantité d'or et autres riches choses"* — certain lands where it was said one might find large quantities of gold and other riches.

During his first voyage, in 1534, Cartier had had no idea of where he was going. His only destination was Riches, and without a specific course to steer he spent his first summer in the New World wandering aimlessly around the Gulf. He found the rugged tundra of the north shore disconcerting, describing it as a land of "frightful and ill-shaped stones and rocks" that "should not be called a new land but the land God gave to Cain." When he met a group of Innu along what is now the Quebec/Labrador coast, he described them in similar terms: frightful and savage.

From Blanc-Sablon he sailed southwest for forty miles to a deep fiord the Innu call Napetic. Then he doubled back, recrossing the Strait of Belle Isle and sailing down the west coast of Newfoundland past Port au Choix to the end of the island. Had he turned left there he would have been on his way back to France, so he turned right, heading southwest across the Gulf past the Magdalen Islands and the tip of Prince Edward Island, and reaching the northern New Brunswick coast around Miramichi in mid-July.

Without realizing it, Cartier had bumped into another country, Wabanaki, which covered most of the Maritimes and parts of New England. A group of Mi'kmaq traders spotted his ships, and showed that they had had previous dealings with European fishermen by trying to hail them from the shore, waving furs on the ends of sticks. Misunderstanding the gesture, Cartier fired the ship's cannon. Then, realizing what was being offered, he pulled in to trade, exchanging knives, combs and small decorative objects for furs.

As the summer wore on, Cartier's zigzagging route around the Gulf was like the path of a blind man feeling his way. The charts he drew at night, by the flickering oil lamp in the captain's cabin, were incoherent — islands became jutting peninsulas, the mainland disappeared and was replaced by islands, bays became rivers, rivers became bays and the extremities faded into the blankness of *terra incognita* — unknown land.

Still, he dutifully made his journal entries, and consulted the declination tables for rough latitude readings, and the slim New World rutters, for basic information on sailing the New World waters, and he pricked the traverse board to plot his track-made-good, knowing all the while that navigation was impossible without a destination.

At the base of the Gaspé Peninsula he came across a broad opening that he mistook for a strait. He entered, hoping that the waterway would lead him to wealth or, failing that, through the New World entirely, to Cathay, the land of the Grand Khan. Disappointment grew as the opening narrowed and finally ended in a river mouth. As he headed back to sea, a storm kicked up out of the northeast and he was forced to retreat to find safe anchorage. He was trapped for ten days while winds raged and the surf beat against the rocks on the windward side of the point.

On one of those drizzly mornings, the watch announced that a group of *sauvages*, a large fishing party, had been sighted on a nearby beach. They looked different from the others — their heads were shaved on the sides — and they didn't have the brazenness of the Mi'kmaq traders. Instead, they hung back near the treeline, curious but cautious. When the longboat was dispatched, Donnacona and the other men watched the landing party row towards them through the mist, while the women led their children to the safety of the trees.

It is hard to overestimate what a shock the physical appearance of Europeans was to the people of the ancient lands. Their clothing would not have seemed that unusual — the tunics and pantaloons of European sailors were similar in shape and cut to the breeches and jackets the Iroquoians wore in winter — but the faces and skin colour would have startled them. Most peoples of the Americas found facial hair bestial, and the Europeans' skin was sometimes compared to the chalky white membrane of a skinned beaver. Their overall estimation of the Europeans approaching them on the Honguedo beach must have been similar to Cartier's description of the Innu at Blanc-Sablon: frightful and savage.

Still, Donnacona stood his ground, with his brother and his two eldest sons at his side, while the strangers walked hesitantly towards them. He noted that the visitors were carrying gifts of knives and decorative combs, the same goods he had seen at Tadoussac trade fairs. This confirmed that they were indeed the ugly pedlars from eastern lands that he had been hearing about since he was a young man. He stepped cautiously forward. Gifts were offered and accepted and, after a safe interval, the women and children came out of the forest to meet the new beings. After the initial hesitation, the Europeans were embraced by the native men and women. By the time Cartier and his men headed back to the ship, they parted with gestures of friendship.

Difficulties between the two worlds did not take long to develop, however. They began the next morning, when another shore party landed on a nearby point and began to erect a thirty-foot cross, as part of Cartier's claim on behalf of his king, François I. Donnacona apparently understood the symbolism, because he, his brother and his sons paddled quickly out to the ship to speak to the leader of the pedlars. In his journals, Cartier said that Donnacona stood up in his canoe some distance from the ship and began "a long harangue, making the sign of the cross with two of his fingers, and then he pointed to the land all around about, as if he wished to say that all this region belonged to him, and that we ought not to have set up this cross without his permission."

When he finished speaking, Donnacona saw a sailor offering an axe to him from the side of the ship. Thinking this was a gift of appeasement, he brought his canoe alongside to accept it.

But what Cartier had in mind was not a gift but a kidnapping. During his summer of wandering aimlessly around the Gulf, he had determined that the only way he could discover riches was to seize some people of the country and force or entice the secrets of the land from them. "One of our men who was in our dinghy caught hold of his canoe," Cartier recorded, "and at once two or three more stepped down into it and made them come on board our vessel, at which they were greatly astonished."

The astonishment was shared by Donnacona's people on shore as they watched the old man, his sons and his brother dragged roughly on board the ship. When Donnacona appeared again, looking worried, his two sons, Domagaya and Taignoagny, were not with him. They had been seized by the strangers. The Stadaconan leader, the Lord of Canada, watched from shore as the ships hauled anchor, unfurled their sails and set off for the east, bearing his sons away.

Historians still debate exactly who the Stadaconans were. The Wendat (Huron) and Mohawk, fellow Iroquoian peoples whose traditional territories also bordered the St. Lawrence, claim them as their own, while most non-native historians describe the Stadaconans as part of a generic "Laurentian Iroquois," a people who have since disappeared.

Wendat, Mohawk or Laurentian Iroquois, Domagaya and Taignoagny became the reluctant discoverers of France that fall. After a long, uncomfortable ocean crossing, the two young men found themselves in the middle of a crowded little French seaport with scores of men loading and unloading ships, and women and children hawking wares from the adjacent market.

They arrived at Saint-Malo on September 5, 1534. With a population of about five thousand, Saint-Malo was three times the size of Stadacona, but it was not necessarily the largest town they had seen. The palisaded city of Hochelaga on Montreal Island is reported to have had a population of six thousand. The largest known metropolitan area in the St. Lawrence/Great Lakes region was Cahokia, in modern-day Illinois. Cahokia reached its peak between 1050–1250 A.D., when it was spread over several square miles, with a population estimated at thirty to forty thousand — larger than London at that time.

Unfortunately, Cartier's journals don't tell us about the Stadaconans' reaction to their new world, France, during the winter of 1534–35, other than the fact that they were put up by Cartier at a boardinghouse. (Cartier later sent François I an itemized bill for their upkeep.) But it is clear from their actions after they made it home that neither Domagaya nor Taignoagny were impressed enough by the new continent to want to return. We know from later accounts that native North Americans found Europeans callous, argumentative and uncivilized in their relations with one another. In fact, the only positive thing one Wendat reported about his sojourn in Europe was the fact that in Paris you could buy roasted meat on the street. At the same time, he found it incomprehensible that people around him were allowed to go hungry. At home, hoarding food or any form of wealth was thought to be a sign of demonic possession.

To be fair, like travellers everywhere, the North Americans misunderstood a good deal of what they saw. An often cited example is the Wendat who, after seeing Parisian women walking their dogs, returned to tell his people of the strange European custom of roping women to dogs which then dragged the poor women hither and yon through the streets.

While they tried to make sense of the bizarre customs and morals of Europe, Domagaya and Taignoagny apparently also spent time figuring out how to get Cartier to take them back home. After the first few months, when they had learned enough French to discern what it was the Europeans were seeking — a land of gold and other riches — they began to tell the adventurer what he wanted to hear. They spun stories describing a mythical Kingdom of the Saguenay where gold lay on the ground like seashells on Honguedo beaches. They promised to show him its whereabouts, if he would just be kind enough to drop them off along the Great River at their home in Stadacona.

The stories worked. After spending the winter in Saint-Malo, the two Stadaconans boarded Cartier's *Grande Hermine* on May 19, 1535, for the journey home. It was a difficult two-month crossing in heavy weather, and Taignoagny and Domagaya spent the time trapped in the crew's quarters, a four-foot-high between-deck crawling with cockroaches and rats. The stench — ripe and acrid from rat droppings mixed with mildew, rot and the odours of never-washed bodies — was so strong that scientists of the day speculated that it was a violent explosion of these shipboard vapours that created ball lightning.

Cartier's lead ship sailed into Blanc-Sablon harbour on July 15, and waited ten days for the other two ships to arrive. On July 29, with Domagaya and Taignoagny showing the way, they headed for the great river that Cartier had somehow missed in his previous summer's wanderings.

After fighting a headwind and putting into various harbours for several days because of bad weather, they reached the southern tip of the 135-mile Anticosti Island. Cartier recorded that "the two savages assured us that this was the way to the mouth of the great river and the route towards Canada."

In one of history's great mistranslations, Cartier had mistaken the Iroquoian *kanata*, which means town or village, for the name of Donnacona's country. From Anticosti, the Stadaconans also told him that "the river grew narrower as one approached their country and that farther up, the water became fresh and that one could make one's way so far up the river that they had never heard of anyone reaching the head of it. Furthermore, that one could only proceed along it in small boats."

When the three ships reached the broad, sandy estuary of the Moisie River, Cartier climbed into a longboat to examine the river mouth. Here he found mythical sea horses, now thought to have been walruses, frolicking in the shallow waters. Near this *rivière aux chevaux aquatiques* he also noted the presence of strange, large white fish with "heads like greyhounds," believed to be St. Lawrence belugas. "The people of this country call them *adhothuys*," he said. "And they tell us they are very good to eat."

While Cartier marvelled at this world of wonders, Domagaya and Taignoagny caught sight of the six islands of Chichedek (Innu for Islands Visible at a Great Distance), which Cartier named Sept-Îles because he mistook the jutting peninsula for a seventh island. After leaving the Moisie, his ships sailed west to the Baie de Sept-Îles, where they pulled in to escape the deteriorating weather. Domagaya and Taignoagny scanned the shore for signs of Uashat, the summer village of their Innu friends and allies. But the Innu, who had likely seen the ships arrive upriver at the mouth of the Moisie the day before, had quietly retreated inland.

Like "Canada," "St. Lawrence" is a mistranslation. The name now borne by the river, gulf and north-shore hills has its origin in a cartographer's error. When Cartier pulled into a small, nondescript bay along the Nitassinan coast, he named it Baie St. Laurent after that day's saint, but on his chart he scrawled the name near the centre of the Gulf. A few years later, in Paris, the map-maker misunderstood the annotation and applied the name to the entire gulf, and the river as well. Later it was extended to include the river valley and the Laurentian Mountains to the north. So the New World began to take shape, from mistranslations, map-makers' errors, misunderstandings and often simple indifference to the old place-names on the part of the European fortune-seekers. Wayne referred to this as "death by cartography." The real maps, he pointed out, were available to any visitor. They existed in the memory of the people, and could be published at any moment with a bit of birchbark and charcoal. As late as 1950, an anthropologist visiting a group of isolated hunters in Nitassinan discovered that they could draw an exceedingly accurate map covering forty thousand square miles of territory, parts of which had yet to appear on government maps. When asked about any particular area within this giant homeland, they could draw inset maps of even greater detail, including most of the lakes, streams and even hillocks.

While we flew along the shore, Wayne remarked on this achievement as he studied the charts on his lap, trying to relate them to the world below, a jagged coastline cut by deep fiord-like gashes and broad bays. He was having difficulty finding out exactly where we were, without even a dirt road for more than a hundred miles in any direction and with no identifiable features but the pattern of the lakes and the twisting course of the rivers. When he thought he had located our position, he held up the map, put his finger in the middle of the whorls of blue and green and read off the names, which reminded us that this area had resisted occupation: Kécarpoui, Cakipi, Checatica, Napetipi.

The land's wild beauty inspired even the writer of a Canadian military report on low-level flying to remark that this land remained "as God made it." The tundra of the northern coast gradually gave way to the taiga of small evergreens growing out of rock crevices, moss-covered basins and water everywhere — dark blue ponds, lakes shaped like butterflies, and broad, fast-moving rivers tumbling over cataracts and plunging into the sea.

Anticosti Island came into view, tilting towards the western shore like a funnel directing travellers to the river mouth. As we flew towards it, the sky began to lower. By the time we spotted the six islands of Chichedek, we had to descend to 1800 feet to stay under the clouds. When we tuned into Sept-Îles tower, the radio was busy with the chatter of approaching and departing aircraft. I called in our position and the harried voice said we were "number one, but two for landing," which meant a faster aircraft was behind us and would catch up and pass us before we reached the airfield. A few minutes later, the tower vectored us south of our track while a Canadian Forces Hercules on final approach passed to the north of us. We were told to follow it in.

We passed over the broad, sandy flood plain of the Moisie River, where Cartier claimed he saw sea horses, and over the nearby Innu village of Maliotenam, ten miles up the coast from Sept-Îles bay. The forests around the city were a mangy patchwork of clearcuts carved with dusty logging roads and sliced by broad swaths where power lines from the northern dams fed a massive aluminum plant across the bay from the city. The land did not look exploited as much as scavenged.

Sept-Îles is, in fact, two towns. On one side is the remote industrial town that grew up to serve the aluminum plant and the region's mines and logging operations; on the other, running along its southern boundary, is the Innu community of Uashat. At first glance the Sept-Îles side looks like a suburb without a city. You enter through the usual North American strip of motels, muffler shops and fast food restaurants, but when you turn off at the sign to *centre ville* you find there isn't one. Instead, you pass through a section of wide avenues lined with tidy middle-class homes and spindly trees. Along the waterfront, where our hotel was located, was a haphazard collection of shops, restaurants and hairdressing salons. There was nothing that looked like a downtown. The heart and soul of Sept-Îles resides in the giant aluminum-smelting plant on the other side of the bay. During the day, its presence is signalled by clouds of black smoke and occasional shooting flames from burn-offs. In the evening, the bright lights of the processing complex, which is served by its own harbour, look more like a city than Sept-Îles does.

We went for dinner at Chez Omer, where a woman who worked at the airport fuelling station had said the seafood was the best on the coast. When we arrived, we saw that she had taken her own advice. The restaurant was crowded, but she was sitting at a table for four in the middle. When she spotted us, she waved us over. Her name was Karen, and she said she was one of the few anglophones in Sept-Îles. She told us she always suggested Chez Omer to the flight crews. "The food is fresh here because Omer has his own fishing boat," she explained. "The others just use the frozen stuff."

I orded a coke, having sworn off alcohol several years earlier. Wayne, who had cut down drinking to a minimum in recent years, also had a coke. Karen, who said she was still a bit wound up from one of the busiest few days she'd ever had at the airport, ordered a beer.

After dinner we spoke mainly about the flooding and the disaster relief operation. A constant stream of military transports and rescue helicopters had been landing and taking off for two days now. Initially they had been taking supplies from Sept-Îles to the devastated cities around Lac St. Jean, but now the town too was running low on food. A couple of the car ferries from the south shore had been pressed into use as grocery barges, bringing in supplies for both the town and the airlift.

We asked Karen about the people of Uashat. She frowned. "People say they're poor," she said, "but I think they've got more money than any of us. You should see the pickups they drive." When Wayne expressed surprise, she continued, "They won't work and they don't pay taxes."

Perhaps sensing that she was on shaky ground, she changed the subject to one safer for English-speaking Canadians: Quebec politics. Everyone in Sept-Îles except her and the Newfoundland guy who worked for her, she said, had voted *oui* in the last referendum on Quebec independence. "They don't realize," she said, "that if independence comes, this place'll be a banana republic." She thought for a moment. "Without the bananas."

Before the dinner ended, Karen returned to the native theme. She compared the local Innu unfavourably to the "natives" she had met during a year she had spent working in Yellowknife, whom she had found much more industrious. "They worked," she said. "And that was where I learned to call them 'natives.'"

When we headed back to the hotel, along the darkened streets of the suburb in the bush, Wayne admitted that he couldn't help wondering what, exactly, she had called her Innu neighbours before she learned to call them natives. He went through the list of names he'd heard when he was growing up in Edmonton. *Bush bunnies, jack-pine niggers* . . . "I can see her in a Yellowknife bar," he said, "with some poor Dene guy trapped at her table while she explains that the *natives* around town are not at all like the *bush bunnies* that hang out around Sept-Îles. . . ."

At a park near the hotel, a summer festival was in progress, with a rock band playing on an open-air stage and a large busy beer tent. This part of the city was only blocks away from the Uashat boundary, but we noticed only one brown face in the crowd and he hung back in the shadows. Wayne said he'd heard that twenty years ago there was a fence between the two communities, and that it was closed at nine p.m., when all the Innu were expected to be back on their own side of the dividing line. Today the fence was gone, but the line remained.

We entered Uashat the next morning, by crossing the boundary road at the western edge of town. The row on row of Department of Indian Affairs cookie-cutter frame houses, with their fake-wood plastic siding, left no doubt about where we were. Uashat looks like any reserve across the country, complete with hand-painted billboards warning about the dangers of drugs and alcohol to the individual and the community. The only differences between this and, say, Whitedog in northwestern Ontario were that in Uashat the signs were in French, and the reserve adjoined a city.

The band council office was a modest brick building in the centre of the community. Inside, the walls were pasted with uplifting Health and Welfare Canada posters and agitprop for Nitassinan, giving the place the feel of a 1960 social movement office. When we arrived, we discovered that the band chief, whom Wayne knew from an Assembly of First Nations committee he had been working on, was in Quebec City. We were led downstairs to meet with the band's land claims researcher, Gloria Vollant.

Gloria was in her thirties. Her basement office was cluttered with local, regional and national maps of Nitassinan. In Innu-accented North Shore French, she gave us a brief sketch of the old order at the time of Cartier.

The people in this region, she said, had traditionally spent their winters inland, hunting caribou, moose and fur-bearing animals, and their summers in coastal villages, fishing and hunting sea mammals — seals, walrus and belugas — which once abounded in the region. In the late summer they travelled to Tadoussac for the trade fair, where they met not only their fellow Innu and the Stadaconans, but Algonquin traders from west of the St. Maurice River and Cree descending the Saguenay to exchange furs and north country manufactured goods (canoes, skis, winter clothing) for Stadaconan corn, beans and tobacco.

Even when she was a child, Gloria said, her father still headed inland in the winter to the family trapline. But in recent years the changes had come quickly. Mines were built in the interior, the forestry companies began clearcutting in earnest and hydro-electric developments, both private and public, began damming the great rivers of the territory. The aluminum plant across the bay, built in the 1980s, was the latest assault on the homeland.

When she spoke about the recent flooding, Gloria chose her words carefully. She felt sorry at the loss of life, she said, "but this is what happens when you try to master nature. You lose in the long run."

We spoke about Sept-Îles and Uashat. The most recent focus of the town's ire towards the Innu, Gloria explained, was a small shopping centre, Les Galeries Montagnaises, that had been built on land the band had leased to a developer. In the beginning the city had collected municipal taxes on the development, but since it was on Innu land, the band had passed its own tax law and now it was collecting taxes from the developer instead. It was the audacity of the local Indians in asserting their rights of ownership, as much as the loss of revenue, that had infuriated the people of the city. Karen had mentioned the issue at supper the night before. She and most white people of Sept-Îles, she said, were refusing to shop at the Galeries because of it.

The Innu had their own grievance in the twenty-year-old deaths of two of their young men. The youths had been fishing out of season on the Moisie River. Provincial fish and game officials went out to arrest them. The next day the Innu were found dead in their canoe. The people of Uashat believed they had been killed by the fish and game officials, who had apparently been the last people to see the boys alive. Even twenty years later, the killings were mentioned at national native assemblies where Innu were present. But the people of Sept-Îles quickly forgot about the deaths and no longer seemed to hear the protests. It was the way of the world. To the victor goes amnesia. The vanquished are sentenced to eternal remembering.

What Gloria found disturbing was the resentment that the people of Sept-Îles had for the Innu. "You hear it all the time on the call-in shows," she said. "They say we're rich, lazy drunks who refuse to pay our share of taxes."

Officially, the people of Nitassinan are largely ignored. The fifty-page local guidebook in the hotel room, which described everything from city government to historical sites, local churches, dry cleaners and service organizations, contained not a single reference to Nitassinan and only one brief reference to the Innu. "*Si vous rencontrez un Innu,*" it suggested, "*dites-lui bonjour dans sa langue: 'Kuei Kuei' . . . il en sera très heureux!*" (If you meet Innu, say hello in their language: "Kuei kuei." They will be very happy.)

But Karen had told us that you rarely saw the natives from Uashat in Sept-Îles because they had their own places. She never said exactly where those places might be.

Gloria knew. Before we left, she unfurled the Uashat land claim, on which the Indian names of the lakes and rivers, mountains and streams, had been meticulously restored. As she gazed at her handiwork, at her old country, she seemed to forget for a moment that we were still in the office. Nitassinan was alive on the page and within her imagination. At Sept-Îles, more than 450 years after Cartier had passed through, the battle of the countries continued among neighbours, with three countries — Quebec, Canada, Nitassinan — struggling to be born, to survive or to rise from the ashes.

CHAPTER FOUR

The Lord of Canada

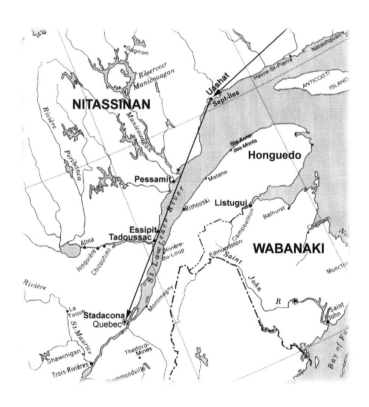

O UR ROOM at the Hôtel Sept-Îles overlooked the bay where Cartier's ships anchored in fog for three days in August 1535, when a trough of warm air over the St. Lawrence was pushed aloft by a cold front swinging down from the northwest.

Taignoagny and Domagaya spent the time with the crew, crammed in the close quarters of the between-decks. There was no room to stand, so the men crouched or sat with their backs against the beams or lay rolled in dirty blankets on the deck. It was almost three months since the two North Americans had left Saint-Malo, and more than a year since they had been seized off the Honguedo beach. The closer they came to Stadacona, the more impatient they were to get home. But when the *Grande Hermine*, *Petite Hermine* and *Émérillon* finally left Chichedek on August 24, Cartier returned to a meandering course around the river mouth. He still wasn't sure, he wrote in his journals, that he could trust the directions the Canadians had given him.

Five days later, the ships put in for the night in the shallow harbour across from the Bic Islands, where two years earlier two hundred Stadaconans had been ambushed in the night by the Mi'kmaq. The ships left the Bic Islands on September 1 and continued their journey upriver to Tadoussac, where the Saguenay

River empties into the St. Lawrence. While Cartier was surveying the river as it issued "from between lofty mountains of bare rock with but little soil upon them," he recorded that "the two men from Canada" had told him that this river would lead him to the Kingdom of the Saguenay, where the riches lay, but that it was not navigable by ships. Beyond that, they had said, this tributary flowed through "two or three large, very broad lakes, until one reaches the fresh-water sea [Lake Huron]."

Four days later the three ships passed Grosse-Île, where the brackish water becomes fresh and where Domagaya and Taignoagny reported that the territory of Stadacona began. Cartier put in at Île d'Orléans, which was only half a day's paddle from their town on the cliff above the river's narrowing.

"After we cast anchor between this large island and the north shore," he wrote, "we went on land and took with us the two men we had seized on our former voyage. We came upon several of the people of the country who began to run away and would not come near until our two men had spoken to them and told them they were Taignoagny and Domagaya. And when they knew who it was, they began to welcome them, dancing and going through many ceremonies. Some of the headmen came to our longboats, bringing us many eels and other fish, with two or three measures of corn, which is their bread in that country, and many large melons."

Domagaya and Taignoagny, the reluctant Stadaconan discoverers of France, had returned home.

Word of his sons' arrival at Île d'Orléans reached Donnacona on the evening of September 8, 1535. Their sudden reappearance seemed miraculous. At dawn he led a welcoming party of twelve canoes, which were quickly joined by a flotilla of well-wishers from surrounding towns, to greet Domagaya and Taignoagny and offer Cartier more gifts of corn, beans, melons and tobacco for their safe return.

"The Lord of Canada, named Donnacona came to our ships," Cartier wrote, "and began to make a speech and to harangue us, moving his body and his limbs in a marvellous manner, as is their custom when showing joy and contentment." Then Cartier claims — although he had no way of knowing what they were actually saying — that Donnacona spoke to his sons and they told him about "the good treatment meted out to them" in France.

The first indication that their reports about the French were far from glowing came when Domagaya and Taignoagny insisted, for several days after their return, on remaining on the far side of the St. Charles River, across from the shallow harbour where Cartier had warped in his ships for the winter. When Cartier sent a group of sailors to enquire why they would not approach, Taignoagny told them that their father "was vexed that the Captain and his people carried so many weapons."

After speaking at length to his sons, Donnacona was preoccupied by more than French rifles and swords. The sudden presence of three shiploads of Europeans presented itself as both an opportunity and a threat. The opportunity resided in potential trade with the newcomers, who his sons informed him had an enormous storehouse of fine metal goods in their country — useful things like knives, axes and kettles as well as powerful weapons. A trade and military alliance with the foreigners could give the Stadaconans a dominant position in the region. But his sons had warned Donnacona that, under no circumstances, were Europeans to be trusted.

While Cartier was supervising construction of a rough fort on the shore, he was also planning a further quick exploration before winter. When he had been examining the young Canadians in France, Taignoagny had told him about a larger city, Hochelaga, a few days' travel up the St. Lawrence from Stadacona. When he had pressed him for details, Taignoagny had become vague. Cartier guessed that Hochelaga was a regional power, and Stadacona one of its dependencies. He asked if Taignoagny would take him there, and the young Stadaconan agreed that he would, but only after he was returned to his village on the St. Lawrence.

Donnacona was not at all pleased when he heard about Cartier's intention to open up relations with the rival town 125 miles upstream. The Europeans were a source of ironwares and possibly weapons, both of which he wanted to keep within Stadaconan territory. To show his displeasure with Cartier's intention to go to Hochelaga, Donnacona descended on the ships with five hundred villagers. He told the European visitor that he was "most unwilling" that Taignoagny should accompany him to Hochelaga. Cartier shrugged him off, replying that in that case he would go alone. A few days later, Donnacona orchestrated what Cartier called "a great ruse to prevent us still from going to Hochelaga."

"They dressed up three men as devils," he wrote, "arraying them in black and white dog-skins, with horns as long as one's arm and their faces coloured black as coal."

Taignoagny then showed he had picked up a smattering of Christian jargon at Saint-Malo by lifting his gaze to the heavens and chanting, "Jesus, Jesus, Jesus." Domagaya joined in with "Jesus, Maria, Jacques Cartier!"

They explained to Cartier that the horned men had been sent by their god, Cudouagny, to warn the French that there would soon be much cold and ice and snow and that all would perish on the upriver journey to Hochelaga.

"At this," Cartier says, "we all began to laugh and to tell them that their god Cudouagny was a mere fool and that Jesus would keep them safe from the cold if they would trust him." The next day Cartier set out for Hochelaga, in the hope that the people there would lead him to the land of riches, the Kingdom of the Saguenay.

The sailors he left behind immediately set about building a shore battery, "with artillery pointing every way to defend themselves against the whole countryside."

Cartier gives a fairly detailed account of his upriver journey to Hochelaga. The trip took nine days, after he became lost in the islands at the west end of the riverine Lake St. Pierre, near modern-day Sorel. Along the shore he counted fourteen towns and villages, all surrounded by large fields of corn, squash and beans. Hochelaga, a heavily fortified town that Cartier estimated to have a population of around six thousand, was situated on Montreal Island, probably somewhere on the plateau between the river and the mountain, near what is now the downtown campus of McGill University. When Cartier landed his longboat, he was welcomed warmly by throngs of people. They brought him gifts "of fish and their bread, which is made of corn, throwing so much of it into our longboat that it seemed to rain bread."

Cartier was then led up to the city, through the gates of the triple palisade to a two-hundred-foot square in the middle of a large residential area of fifty longhouses, some of them two hundred feet long. While the people seated themselves, the headman, who was apparently suffering from a neurological illness that deprived him of the use of his limbs, was carried out to meet him. It is unclear why, but for some reason Cartier assumed the headman expected a faith-healing ritual, so he obliged by rubbing his palsied limbs.

After a prolonged period of gift-giving, smiling, nodding and mutually unintelligible speech-making, a group of Hochelagans offered to take Cartier up the steep slope of the adjacent hillside, which Cartier named Mount Royal. From there, Cartier records, he could see almost a hundred miles of territory, including the Laurentian Mountains to the north and the foothills of the Adirondacks to the south. Between the two lay the Laurentian Valley and the southern Kentaké plain, which he described as "the finest land it is possible to see, being arable, level and flat." Looking down to the river, he then saw "the most violent rapid it is possible to see."

It was the sight of the Lachine Rapids that confirmed he could go no farther that year. After establishing through pantomime that the Kingdom of the Saguenay lay beyond these rapids, Cartier headed to his boats for the return trip to Stadacona.

The Hochelagans were, it turned out, an obliging people. Cartier recorded that when some of his men, who were dressed in full fighting armour, tired on the trip down the mountain, his hosts picked them up and carried them on their shoulders to their boats. It was now early October. The days were shortening and a chill had crept into the air. As Cartier headed downriver, past the farming towns and the splendidly coloured autumn forests, he had a sense of having arrived in a wondrous country, one that must have its own source of riches to trade for or plunder. His plan was to winter with Donnacona and his people, then set out in the spring to search for the city of gold, the Kingdom of the Saguenay.

When we took off from Sept-Îles, our airspeed indicator read zero, and it continued to read zero as we made our way west. This mechanical glitch would make landing tricky, but en route it only added to the sense we had that day of flying over an infinite country.

While we were reaching the point where the Gulf begins to narrow into the river, Wayne wondered if there was an identified Canadian syndrome, like the so-called European syndrome that affects tourists who become overwhelmed by Florentine splendours. There were moments when the beauty of the land, with lakes, rivers, beaches and forests bending into the distant horizons, caused a kind of light-heartedness, even light-headedness, as we watched our shadow-plane silently tracing its course over the treetops and waters below.

Just west of La Tête de Chien, we passed over the first washed-out section of the highway where five people had drowned a few days before in the rushing waters of the Pentecôte. Below, we could make out road crews with heavy equipment suturing back together the thin black vein of pavement between the river and the vastness, reasserting a measure of authority over the land.

As we continued west, Wayne pointed out the Bic Islands, lying just off the south shore of the St. Lawrence. The smallest island, where the killings took place in 1533, is known locally as Île du

Massacre. But the non-native version has the slain Stadaconans still haunting the island on summer evenings with torchlight processions. During one of these nights, a young lighthouse keeper is said to have died of fright when he heard sounds of "a tomahawk beating against the walls."

Just up from the Bic Islands is Tadoussac, which means breasts in the Innu language, referring to the two bare, rounded hills at the river's entrance. The Stadaconans' assertion that this was the route to the Kingdom of the Saguenay, and great quantities of shiny *caigneldaze*, was essentially true, though the metal was copper, not gold. The copper-producing area was on the north shore of Lake Superior, fifteen hundred miles to the west. But during times of conflict with the Mohawk, the Stadaconans could only reach these lands by a circuitous route that passed up the Saguenay River, through a series of lakes and rivers and long portages, to the Gatineau River in northwestern Quebec, which flows south into the Upper Ottawa. From there they followed the ancient trade route to the Mattawa River, across Lake Nipissing to the French River and into Lake Huron at Georgian Bay.

By the time we passed over Grosse-Île, where Cartier recorded that "the province and territory of Canada begins," the land had softened into the green carpet of rich agricultural lands that surround Quebec City. Here, he noted, the lands "were very fertile and covered with magnificent trees of the same varieties as in France, such as oaks, elms, ash, walnut, plum-trees, yew-trees, cedars, vines and hawthorns bearing a fruit as large as a damson."

This was the home that the two men Cartier called Canadiens had thought of with nostalgia during their long months in Europe — a coherent world to which their ancestors, contemporaries of the Maritime Archaics, had moved behind the glaciers, after lichens and mosses had enriched the rock and gravel with enough soil to support sedges and grasses. Here the people lived through the slow warming that brought dwarf willows and birches, and then the stunted black spruce and reindeer moss of the taiga, and then the boreal forest inching up from the south and, finally, the deciduous trees that Cartier discovered upon his arrival. The people had, in a very real sense, grown up with the land.

In the distance, Quebec City loomed into view. Perched on the edge of the cliffs overlooking the narrows, the *vieille capitale* is built on the spot where Stadacona had been situated in Donnacona's day.

Without an airspeed indicator, landing was tricky. My guesswork on approach must have been close, because the landing was only a little rough, a couple of bounces. After parking at the aviation Esso and arranging for repairs, we headed downtown in a rental car. As we neared the old town, we were caught in the afternoon traffic jam.

In mid-July most of Quebec's civil servants are off to their cottages in the north, but the city throbbed with Canadian, American and European tourists, blocking roads and filling the outdoor cafés that lined one side of the street. On the other side we inched past the manicured lawns of the Plains of Abraham, now a national park, where the decisive battle between the British and French was fought in the fall of 1759. Today, the best guess of historians is that this is also where the town of Stadacona stood.

Although he spent a winter in its shadow, Cartier records only one visit to the Stadaconan capital. On October 13, just back from his visit to Hochelaga, he assembled a force of fifty marines and marched up the path and through the recently harvested cornfields to the town. After Cartier was met at the edge of town by hundreds of curious Stadaconans, Donnacona took him on a tour of the longhouses.

Inside each, there was room for several extended families, with fur-lined sleeping platforms built into the walls, and fires in central hearths providing warmth. The longhouses were at least as comfortable as the accommodations of the average European of the period, with the added benefit that, unlike the country people of Europe, Stadaconans didn't have to share their living space with their pigs and chickens. For Cartier, who had reached a relatively high station in life through a strategic marriage, the longhouse would have been a decided step down. But for most of his sailors, accustomed to living in peasant huts or port city slums, such accommodation would have seemed more than comfortable. Cartier, who was wondering how he was going to feed his hundred-man crew that winter, noted with interest that the longhouses were well provisioned with corn, beans, melons and dried fish.

During the tour, Donnacona made a half-hearted attempt to draw Cartier into a military alliance against the Mi'kmaq by showing him five of their scalps and relating the story of the massacre at the Bic Islands.

Misunderstanding or choosing to ignore the solicitation of support, Cartier concluded: "After seeing these things, we returned to our ships."

During the late fall and early winter, the French captain had time to record some observations of day-to-day life in the country. But since he worked out of a rough fort in a small clearing, with no understanding of the language and little interest in the culture, his Canada was fashioned from fragments of knowledge, and shaped by his own fears and yearnings. Like the Wendat in Paris who reported women roped to their dogs, he had some absurd misconceptions. The difference was that Cartier's misunderstandings were recorded as history, and even today they shape the way we view the ancient lands. A good example was his interpretation of Iroquoian sexual customs, which allowed relative freedom to the unmarried. To ensure that women weren't pressured into sex in Iroquoian society, men showed interest by discreetly offering a small token gift. The woman could then either have it quietly returned, to indicate a lack of interest, or accept the gift and the man's attentions. From this face-saving method of carrying on intimate relations, Cartier surmised that the gifts were used to purchase sexual services, and he wrote that the young women of Stadacona served as whores to the men.

In many other instances, Cartier's journals portray the people of the land in the worst possible light. During the research, Wayne pointed to a section in the journals where he describes the Stadaconans' ability to withstand severe cold, even with bare flesh exposed, as "incredible." But instead of attributing this, in a human way, to their self-discipline and fortitude, he concludes that "men, women and children are more indifferent to cold than beasts."

In the first few weeks after Cartier's return from Hochelaga, the Stadaconans came to the ships frequently to trade fish and other foodstuffs for knives and kettles and novelty goods. At some point, Domagaya and Taignoagny told the people that in France such items were commonplace, and that they were being shortchanged. Soon they began asking for hatchets rather than knives and trinkets, and Cartier labelled his former kidnapping victims "rogues and traitors" for telling their people the truth about the French goods.

This incident, coupled with the refusal of Taignoagny to accompany him to Hochelaga, appears to have fed Cartier's mistrust of the Stadaconans. "Sensing their malice," he wrote, "and fearing lest they should attempt some treasonable design and come against us," he gave orders "for the fort to be strengthened on every side with large, wide, deep ditches and with a gate with a drawbridge." A twenty-four-hour watch was instituted, with trumpets sounded every eight hours to signal the changing of the guard. Once again North Americans and Europeans had come together, and neither seemed to know exactly what to make of the other.

Konrad Sioui, an old friend of Wayne's, was living in Wendake, a two-hundred-year-old Wendat (Huron) community that in the past twenty-five years has gradually become surrounded by Quebec City's urban sprawl. When you enter it along Boulevard de la Rivière, Wendake looks like a typical old Quebec village, with narrow streets, stone buildings, neat little cafés and shops and a church with a large spire overlooking the cascading falls that tumble underneath the main-street bridge. At first glance, the only things that mark this as an Indian town are the native craft shops and the Iroquoian names on the streets.

Konrad Sioui's house was in a small suburban development a few blocks from the village. He met us at the door with a cheerful greeting and led us to his downstairs study. He'd just arrived back from Labrador, he said, where he was working with the Innu Nation, the tribal council of the Labrador Innu. "I like working with the people up there," he said, "because they're still connected to the land."

Konrad's face and voice were familiar from television. During the 1980s he had been the Quebec leader of the Assembly of First Nations, and in 1991 he had been one of the leading contenders for national chief. He'd come across well during the campaign, as a man who could articulate a vision, but our friend Dana Williams had told me, "He'll never win. He looks too white." It was true that Konrad was fair-skinned — like many Wendat, who had been intermarrying with the French for centuries.

Wayne had already told him a bit about our travels on the phone, and Konrad had obviously given the issues some thought. Leaning forward at his desk, he indicated that he wanted to begin at the beginning. "I hope you guys aren't planning to repeat all those lies about the Bering Strait," he said. "That's not history, it's *twistory*."

Origins are a sensitive subject. The archaeological record is murky before the last ice age, and the official theory is still that the native North Americans crossed over from Asia 12,500 years ago, when there was still a bridge of land across what is now the Bering Strait, and travelled down the ice-free west coast. From the southwest interior of the continent, this theory says, they moved north and east as the ice receded.

A reminder that the last word on origins is far from written came during our summer travels, when archaeologists in Alberta discovered evidence of human occupation that they dated at twenty thousand years ago. A few months later, an even more surprising discovery was made in southern New England, indicating a human presence in the Americas as much as fifty thousand years ago — which would mean that people were living in the Americas before the last ice age even began.

According to Wendat legend, the world began with an accident in the sky when Aataentsic, a female spirit, suddenly slipped through a hole in the sky and fell towards earth, then a watery planet inhabited only by aquatic creatures. Seeing the sky woman falling to the fathomless waters, the great tortoise positioned himself to break her fall, and the other aquatic animals piled mud from the deep on his back to soften her landing. Aataentsic, who was pregnant at the time, landed on the earth-covered turtle's back without injury. Before giving birth to two sons, she made the turtle's back expand into what became North America, the Turtle Island of many indigenous peoples' mythology. One of Aataentsic's sons, Iouskeha, released people and animals on the land, and the various peoples then headed to their appointed countries.

Konrad Sioui brought us up to date on the Wendat, beginning sometime after creation, when they had been given territory somewhere in Central America. As people of the corn, they had been sent north, presumably by Iouskeha, to bring the food of life to the hunting peoples.

So the corn people worked their way north over time, moving up the Mississippi into the heart of the continent, teaching the locals how to sow and harvest all the varieties of corn, as well as beans, squash, melons and tobacco. Some of the Wendat ended their journey on the shores of Georgian Bay, which became the seat of the Wendat Confederacy. Others settled along the northeast shore of Lake Ontario and along the upper St. Lawrence. The Stadaconans, according to Sioui, were the northernmost arm of the Wendat nation, living along the St. Lawrence at the very limit of the corn-growing area.

As he recounted the Wendat version of history, Sioui's story took a few twists of its own. In describing the limits of old Wendake, he connected the dots of the relatively small Wendat farming countries to a vast Wendat land that stretched from Stadacona, including within its boundaries large sections of land that were also claimed by the Mohawk and the Ojibwa as parts of their ancient territories.

Wayne asked about Jacques Cartier's arrival in Stadacona. On this subject, Konrad was brief. "They wouldn't have made it through the winter without our help," he said. "They were sick and weak, from a dying continent. We gave them food and medicine and then they turned around and tried to destroy the Old Order. So we drove them off."

The Europeans' first recorded winter on Canadian soil turned out to be a disaster for them and unpleasant for the Stadaconans, with Donnacona later complaining of instances where Frenchmen "sharpened their swords on the flesh" of his countrymen.

Cartier makes no mention of the bloodletting; he was preoccupied with the suffering imposed on him and his crew by Cudouagny's revenge, the intense cold, the deep snow and the ice that coated even the inside walls of the fort and the ship. Just when the cold seemed almost unbearable, a terrifying disease began stalking the Europeans — one that began with a swelling of the limbs and a rotting of the gums and ended with the flesh turning purple as the body wasted away.

By the middle of February, 100 of Cartier's 110 men were suffering from this grotesque condition. The men were dying at a rate of several a week, and Cartier faced the possibility of losing his entire crew to the winter plague. Trying to hide the mysterious disease, for fear the Stadaconans would take advantage of his crew's weakened state by launching an attack, he ordered the few healthy men to spend their days making enough noise for a hundred.

Then one morning, when twenty-five sailors were dead and eighty more were near death, Cartier met Domagaya outside the fort. As soon as the Stadaconan learned of the illness affecting the French, he arranged to have two women gather *annedda* (cedar) bark and boil a large pot of healing tea for Cartier's men. Within days, the vitamin C in the brew cured everyone of the dreadful disease — which we now know as scurvy.

Cartier marvelled that "all the drugs of Alexandria could not have done so much in a year as did this tree in three days." But instead of thanking Domagaya and the Stadaconans, he offered a "Thanks be to God, Who in his divine grace had pity upon us and sent us knowledge of a remedy which cured and healed us."

After barely surviving the winter, Cartier gave up his plan to spend the following summer searching for New World treasures. Instead, he faced the prospect of returning to France with a quarter of his men dead and buried and absolutely nothing to show for his trip except more vague stories of the Kingdom of the Saguenay. Sometime while the snows were melting and the current was dislodging the ice from the river, he decided to grab Donnacona, the Lord of Canada, and take him back to France, as a kind of walking souvenir and a source of more information about the Saguenay riches.

He laid his trap by inviting the people of Stadacona to a good-bye party. They came but, suspicious of his motives, hung back near the trees at the edge of the clearing. When Cartier strode out and invited Donnacona to come into the fort with him for a farewell drink, both Domagaya and Taignoagny warned their father that under no circumstances should he go near the fort. When Donnacona heeded his sons' advice and declined the offer, Cartier ordered his marines to seize Donnacona, Taignoagny, Domagaya "and other headmen." While they were being wrestled to the ground, Cartier ordered his company to drive away the other Stadaconans. "The Canadians," he noted, "began to flee and scamper off like sheep before wolves."

When the ship sailed, Cartier had on board the "Lord of Canada," his two sons, Domagaya and Taignoagny, three other leaders and a young Stadaconan girl. After docking in Saint-Malo, he took the "Lord of Canada" to Paris to meet François I, amid the splendours of the imperial court. Like his sons two years earlier, Donnacona tried to convince the French that he would lead them to the Saguenay riches if they would only take him and his people back home. To make the prospect even more enticing, he described other marvels he could show them in his homeland, including a country where people had only one leg and had to hop to and fro, and another where people could eat no solid food because they had no anuses. There was even a nearby land, he said, where people had bats' wings and flitted from tree to tree. A few court skeptics challenged some of his more outlandish tales, but the King quelled their protests by pointing out that Donnacona had sworn to their veracity on a bible. The royal gullibility held sway and, for a time, drawings of one-legged people and bat-winged people were faithfully recorded in the blank areas on maps of Canada.

Unfortunately, by 1541, when Cartier was finally ready to make his third voyage to the mythical land of marvels and riches, all of the adult Stadaconans, including Donnacona and his two sons, had died from European diseases. There is evidence that the young girl survived beyond that date, but there is no further record of her.

When Cartier returned to the St. Lawrence, he cautiously made camp several miles upriver from Stadacona, at Cap-Rouge. When the Stadaconans came to enquire about the whereabouts of their countrymen, he said they were so happy in France that they hadn't wanted to return. The Stadaconans, who'd already heard Domagaya and Taignoagny's dark description of life in Europe, looked at Cartier incredulously but said nothing. During the winter, Frenchmen who strayed into the woods beyond cannon range to hunt were killed. Those who went in search of firewood in the bitter winter cold, were killed. Those who came searching for their missing comrades, were killed. In all, thirty-five men died from Stadaconan arrows or war clubs.

Having failed to discover any of the wondrous lands described to him — or the route to Cathay — Cartier fled the country for good as soon as the ice left the river. The legacy from his three voyages would be some sixty or so Europeans buried in Canadian soil, and eight Canadiens buried in France.

The spot where Cartier had wintered in 1535–36 is now a city park with a full-sized replica of the *Grande Hermine* dry-docked on the lawn. On the hillside overlooking the display, a thirty-foot cross still claims the land for the greater glory of François Primer. But after Cartier's Canadian disasters, the French were in no hurry to establish themselves in their new acquisition. It would be more than half a century before any major expeditions penetrated the river beyond Tadoussac. By then, Stadacona had disappeared. According to Konrad Sioui, the Stadaconans had shifted to the west due to crop failures and rejoined their Wendat countrymen along Georgian Bay. Around the same time, the Hochelagans had also retreated. Mohawk sources say that the Hochelagans moved south into the heart of Kanienke, either because of crop failures or because of an outbreak of war between them and the northern hunting peoples. This was apparently a common enough occurrence. In Mohawk, the name for Montreal Island is Kawennote Tiohtià:ke, Land where the Peoples Divide, and the St. Lawrence River served as the frontier between the Mohawk and their Algonquin enemies.

 As it passed from Iroquoian control, Stadacona became Kebek, the Innu word for "the narrows," and the Innu began to travel down the St. Charles River in the summer, portaging around the falls upriver, where Wendake now stands, and paddling down to the St. Lawrence to fish for eels. On the cliffs above, the abandoned longhouses rotted and collapsed; the untended cornfields were gradually swallowed up by the encroaching forest. The land, under cultivation for a thousand years by Iroquoian farmers, rested in silence under the summer sun and winter snows.

CHAPTER FIVE

An Outpost on the River

NITASSINAN

St. Maurice

Kebek
Quebec

Attikamek

Trois Rivieres

TENAKIWIN

Hochelaga

Montreal

Kentaké

Veskarini Kanesatake

Kahnawake

River of the
Iroquois

Cowasuk

Akwesasne

KANIENKE

Lake
George

T HE CLIFFS on the Plains of Abraham, where Stadacona was likely located, overlook the St. Lawrence narrows. From here, Donnacona's people would have witnessed the arrival of Cartier in their country in 1535 and his hasty final departure in 1542. For the rest of the century these channels would remain largely empty of ships, as Europeans all but gave up on exploration of the interior countries. The New World remained predominantly a place to fish, its prodigious stocks of groundfish drawing hundreds of ships to the Grand Banks each year from Britain, France, Spain and Portugal.

The fur trade gradually emerged during this period, beginning as an indigenous initiative, with European fishermen being hailed from the shore, as Cartier had been, by Mi'kmaq or Innu traders waving furs on sticks. By the end of the century, fishermen were finding the fur trade a lucrative business in its own right, and the Basques established a small summer trading post at Tadoussac. There were a few European forays up the river during this period, including a reconnoitring trip by Samuel de Champlain in 1603, but no permanent trading posts were established until Champlain's return in 1608.

By then, Champlain had considerable experience in the Americas. After serving in the quartermaster corps in Marshal d'Aumont's army in the French–Spanish wars in the 1590s, he shipped out with the Spanish to the West Indies and made his way to the old Aztec capital at Mexico City. At Tadoussac, in 1603, he followed the tradition of Cartier by taking a child back to France with him. Champlain's biographer, Morris Bishop, tells us that Champlain gave the boy to the French Crown, and that the Innu youngster ended up — dressed in a blue coat and bonnet — as a gift for the three-year-old Dauphin Louis. He called the Innu boy "Canada" and is reported to have sent him "the soups and jellies he refused to eat." Canada died of European diseases a year later, in June 1604.

After his 1603 trip to the St. Lawrence, Champlain became involved with a settlement and fur-trade venture along the coasts of Nova Scotia and New England, but they were abandoned after several harsh winters. In 1608, armed with a Crown monopoly on the furs of the interior, he arrived at Kebek with cannon and mercenaries to build the first permanent post in the New World. He dragged his longboats onto the beach below the cliffs on July 3 and immediately set his men to clearing the land for his *habitation*, which consisted of three two-storey buildings and a single-storey warehouse with a deep cellar. The perimeter was fortified with a moat, interior and exterior palisades, cannon platforms, and a drawbridge for entry.

The local Innu who had moved onto the abandoned Stadaconan lands deduced from all this construction activity that the French were planning to stay awhile. But it is unlikely that this caused them much concern. During the past five years, Basque trade out of Tadoussac had allowed the Innu to exchange their furs for European axes and kettles. This new post at Kebek would be more a shopping convenience than an invasion. In fact, at no time over the next quarter-century would there be more than a hundred Europeans in the vast territory between Tadoussac and Lake Superior. It would be over a century before Europeans were able to move beyond the Great Lakes and onto the plains.

While the fort was being constructed, the Innu had a troubling glimpse into the Europeans' character. The incident began with angry shouts from within the half-completed palisade. They watched as four of Champlain's men were seized, and put in chains and dragged off into the warehouse. Sometime later, one of the captives — a locksmith by the name of Jean Duval, who was accused of conspiring with Basque whalers at Tadoussac for the takeover of Kebek — was dragged outside to the nearest broad-limbed butternut tree, strung up and hanged. When he continued to twitch after being cut down, a French sailor fell upon him and strangled him. Duval's lifeless body was then dragged over to a stump at the edge of the clearing and his head was severed from his body. The bloodied head was carried to the palisade and stuck on one of the spikes, and left to stare blankly at the people of the country.

The Innu watching from the ridge were deeply disturbed — not so much at the cruelties as at the fact that the French had inflicted them on one of their own. But Champlain had learned the art of managing men as a soldier under Marshal d'Aumont, who had once hanged twenty-eight of his own troops in a single morning for breaches of military discipline. In Canada, Champlain had come prepared, as the indigenous people sometimes said mockingly, to make war on the beaver. The military code would apply.

When we took off for the ninety-minute flight to Montreal, the air was calm, with only a slight summer haze. The Quebec City/Montreal leg is one I have flown many times, but it's always a pleasure, offering a vista that includes river, northern and southern mountains and a broad plain.

The great river, the conduit between the freshwater seas of the interior and the salt water of the Gulf, dominates the scene, widening and narrowing as it passes through a series of riverine lakes like a serpent bulging and contracting around swallowed prey. Along this section of the St. Lawrence, more than anywhere else, the ancient national territories were tucked into the contours of the land. On the north shore the land rises quickly from an elevation of two hundred feet to as high as three thousand. This is still part of the vast Innu territory of Nitassinan, which stretches as far west as the St. Maurice River at Trois Rivières, where Tenakìwin, the land of the Algonquins, begins. To the south, the valley widens into the broad Kentaké plain, which forms the northern frontier of Kanienke, land of the Kanienkehaka (Flint People), known as Mohawk.

As we passed Trois Rivières, with the dark hills of Tenakìwin off to our right, Wayne mentioned that the Algonquin had something of an identity problem: they are often lost within the larger group of Algonkian-speaking peoples. The Algonquin call themselves Màmìwininì, but they also consider themselves part of the larger Algonkian family of hunting peoples inhabiting the Laurentian Shield and Great Lakes region. These include the Innu, Cree, Ojibwa, Odawa, Potawatomi and Mississauga, all of whom spoke a dialect of what linguists call the Algonkian language.

This naming problem is part of the general confusion about peoples of the ancient lands that began in Cartier's time and persists to this day. Part of the problem resides in the fact that, as Wayne pointed out, the indigenous peoples tended to call themselves something that translated as "human beings," and to call neighbouring nations they were on unfriendly terms with something akin to "assholes."

When Champlain arrived at Tadoussac in 1603 and enquired about the people upriver on the south shore of the St. Lawrence, the Innu said they were "Mohawk" (Cannibals) and were part of a large group of "Iroqu" (Snake People). In fact, among themselves the Mohawk are Kanienkehaka (People of the Flint), and they consider themselves not Iroquois but part of the Rotinohshonni (People of the Confederacy or, literally, Longhouse). Similarly, when later Dutch and British traders moving up the Hudson River asked the Kanienkehaka about the peoples living to the north and east of them, they dismissed them all as Adirondacks (Bark Eaters) because they were people without corn. For the next century the

Algonquins to the north and the Maliseet and Mahicans to the east
were known as Adirondacks to the British and Dutch.

To make matters more complicated, Europeans added a few
names of their own — like Huron (Ruffian) for Wendat — and
mangled and mispronounced some difficult names, often beyond
recognition. The best example of this was the Kenistenaag people
living around James Bay. The French first mispronounced their
name as Kristinaux and then shortened the misnomer to Cris,
which the English then rendered Cree. And so it went. The settled
order of the ancient lands blurred out of focus with the chaos of
misnaming, mispronunciation and mistranslation. By the time
Europeans arrived in Danaiiwaad Ojibweg, the country to the immediate west of Tenakìwin, their confusion had reached the point
where they had more than a hundred names for the Ojibwa people; in many cases, historians are still confused about whom, exactly, the early record-keepers were referring to.

The indigenous custom of giving colourful and descriptive
names to neighbouring peoples also extended to the new arrivals.
Most indigenous peoples named Europeans for the goods they
peddled, so the names were often something like People of the
Ironwares or Men who make Kettles. But his favourite, Wayne said,
was the Passamaquoddy name for Europeans. The direct transla-
tion was the ominous-sounding Somebody's Coming. The most
colourful and insulting, though, came from the Arapaho, whose
name for Europeans translated as People the Colour of Piss-stains
on a Horse's Tail.

Twenty minutes after passing Trois Rivières, we were over the
Richelieu, the river known during Champlain's time as River of
the Iroquois. From there we had our first view of Montreal Island
and the cluster of skyscrapers ringing Mount Royal, where Cartier
had stood during his brief visit in the fall of 1535.

As we neared St-Hubert airport on the south shore, we passed
the Jacques Cartier Bridge, with the Champlain Bridge a few miles

to the west. On the other side of the Champlain we could make out the frothy waters of the Lachine Rapids, the barrier that no European crossed until the summer of 1610 — 113 years after Cabot's landfall.

We began our descent towards the old military airbase on the Kentaké plain to the south of the city. Landing, especially in a busy airspace like the one around Montreal — where the radio is constantly crackling in two languages — requires a degree of alertness. Wayne rarely spoke when we were on final approach, thinking it better to leave me to the job at hand. But he said later that when we were descending into Montreal, he had a sense of Tenakìwin slipping away to the north, and Kanienke to the south, as the broad outlines of the ancient lands were replaced, at 1500 feet, by the strip malls, muffler shops and fast-food joints of Chambly Avenue. Entering Montreal after travelling almost a thousand miles from Newfoundland, mainly over wilderness, felt like entering the belly of the beast.

My wife, Betsy, and I had dinner with Wayne that evening on a waterfront terrace in Ste-Anne-de-Bellevue, which overlooks the small Ste. Anne's rapids. The boardwalk in front was crowded with people out for an evening stroll. A flock of terns flitted above the eddying pools at the base of the rapids. With remarkable agility, they would suddenly lower their heads and dive in an accelerating spiral, hitting the water without a splash, like a bullet. A moment later they would emerge with tiny perch in their beaks.

From where we were sitting, across from the rapids, we could see the base of Lake of Two Mountains to the north and the opening to Lake St. Louis to the southeast. Wayne pointed out that the fact that the Mohawk community of Kanesatake is north of the island, on the shore of Lake of Two Mountains, is a source of resentment among some Algonquin. In the seventeenth century, it had been the site of an Algonquin community called Occaw (from the Algonquin word for walleye). In the eighteenth century the

French priests moved a large group of Mohawk into the community to take them away from the influences of Montreal, and the village had slowly been transformed into Kanesatake.

Many Algonquin, Wayne said, have difficulty accepting the fact that Mohawk are living within the traditional borders of Tenakìwin. When the Algonquin chief Jean-Guy Whiteduck, from Brenda's community of Kitigan Zibi, drafted a land claim for the Algonquin nation, he not only included within its borders the land around Kanesatake, but kept his pen running south onto and across the Kentaké plain and into the Adirondack Mountains of northern New York State. A Mohawk friend who had seen Whiteduck's claim, Wayne said, had scoffed at it. "If Whiteduck thinks the Algonquin are going to get Kanesatake and Kahnawake," he said, "he's dreaming."

These tussles over traditional boundaries are sometimes portrayed with amusement in the press, with Indians gently mocked for serving one another with imaginary land claims for imaginary countries. "But as Canadians and the Québécois know," Wayne said, "countries exist first in the imagination. Political and other struggles make them appear or disappear, but as long as they continue to live on in the peoples' imagination, there's always hope. Look at Eastern Europe. With the collapse of the Soviet empire, old European countries are emerging again. Changes can come quickly. Maybe the Canadian empire will be the next to go."

According to Algonquin legend, it was sometime around 1570 that their armies drove the Cannibals from Hochelaga, across the broad Kentaké plain and deep into the southern hills. This was the greatest victory in Algonquin history, giving them undisputed control of the Great River and the island and the Lachine Rapids and extending the borders of Tenakìwin deep into traditional Mohawk territory.

But the Algonquin were never able to consolidate their hold. Within a matter of years, the Mohawk and their Five Nations allies were sending troops beyond the Adirondack Mountains and back up the River of the Iroquois (Richelieu River) to attack the Algonquin summer villages that had sprung up along the St. Lawrence.

By the time Champlain arrived, the Algonquin had been pushed back up the Ottawa to the Rivière Rouge, where they had settled above a twelve-mile rapid. The St. Lawrence lowlands had once again reverted to a no-man's-land where both Algonquin and Kanienkehaka (Mohawk) sent spring and fall war parties.

That was the situation when Iroquet, a soft-spoken hunter, was called upon to lead his Algonquin people. According to tradition, he was summoned to the centre of the circle during the leadership ceremony and the staff of leadership was handed to him. As it turned out, his people had chosen wisely. The defence of a heartland country like Tenakìwin required courage and ability not only in war but also in diplomacy. Iroquet showed himself to be a master at both as he forged an alliance that would lay the foundation for a generation of peace and prosperity, for his people and their allies.

Iroquet's people were at the mouth of the Rouge River, on the lower Ottawa, in the summer of 1603 when Champlain made his first brief appearance at Tadoussac. Iroquet heard about Champlain's arrival from Tessouat, the one-eyed chief of the Kichesipirini Algonquin, who controlled the lands around the upper Ottawa near modern-day Pembroke. Tessouat had been in Tadoussac that summer, celebrating a joint Algonquin/Innu military victory against the Mohawk, when a three-masted ship appeared at the mouth of the Saguenay and Samuel de Champlain had rowed ashore for his first visit to Canadian territory.

By this time, European fishermen and a few pedlars were already making regular trips to the Gulf of St. Lawrence. So when Champlain stepped ashore, the Innu chief, Anadabijou, had him brought to sit beside him and share in the feast of moose, beaver, bear, great quantities of wildfowl and, in honour of the recent victory against the Cannibals, dog meat.

When all had eaten their fill, the ceremonial dances began, with the women, as Champlain noted with some dismay, dropping their mantles and dancing naked. While they danced, Chief Tessouat wandered over to Champlain and suggested through the interpreter that he would be able to celebrate with them, if he joined them in battle. "You must do this," Tessouat said, "in order to please us."

In 1608, when Champlain had been back in the country for only a matter of weeks, Iroquet sent his son to scout out the French fortification and ordnance, and to sound out the French commander on the possibility of a military alliance. Champlain didn't make a commitment at the initial meeting, but he listened with great interest to the suggestion that it was essential to any future trade that the river be kept clear of Mohawk raiders.

When his son reported back to Iroquet that Champlain seemed interested in close relations with the people of Tenakìwin, Iroquet himself headed down the river. Champlain welcomed him respectfully, and listened while Iroquet explained that the river was too dangerous to carry large-scale trade, since the Mohawk made regular forays up from the south along the River of the Iroquois to launch attacks on Algonquin traders. They could strike the traders on the way down to Kebek to steal their furs, he said, or they could hit them on their way back to steal their trade goods. What Iroquet proposed was that Champlain and his soldiers undertake a joint campaign with Iroquet's people and their allies that would drive the Mohawk to the south, far into Kanienke. With the promise of acquiring a monopoly on the Tenakìwin fur production, Champlain agreed. The attack was set for the following summer.

After Iroquet left Kebek, he stopped briefly in his village on the Ottawa, then continued up the river on a six-hundred-mile journey to consult with his western allies, the Wendat, on Georgian Bay.

On his way, Iroquet stopped to visit the Algonquin tribes along the route: the Matouweskarini thirty miles upstream; the Keinouche, living near the site of modern-day Ottawa; Tessouat's Kichesipirini, who controlled the upper river and levied a toll on all who passed; and the Ottagoutouemin, who lived near the juncture of the Ottawa and Mattawa rivers. After paddling up the Mattawa to Lake Nipissing, he stopped for a long consultation with the Nipissing people, who were closely related to the Algonquin but had been falling under Wendat influence, to the point of adopting many Iroquoian customs, such as the Feast of the Dead. Their support, which was readily offered, was key to his plan for a new alignment of forces in the St. Lawrence/Great Lakes region.

After consulting the Nipissings, Iroquet left their country, paddling along the French River to Lake of the Attignawantan (Lake Huron), named for the leading nation in the Wendat Confederacy. From there he headed south to the Penetanguishene peninsula, the western homeland of the Wendat Confederacy, which was made up of four Wendat-speaking nations — the Attignawantan (Bear Nation), Attigneenongnahac (Barking Dog Nation), Arendarhonon (Rock Nation) and Tahontaenrat (Deer Nation).

Iroquet's people were most closely aligned with the Arendarhonon Nation, which had arrived in Georgian Bay only in 1590. They are said by today's Wendat to be made up largely of the Stadaconans who left home after the upheavals of the mid-1500s, so the relationship between the Arendarhonon Wendat and the Weskarini Algonquin may extend back to the time when they were neighbours along the St. Lawrence. When he arrived on Georgian Bay, Iroquet went to the southern Arendarhonon capital of Cahiagué, to see his friend, Ochasteguin.

Cahiagué was an impressive town, with a population of somewhere between three and six thousand. It was fortified by a massive palisade that enclosed the village, in the middle of which was a large plaza paved with stones. The walled city was surrounded by more than a thousand acres of cornfields.

By this time, the Wendat were aware of the European presence from the trade goods that were beginning to reach them. Ochasteguin listened closely to Iroquet's account of the fortified post at Kebek, the European weaponry and the discussions with Champlain.

In the complex political situation in the Great Lakes/St. Lawrence region at that time, there were many strategic implications — economic as well as military — to an alliance between the Algonquin, Wendat, Innu and French against the powerful Five Nations Confederacy, which controlled most of the lands to the south of Lake Ontario. Over the winter, Iroquet and Ochasteguin discussed them not only with the headmen of Cahiagué, but in other Wendat towns and cities across the peninsula. Few could find a reason to object to an expanded military and trade alliance, since the French were safely camped six hundred miles away, in someone else's country.

Among the Wendat, the main issue became how to regulate the potential trade among their own four peoples. Over the winter's discussions, the Attignawantan, the leading trading nation in the Wendat Confederacy, asserted its right to manage the trade. This dispute would be resolved two years later, when the Arendarhonon accepted the title "Initiators of Trade with the Iron Men" while the Attignawantan quietly took control of its operation.

After the initial trade discussions, the winter of 1608–09 passed pleasantly enough. Iroquet stayed over at Cahiagué until spring break-up, enjoying the winter festivals, the days and nights of gambling and the deer hunts in the rolling hills above Lake Simcoe.

This was in stark contrast to Champlain's winter in Kebek. Europeans were still mystified by scurvy, but Champlain's own theory was that it was caused by "eating too much salt food and vegetables, which heat the blood and corrupt the inward parts." His suggested cure of eating lots of fresh meat ensured that eighteen of his twenty-four men came down with the disease. By the end of May, ten of them had died, along with two others from dysentery. With Duval's execution and the carting off of three others to Europe for hanging, that left only eight of Champlain's men alive after the first winter of his command. In France, Canada was getting a deservedly gruesome reputation as a land to which many sailed, but from which few returned.

Iroquet and Ochasteguin's journey from Georgian Bay in the late spring of 1609 took on the form of a procession. Ochasteguin brought with him only a small number of fighters and a number of traders and their families. But as they travelled south and east to meet Champlain, Algonquin villages along the way sent local fighters and traders to accompany them, until, by the time they reached the Lachine Rapids, there were almost three hundred people travelling in fifty canoes.

They ran into Champlain and a group of French reinforcements from Tadoussac near the Batiscan River, sixty-five miles west of Kebek. The French commander was surprised when the Algonquin and Wendat party insisted on continuing downriver to visit his trading post before heading to war. They spent almost a week feasting there, holding friendship ceremonies and trading with the French, while Ochasteguin had an opportunity to inspect the French fort and weaponry. When both he and Iroquet were satisfied that they could have confidence in Champlain and his men in the upcoming battle, the multinational force of Algonquin, Wendat, Innu and French broke camp and headed upriver.

When they reached the River of the Iroquois, the traders and their families left the war party to continue home to their country. Misunderstanding this, Champlain thought they were abandoning the fight and accused them, in his journals, of cowardice. But these were not warriors; they were traders who had only intended to go to Kebek to shop.

The fighters continued up the River of the Iroquois and the battle took place deep in the heart of Kanienke, at the mouth of the river at Lake George. It began one evening when Ochasteguin and Iroquet's forces spotted a Mohawk war party on the river. The Mohawk paddled quickly to the shore and began erecting a rough barricade while the allies set up camp on the opposite side. It was too late in the day for an attack, so two Mohawk warriors paddled across the river mouth to suggest they put off the fight until morning. Both sides spent the night drumming, singing war songs and hurling insults across the river, with many of the veterans knowing their opponents by name and reputation. Like so much else in the ancient countries, war was an intimate act — a personal contest of courage and honour as much as a struggle for territory.

But the encounter that morning near Lake George was like none they had seen before. When the allied forces approached, the Mohawk, a people known for their courage, left their barricades to prepare to fight in the open. But then Champlain stepped forward and fired his arquebus. In a thunderous instant, two of the leading men were killed. Other Frenchmen began firing from the trees. It was the Kanienkehaka's first contact with Europeans since Cartier had spent a few hours at Hochelaga seventy-four years earlier, and nothing in their lives had prepared them for that explosive reintroduction. Their formation broke, and when they fled into the forest, Champlain pursued them and "laid low several more."

The allies celebrated their victory that evening. A dozen prisoners had been taken, and the sacrifice began with the setting sun. A fire was lit and each fighter took a brand and burned the flesh of one of the prisoners. They tore out his fingernails and applied the torches to his genitals. Then they scalped him, poured burning spruce gum into the wound. Champlain observed that while the victim occasionally uttered strange cries, "he bore it so firmly that one would have said he felt no pain."

Champlain finally offered to shoot the man to put him out of his misery. The allies resisted, since ritual required that the prisoner be kept alive until dawn. But finally they decided that since the Frenchman had played such an important role in the battle, he should be allowed to practise his own customs on the first prisoner. Apparently, that custom was to step up and blow the man's head off with an arquebus shot. After Champlain had dispatched him, the allies cut out the victim's heart and tried to force the other prisoners, one of whom was the victim's brother, to eat it. As Champlain noted, "they refused to swallow."

In his journal, Champlain, an old soldier, expressed offence at this brutality towards someone he considered a prisoner of war. As historian Bruce Trigger has pointed out, however, he likely wouldn't have been bothered if the torture had been enacted against someone accused of "treason, heresy or sexual deviancy." It wasn't the cruelty Champlain objected to, but the violation of the European codes of war.

While we were working on the research, I sent Wayne a folder on Iroquoian tortures, taken from the Jesuit accounts. He sent me back an account of drawing and quartering, which was a common practice in Europe during the same period. Those who received this sentence were hanged, then cut down before they were dead; while they were still conscious, their bellies were slit open, and their bowels pulled out and tossed into a fire. According to British law, it was decreed that "their heads then be cut off" and their body sliced into four quarters "to be at the King's disposal." Champlain's own grim measures against Duval, the traitor, had been a short form of this European ritual.

In the ancient lands, evidence suggests, the practice of torture began among the Iroquois seven centuries earlier and gradually spread to their immediate neighbours. Among Iroquoian peoples it was accompanied by elaborate rituals. When later missionaries asked the neighbouring hunting peoples why they practised the dark arts, their answer was simple: "Because they do it to us."

CHAPTER SIX

People of
the Longhouse

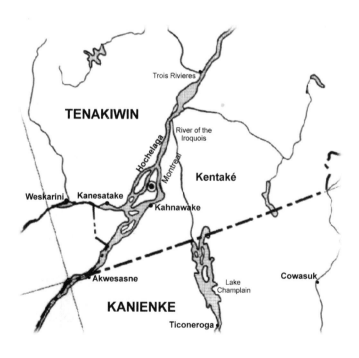

WHEN HE WAS LIVING IN OTTAWA, Wayne went out with a Mohawk woman who was working at the Assembly of First Nations, and they often travelled to Kahnawake on weekends to stay with her family. During that period, he said, he had developed a deep admiration for the Mohawk people. They had managed to keep their language and culture alive to a large degree, even though they lived just across the river from one of Canada's largest cities. They also had what seemed like an unshakeable pride in their Iroquois heritage, and many held to the belief that Kanienke, their homeland and the eastern door of the Iroquois Confederacy, would someday, somehow, rise again.

In the 1980s these feelings were particularly strong. The local economy was booming from the illicit cigarette trade, and a militant form of nationalism was growing under the guidance of Karoniaktajeh (Louis Hall). Hall had founded the Mohawk Warriors' Society in the 1960s and served as its philosophical leader and main strategist until his death in the early 1990s. His works included *Rebuilding the Iroquois Confederacy* and the *Warrior's Handbook*, which contained the Warriors' ten commandments. The commandments urged the young men to "Be Brave and Fearless for there can be no peace on earth for those who live in fear." They also warned them to "Respect nature's law of Self-Preservation and stop any traitor seeking to destroy you and your people." The slogan for the Warriors' Society was equally forthright: Peace, Righteousness, Power.

Wayne said he noticed the growing influence of the Warriors' Society during his New Year's visits to Kahnawake, where it was a long-standing tradition to fire rifles into the air at midnight. In the mid-1980s, the *feu de joie* had consisted of scattered shots from a few dozen .22s. But each year the number and the calibre of the rifles had increased. By 1987 you could hear the reports of larger-calibre semiautomatics. The following year, the air rang with the rattle of automatic rifle fire. By New Year's Eve 1989, the cold night air exploded in a cacophony of ordnance that included assault rifles and .50 calibre machine-guns.

The following summer, two Mohawk communities, Kahnawake and Kanesatake, were under siege, ringed by armoured vehicles, razor wire and thousands of Canadian soldiers and provincial police officers.

The so-called Oka Crisis had begun innocuously enough that spring with Mohawks and environmentalists blocking a side road to the Oka municipal nine-hole golf course, adjacent to Kanesatake. The Oka town council intended to expand the course to eighteen holes by cutting down a large stand of pines and moving a small cemetery. The pines were on land claimed by the Kanesatake Mohawk and the cemetery was their burial ground. The blockade remained peaceful, almost unnoticed, for four months, until the Oka mayor called on the Sûreté de Québec, the provincial police, to intervene. In response, the people of Kanesatake called in the Warriors. For three days armed Mohawk slipped into the forest and took up positions behind the barricade.

Before dawn on July 11, 1990, the police massed on the nearby highway. At six a.m. they fired concussion grenades at the native protesters, who included women and children. Panic caught hold when the grenades exploded. No one knows who fired the first shot, but within moments the police and Mohawk were in a fierce gun battle. One of the police officers, Corporal Marcel Lemay, fell, mortally wounded. By this time the police, surprised by the intensity of the return fire, were also in disarray. They gathered up their fallen comrade and made a hasty retreat down the hill towards the town. The Mohawk used the police's front-end loader to overturn an abandoned police cruiser and build up a new barricade on the highway. When news spread to Kahnawake, the Warriors quickly blocked Mercier Bridge, a central artery onto the island of Montreal. All this happened on the morning of July 11. Not until late September would the rifles be laid down and the barricades dismantled.

For the Mohawk Warriors it was a heady time. Behind the barricades, they were exuberant at having defeated the Sûreté de Québec, and two weeks later at finding themselves standing down the Canadian army.

I was covering the conflict for a national magazine, and during a rainy night in a plastic-covered foxhole I chatted with one of the young Mohawk, who went by the unusual *nom de guerre* of 7 Eleven. He'd chosen the name, he said, because he spent most of his time hanging out at the convenience store at his home in Akwesasne. He was only fifteen years old, but he said he saw this as just one battle in a long war. What they were going to rebuild, he said, was an Iroquois state that would stretch from the St. Lawrence across the old Kentaké plain and into the Mohawk Valley in upstate New York. I asked him about the Warriors and about Louis Hall. He told me that some people believed Karoniaktajeh was the reincarnation of Dekanawida, the law-giver of the Five Nations. "I'm not sure if it's true," he said, "but that's what some people say."

By the summer of 1990, the Iroquois had been living under Dekanawida's Great Law for more than five and a half centuries. His thought had not only revolutionized the political alignment of forces in the region by giving birth to a powerful confederacy; it had also reverberated in Europe centuries later, when European political philosophers like Jean-Jacques Rousseau were casting about for a model for a democratic state to replace the divine right of kings and the rigid class systems of Europe.

Dekanawida was born sometime around 1400 in Ka-ha-nah-yenh, a Wendat (Huron) town on the north shore of Lake Ontario near present-day Kingston. At the time, the Iroquois nations to the south of the Great Lakes, the Mohawk, Cayuga, Oneida, Onondaga and Seneca, were at war with one another as well as with the Wendat to the north and the other smaller Iroquois nations to the west.

Dekanawida, whose name means Two Rivers Flowing Together, is said to have begun life in messianic fashion, with a virgin birth. In a dream after she became mysteriously pregnant, Dekanawida's mother was told that her child would leave the Wendat to live among the enemy Flint People (Mohawk), and that he would be recognized as a great man. But as Dekanawida grew, the people of Ka-ha-nah-yenh watched him develop into a peculiar young man who seemed lacking in the social graces the Wendat were known for. He spoke with a directness that the people around him found disconcerting, and he appeared to live by no counsel but his own. So it was almost with relief that they learned he intended to leave them to go live among the Mohawk on the south side of the Beautiful Waters (Lake Ontario). When he said he would cross the lake in a stone canoe, they were convinced the young man was mad. Even if he made it to Kanienke, he would face almost certain death at the hands of their Mohawk enemies. But Dekanawida shrugged off their warnings and set off across the lake.

Mohawk fishermen discovered the young Wendat a short distance from their village, sitting under a tree, smoking his pipe. They fetched their headmen, who came to question him. Dekanawida answered all their questions with his usual directness. When they asked who he was, he said he was a Wendat from Ka-ha-nah-yenh, the son of a virgin woman.

When they asked him why he had come to Kanienke, Dekanawida launched into a strange speech. "The Great Creator from whom we all are descended sent me to establish the Great Peace among you," he said. "No longer shall you kill one another, and nations shall cease warring upon each other. Peace and comfort are better than war and misery for a nation's welfare."

The words struck a chord. The wars between the five Iroquoian peoples to the south of the lake were not only inflicting terrible wounds on each nation; they were also leaving them at the mercy of the Bark Eaters (Adirondacks) who surrounded them. But despite the obvious wisdom of his words, there was something preposterous about a young man from an enemy nation appearing out of nowhere to lecture them about how to manage their affairs.

After conferring for a moment, the headmen decided to put this strange man from the enemy nation to death. He was told to climb a tall tree standing beside a great waterfall. When he reached the top branch, the young men chopped it down. Dekanawida was hurled over the edge of the gorge and disappeared into the angry waters.

The next morning the Mohawk saw smoke curling up from the chimney of one of the guest cabins outside the gates of the town. When some of the young men poked their heads in, they found Dekanawida hunched over the hearth, cooking his breakfast.

After performing such a feat of survival, he was permitted to take up residence among the Kanienkehaka (Mohawk), and he continued to spread his teachings among the Iroquoian nations. His message was taken to heart by Hiawatha, an Onondaga chief who had lost his seven daughters in war. When Hiawatha told Dekanawida his story, the Wendat prophet listened sympathetically. "Dwell here with me," he said. "I will represent your sorrow to the people." Together, the Wendat exile and the Onondaga chief began to spread the Great Law of Peace among the five nations, which included, along with the Kanienkehaka (People of the Flint) and Onondaga (People of the Many Hills), the Seneca (People of the Mountain), Cayuga (People of the Landing) and Oneida (People of the Standing Stone).

The Great Law not only dealt with the need to end the constant warfare among the five nations, but also codified Iroquoian democratic principles and set up a detailed structure for the federation. In Iroquoian tradition, land ownership belonged to the women, and political power ultimately resided with the clan mothers. It was they who were responsible for placing the deer antler crown on the hereditary chief's head, and in the case of wrongdoing on his part they had the power to dehorn him (remove him from office). But along with hereditary chiefs, Dekanawida's system made provision for the emergence of Pine Tree Chiefs, men of talent and wisdom who sprang from the people and were given equal place at the chiefs' council with the hereditary chiefs.

While each nation retained its independence, Dekanawida placed the five nations within a common government, symbolized by the longhouse, with the Seneca guarding the western door, the Mohawk guarding the eastern door and the Onondaga, in the middle, designated as keepers of the council fire. The Cayuga and Oneida were "little brothers" of the Confederacy. This Five Nations parliament met on a regular basis, and between sessions the chosen representatives, or sachem, held local meetings to discuss the issues of the day within the nation and individual clans. The Great Law also decreed that whenever an important issue arose, or the people were faced with a situation that threatened their security, a general council of all the citizens of the nation must be called. Their decision would be final.

While the establishment of formal democracies came quickly to the Rotinohshonni, the process of actually merging the five nations was slow and difficult. Initially the Mohawk and Oneida came together in the east, and the Seneca, Cayuga and Onondaga in the west, but the Confederacy remained weak and uncoordinated. The importance of strengthening it was hammered home in 1570, when Iroquet's people swept down from the north, razed Hochelaga and drove the Mohawk deep into the heart of Kanienke. After this, the Five Nations pledged an all-out effort to join forces and enforce the Great Law, not only among themselves but among all their neighbours.

Front-line peoples like Iroquet's Weskarini Algonquins had reason to fear this new Iroquois resolve. As is often the case, democratic principles at home are not necessarily reflected in policies abroad. The Bark Eaters would have a place in the Confederacy, the Five Nations decided, but it would be as suppliers of meat, hides and northern manufactures. They would be given almost nothing in the way of political rights. To their fellow Iroquoian people — the Wendat, Attiwandaronk, Tionontati and Erie, to the north and west — the Five Nations would be more generous. They could be admitted to the Confederacy, but would not be given a vote at council because they, "not knowing all the traditions of the Confederacy, might go against its Great Peace."

In both cases, once the Great Peace was established, the Five Nations war chief would "cause all the weapons of war to be taken from the nation." In this way, the nation would "observe all the rules of the Great Peace for all time to come."

To bring the "rebellious" neighbours to heel, the diplomatic strategy of the Five Nations would begin with speaking quietly and end, literally, with a big stick. If a neighbour refused to submit to the Great Law, its leader would be invited to a council where the Iroquois war chief would stand up and three times repeat the offer. If the third request was met with refusal, the "War Chief . . . shall bound quickly forward and club the offending chief to death." That act would signal the beginning of a war to enforce the Great Peace on the offending neighbour.

By the time Samuel de Champlain arrived on the St. Lawrence in 1608, the Five Nations were in a period of expansion. They had not yet re-established their northern capital at Kawennote Tiohtià:ke, but they had driven Iroquet's people and the other Algonquins out of the St. Lawrence Valley. As it turned out, French fire power would only stall their advance.

In the morning we drove from my house at Senneville, on the western tip of the island, along Lakeshore Road, which skirts the shore of Lake St. Louis to its discharge at the Lachine Rapids. We parked on the riverside road and followed a muddy trail to the shore. The rapids have been called Lachine since the mid-1600s, when René-Robert Cavalier de La Salle passed through on his quest to reach China by an overland route. Even in the late seventeenth century, almost two hundred years after Cabot's landing, Europeans were still unsure of where they were in the world.

When Champlain visited the rapids during his brief upriver reconnoitring mission from Tadoussac in 1603, he said that he "never saw any torrent of water pour over with such force as this. . . . it descends as it were step-by-step; and wherever it falls from some small height, it boils up extraordinarily."

In some places the rapids stretch a mile across, and they thunder downriver for more than ten miles, from the first steep ledge at the east end of Lake St. Louis to the basin near Nuns' Island, where their rage gradually subsides.

We had walked along the turbulent waters for half a mile when we came upon a Mohawk fisherman, who looked to be in his sixties, casting from a large, flat stone projecting into the rapid. When we approached, he pointed to a three-foot-long, snakelike fish tethered to a stringer in a quiet pool. It was a sturgeon, recognizable by its flat head, brown scaleless skin and large feelers protruding from the side of the head. Sturgeon, which can grow to a length of six feet or more, were once plentiful in these waters, and were prized for their roe as well as their flesh.

"I've been fishing here for forty years," the man said. "I haven't caught one of these in more than twenty years."

Seeing Wayne leaning over to examine it, he flipped the sturgeon onto its back, exposing its white belly and sucking mouth. "They're the oldest fish in the world," he said. "As old as dinosaurs."

There was an old Mohawk legend about the sturgeon that Longfellow had written about in *Hiawatha*. It began with Hiawatha challenging a great sturgeon to take his line. After being taunted for several minutes, the fish struck, breaking the water and swallowing

Hiawatha and his canoe in one bite. They tumbled down the rapids with Hiawatha inside, beating his fists against the massive heart of the fish, until the fish was forced to cough him up.

The Mohawk people appeared to have adopted Hiawatha's strategy. From the jutting rock on the rapids, we could see the steel frame of the Mercier Bridge cutting through Kahnawake territory. Dekanawida had warned that great trials might be ahead for the People of the Longhouse. In his parting speech, he said that if they abandoned the Great Law, "the white panther (fire dragon of discord) will come and take your rights and privileges away and you will be reduced to poverty and disgrace" and other nations would say scornfully that the Iroquois were "a proud and haughty people once." But Dekanawida also had a warning for the mockers of the Confederacy. Before they've gone too far, he said, they will find themselves "vomiting blood."

CHAPTER SEVEN

Beyond the Rapids

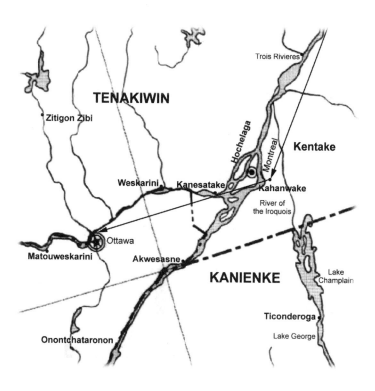

IROQUET KNEW OF THE POWER of the Five Nations, and he feared it. Since the great Algonquin victory of 1570, the Confederacy had been relentlessly pushing its way back into the north seeking to reduce Tenakìwin to a Five Nations protectorate. But when Iroquet first turned to the Europeans to help fend them off, the arrangement he sold to his fellow Algonquin leaders, and to Ochasteguin and the Wendat, did not include the newcomers moving inland past the Lachine Rapids. It was expected that they would remain based at Kebek, using their advanced weaponry to help keep the river clear of Iroquois raiding parties, while native traders met them at the rapids in the spring and summer, or at the Kebek post in the fall.

The first breach of this plan came in 1610, when the allies amassed at the mouth of the River of the Iroquois, and Champlain insisted that one of his young men be allowed to accompany Iroquet into his country for the winter.

By this time Champlain was a little clearer on the concept of combining trade, friendship ceremonies and military activities, so he came to the rendezvous, on a large flat island at the mouth of the River of the Iroquois, with four pinnaces loaded with knives, axes, kettles and decorative goods. Iroquet and Ochasteguin still hadn't arrived from Cahiagué, but before Champlain's ships were unloaded, an enemy war party was spotted upriver. This time the Mohawk, caught by surprise, were trapped inside their makeshift fort. In a short, fierce battle, Champlain was lightly wounded by an arrow in the neck, but once again French firepower played a decisive role. After the Algonquin fighters breached the Mohawk barricade, Champlain told his allies to stand back so he and the other Frenchmen could engage in a kind of turkey shoot on the trapped enemy, so they "might have their share of pleasure."

In the end, fifteen Mohawk were taken prisoner; the rest were killed by "arquebuses, arrows and swords," or drowned in the river while trying to escape.

Iroquet and Ochasteguin arrived the following day and were disappointed at having missed the second allied victory in as many summers. Champlain was pleased to see them. After a day of Indian fighting, he was ready to get down to the business of trade. Taking the Algonquin chief aside, he made the proposal of sending one of his young men, Étienne Brûlé, to spend the winter with Iroquet's people to learn the language and the lay of the land beyond the Lachine Rapids.

Iroquet's immediate response was to tell Champlain, diplomatically, that he would not oppose such a request, but that he had to consult the other Algonquin and Wendat leaders. Their first reaction was a firm no. Permitting the Europeans past the Lachine Rapids into Tenakìwin and beyond had never been part of the deal. They sent Iroquet back to Champlain with the excuse that they feared that, if any harm came to Champlain's emissary while he was in their care, it might jeopardize their friendship.

But Champlain was adamant. It was not like "a brother or a friend," he said, to deny such a request, particularly when it was made for the purpose of increasing their friendship.

Champlain had put them in a spot. The past two years had shown the usefulness of European trade goods, and of the French military alliance for keeping the river clear of Five Nations raiding parties.

After a final consultation, Iroquet stepped forward and announced to Champlain that he would take the young Frenchman into the country with him, but that in return Champlain was asked to take the younger brother of Tregouaroti, a Wendat chief, back to France for the winter. Champlain agreed, and eighteen-year-old Étienne Brûlé and the young Wendat, who became known as Savignon, were brought forward to exchange places. When they parted, Savignon headed east to Kebek and on to Paris. Étienne Brûlé, a farm kid from Champigny, a small peasant village south of Paris, headed west to the unknown lands beyond the Lachine Rapids.

Étienne Brûlé had arrived at Kebek with Champlain in 1608, when he was only sixteen, and had survived that first disastrous winter when scurvy, dysentery and executions almost wiped out the company. Since then, he had been trained as an interpreter, spending most of his time living with the local Innu at Kebek, learning their language and customs so he would be in a position to promote trade.

Now that he was heading upcountry, beyond the mighty rapids and into unknown lands, Champlain's instructions were more explicit. Brûlé was told that he must also observe the country, its rivers and transportation routes; locate any Indian mines and "if possible, make your way westward to the great lake [Huron] and on your return make a good report of what will be useful to us."

Brûlé's first trip into the country began with a full day's portage of canoes, sleeping mats, cooking implements, weapons and the newly acquired trade goods along the ten-mile length of the Lachine Rapids. It was late afternoon when the Algonquin and Wendat party finally floated their canoes in the calm waters of Lake St. Louis. There was only enough time left in the day for the two-hour paddle to a campsite at the tip of Montreal island, along a flat section of land just above the small St. Anne's Rapids.

While the canoes were being unloaded, not far from the terrace where we had had dinner with Betsy, a few of the men headed out to fish. Others set out to find quick-burning wood for the cooking fire, while the cook headed into the nearby bush to retrieve birch-bark containers of ground corn that had been stashed at selected spots on the downriver run.

By the time the cook had recovered the food, the fire-maker had the tinder smouldering and the first armfuls of dry wood were being added. Food was still prepared in the old way of heating small stones until they were red-hot, then dropping them into a birchbark container of water until it was gradually brought to a boil. Cornmeal — as well as fish, meat, wild vegetables, whatever was available — was added, making a kind of all-purpose porridge which the Wendat called *sagmité*. This had been their travelling food for centuries, and it was increasingly becoming the travelling food of the people of Tenakìwin, who traded for Wendat corn and had begun planting small cornfields of their own.

It was while they were eating supper on the narrow beach that Iroquet came over to speak with Brûlé. The young Frenchman was surprised when Iroquet told him that they were not going to spend the winter in Iroquet's village, as Champlain had been led to believe, but were going to Ochasteguin's country on the shores of Lake Attignawantan (Lake Huron), six hundred miles away. This had apparently been the plan all along, since the young man exchanged for Brûlé was Wendat, not Algonquin. Neither Iroquet nor Ochasteguin had volunteered this information to Champlain.

When darkness fell, the travellers lit smudges to keep the mosquitoes at tolerable levels and climbed under their canoes to catch a few hours of sleep. It was still dark when Brûlé awoke to movement around him. The canoes were being loaded. The Algonquin and Wendat were on the Ottawa River before dawn, to begin the three-week journey, that included thirty-five portages, to Lake Attignawantan.

By late afternoon they reached the twelve-mile-long shallow rapids the French called the Long Sault, which could be traversed using ropes to drag the canoes through the most turbulent patches.

While they worked, sentries were posted to watch for Five Nations war parties, which had in the past surprised a number of Weskarini travellers by lying in ambush on the ridge above the riverbank. When they finally cleared the rapids, they were only a few hours' paddle from the Weskarini summer village.

Word of their victory against the Mohawk and their acquisition of a large haul of trade goods from Champlain had preceded them, and they were met at the mouth of the Rouge with much ceremony. The feasting and dancing and storytelling lasted three days. On the third evening, when the celebrations were beginning to wane, Iroquet told young Étienne Brûlé to prepare to leave at first light.

By the time the sun had fully risen above the horizon, Iroquet, with Brûlé and a small group of Algonquin, and Ochasteguin and his Wendat soldiers and traders, were on the river for the long journey through Tenakìwin to Georgian Bay. The first night, they camped at the mouth of the Gatineau.

The next morning they reached Rideau Falls, named for the curtain (*rideau*) of water that drops into the Ottawa from a height of thirty feet. In the old tradition, each of the canoe crews tried to paddle through the narrow space between the rockface and the cascading waters without getting drenched.

These curtain falls marked the beginning of a stretch of river that was among the wildest, most beautiful and most spiritually significant anywhere in the ancient lands. It was the gateway to the lands of the great manitou, or spirit, Nana'b'oozoo, which stretched for almost a thousand miles, to the western shore of Lake Superior, where Nana'b'oozoo is still said to lie in the middle of a nine-hundred-year sleep. Among the Algonquins, and all the Anishnabe peoples, Nana'b'oozoo held a special place. He had taught the people many of the skills they needed to survive in the country, and had given them the gift of tobacco. But he had also re-mained with them to help in their battles with the Weendigos, who brought madness and starvation. He was not always successful, since he had human failings: he could be impulsive, arrogant and afraid. But his failings only endeared him to the people, and gave them a rich source of instructive and often amusing stories.

Even before they arrived at the Rideau, they could hear the roar of what Iroquet told Brûlé was the Asticou, the Boiling Kettle, where the waters tumbled out of the north and crashed through a series of whirlpool basins that were topped by rising circles of mist. The basins were said to have been formed by Nana'b'oozoo's footsteps when he was (according to various stories) either chasing off the Weendigos or being pursued by them.

Because of a jutting point at the base of the Asticou, paddlers could make their way to within reach of the spray by hugging the north shore. The portage began with a steep, almost hands-and-knees crawl up the slippery rock face. But after the canoes and supplies were laboriously passed up to the ridge, it was a short carry along the edge of the falls to the spot where a stone effigy of Nana'b'oozoo stood in the middle of the onrushing waters with arms outstretched in supplication.

In the summer of 1609, Brûlé became the first non-native to witness the gift-giving ceremony. A wooden platter was passed around, with each man pulling a few finger-widths of tobacco from his pouch. When all had made their contribution — including Brûlé, who had adopted the smoking habit during his two years with the Innu — the collector took the plate to the edge of the cliff face and tossed the offerings into the rushing water in the direction of the stone effigy. With Nana'b'oozoo's needs met, the travellers sat down to smoke their own versions of the *panaugun* (pipe) Nana'b'oozoo had given to humans. For travellers, it was said, the gift of tobacco to Nana'b'oozoo, and the ceremonial smoke, brought a safe and profitable journey.

If it had been a longer flight, we probably wouldn't have left Montreal that day. On the tarmac at St-Hubert a light rain was falling from a leaden sky. Mount Bruno was in sight to the south-west, so visibility was more than the minimum three miles. But beyond that the land dissolved into a gauzy curtain of mist. It was the type of day when pilots say that it's better to be down here wishing you were up there, than up there wishing you were down here. But Ottawa was less than a hundred miles to the northwest, over terrain I knew well, and we had arranged to meet the national chief of the Assembly of First Nations, Ovide Mercredi, early the next morning, so we decided to take off to see what *up there* looked like.

It seemed flyable. Barely. To stay under the broad, flat stretch of stratocumulus cloud, which weather radar showed covering the land for almost five hundred miles in every direction, we would have to fly at fifteen hundred feet, five hundred feet below the minimum altitude for overflying populated areas. So we skirted the towns, heading west over the large farmers' fields at the northern edge of the Kentaké plain. When we passed the end of the island, we swung north over the western shore of Lake of Two Mountains to the mouth of the Ottawa. Wayne struggled to pick out landmarks in the small semicircle of land visible in front of us. He would spot a tiny section of railway track, what looked like a power line running just beyond the edge of the gauze curtain, roads crossing and disappearing into the mist, a shoreline that might be the lake or the north channel around Salaberry Island.

I radioed ahead to Ottawa International Airport for the field conditions. A French-accented woman's voice responded. It was overcast, she said, winds calm, visibility five miles in light rain. But at 1700 Zulu (one p.m. local time) they were forecasting the possibility of heavy rain with visibility temporarily dropping to one to three miles. Our ETA was half an hour before that. We pressed on.

The lake narrowed into the river. We passed the Carillon Dam, where the Long Sault rapids once tumbled in a twelve-mile stretch of wild water but now lie quietly behind the turbines, waiting to pass through the concrete flow-way.

A few minutes past Carillon, we were across from the site of Iroquet's village at the mouth of the Rouge, which was protected by a small archipelago and a long sandy point. Just past the Rouge, the Ottawa River bends to the east, and we began to pass over the broad section of the Ottawa Valley which, in another century, was stripped of its valuable white pine forests and sectioned into the small irregular farm plots that formed a soggy patchwork below us. Wayne searched the fields for landmarks. He found none, so we departed from our charted route to follow the twists and turns of the river.

When Ottawa tower radar identified us as thirty miles out, we both noted an element of concern in the air traffic controller's voice. She said that the rain over Ottawa International was heavier now, with visibility slipping to three miles, the minimum allowed for visual flight plans like ours. I asked Wayne to check the chart for an alternate airport. He said Gatineau was closest, and began looking up runway data in the bulky Flight Supplement manual.

Then the world disappeared. We were engulfed in the gauze. When a small aircraft like ours flies into cloud, the procedures are clear: note your heading and the reciprocal, and make a one-minute, twenty-degree turn, which should get you back to clearer flying. But my mind, as well as the plane, was wrapped in the fog. I began to turn without settling on a direction, and I turned more sharply than I should have. The nose dropped. I raised the nose and the wing dropped. I raised the nose farther and the speed began to drop. I lowered the nose, still without straightening the wing, and we dropped three hundred feet before I raised the nose again. And all the time we were still turning blindly, engulfed in the cloud. The woman was watching this performance on the radar: a pulsating dot going in circles, with altitude slowly bleeding away. There was alarm in her voice.

"Have you lost VFR, sir?" she asked.

"Yes," I said.

"Straighten it out," Wayne said. We were still turning.

I didn't respond right away. I was still trying to get back into level flight. "Straighten it out," he repeated, this time more insistently.

I straightened it out.

It was now raining heavily in Ottawa, the woman told us. Visibility was down to one mile. I asked for field conditions in Gatineau.

"Five miles in light rain," she said, and gave us a heading. I turned onto it, continuing to scan the instruments as we flew through the cloud. For a moment there was no sensation of moving; we were suspended in the gauze. Finally Wayne said, with palpable relief, "I can see the river." We still had no forward visibility but we could see below.

As we crossed the Ottawa, conditions improved slightly. It was still raining hard but we could see the airstrip ahead. I pulled off the power and put on full flaps to make a steep descent, and we touched down more than a third of the way along the runway.

While we were unloading the gear, Wayne said, "Good job." It was a generous statement. I had come close, in the first few minutes, to losing control of the airplane. From the tone of her voice, I knew that the air traffic controller had been aware of this. The blip on the screen had been showing all the signs of a blinded airplane tumbling into a spin at an altitude too low for recovery. When I dream of plane crashes — which all pilots do — they are always in these conditions: confusion in a cloud, a wing dropping, a spin, a spiral dive, like a tern plunging for a fish. But unlike the tern, the airplane does not rise again.

From Gatineau I called Ottawa tower to close my flight plan and I was surprised when the same woman answered the phone. "It was pretty bad conditions for VFR," she said reproachfully. "You should check the weather more carefully."

On our way into town, I asked Wayne about our interlude in the cloud. "Were you worried?"

"I'm surprised," he said, "that you've gotten us this far."

The rain let up later that afternoon, and Wayne and I went down to the river, where a half-mile or so of the ancient portage can still be found. Along the way, we stopped at the Asticou on the Ottawa side of the bridge, just beyond the Parliament Buildings. Today much of the Asticou's legendary force has been harnessed by a hydroelectric dam that spans half the river. But even at one-tenth their former power, the falls are impressive. The rushing waters, filtered through giant turbines, still thunder over steep ledges and swirl in the boiling kettles at the base of the falls before crashing into Devil's Hole.

The surviving section of the portage lies across the bridge, on the Hull side, along a hundred-yard-wide strip of bush between a set of railway tracks and the cliff running along the edge of the Upper Chaudière Rapids. It took us twenty minutes to find the trail, which over several millennia, had been worn into the granite by millions of footsteps. When we stopped for a smoke at a point where the trail travelled along the cliff's edge, Wayne said he was surprised that there was nothing around the Asticou, or Chaudière, or here on the ancient trail, to indicate that the river and the trail had been important passageways in the old countries. "Especially in Ottawa," he added, "where the government puts a plaque on anything that doesn't move."

He took out another cigarette, emptied the tobacco into his palm and tossed it into the fast-moving river. It was carried swiftly between the two sets of rapids, passing over the stone effigy of Nana'b'oozoo, now submerged under the backwash of the power dam.

In the morning we stopped off at the Assembly of First Nations office, on the edge of Ottawa's typically tidy and well-ordered market district, to see Ovide Mercredi. Wayne had worked at the AFN with Mercredi in the early 1980s. He said he had always found him a complicated character who combined a strong inclination towards spirituality with a talent for cold and calculated backroom manoeuvring. Lately Ovide was being forced to rely on both sides of his personality, as he fought to control ideological splits in the Indian movement. On one side was a small radical element, like the people behind the Oka and Gustafsen Lake shootouts, which tended to see men like Mercredi as sellouts who played by the white man's rules. On the other side were a series of powerful regional chiefs, generally from the wealthier reserves, who had decided that it made more sense for them to deal with the government directly than through Mercredi's organization. Mercredi's response to the militant side had been to preach Gandhian nonviolence; to those who wanted to make concessions, his message was "no surrender." The result was political paralysis. In his television appearances recently he had looked haggard and defensive, and at one point he had blurted, to the surprise of his allies and the delight of his enemies, "I am becoming irrelevant."

When we arrived at his large L-shaped office that morning, however, Mercredi was upbeat. He was just ending a meeting with a group of Northern Ontario Cree who had come to see him about a local grievance, and as he ushered us towards his large oak desk he said, "Sovereignty, sovereignty, everyone wants sovereignty. Except me." He smiled. "I am sovereign."

After Wayne introduced me, Mercredi picked up a small stone from his desk and showed it to us. "What do you see?" he asked.

Wayne squinted and stared at the vague markings on the stone. "A buffalo?" he guessed.

"Right," Mercredi said. Then he rotated it. "And now?"

Wayne stared for another long moment, then gave up.

"It's an elephant," Mercredi said. "See? There's the trunk."

He had found the stone along a Lake Winnipeg beach, and said it had presaged his visit to India, which had been covered in the national press as a pilgrimage to Gandhi's birthplace, but made fun of in native circles as Mercredi looking for Indians, any kind, to take him seriously. While he and Wayne chatted about the India visit, I glanced around the room, which was filled with fine native North American artwork. On the floor in front of his desk was a square red cloth with a glazed clay smudge-pot used in sweetgrass-burning ceremonies.

Wayne told him about our trip. When he mentioned the Cabot quincentenary and the planned government celebrations, Mercredi thought for a moment, then said that he believed we were on the verge of a new era, "when the indigenous peoples, not just in Canada but around the world, are going to stand up and demand their rights. And they're going to get them. Sooner or later, oppressive regimes always collapse."

But the longer he spoke, the more his initial sense of optimism about the First Nations marching off together to their singing tomorrows faded away. He spoke about the Canadian government with bitterness for its refusal even to discuss what he called "the big questions," the sovereignty of First Nations on Canadian territory. "The government only cares about the big companies, the banks, profits," he said. "They want to turn our homelands into real estate."

Mercredi then admitted that this was a road some of his own people were willing to take. A few of the regional leaders were quietly signing agreements that gave up a measure of sovereignty in return for local economic benefits. "Our people don't understand what they are giving up when they sign," he said. He pointed to the portrait of the legendary Cree leader Big Bear on the wall beside his desk. "Big Bear refused to sign," he said, "and it's because of leaders like him that we still have our rights."

It was clear that Mercredi had made this plea many times before, but that it was falling on deaf ears. Wayne had heard rumours that many of the most powerful chiefs were organizing against Mercredi for next year's election.

On our way out, I mentioned to Wayne that I'd noticed two books pulled out of the extensive library against the back wall of Mercredi's office. On his desk was a paperback copy of a Hindu spiritual guide with a bookmark from a local esoteric bookstore. On the coffee table in the side room was Pierre Vallières's *White Niggers of America*, a Québécois revolutionary tract. Wayne had noticed them as well. "Like I said, Ovide's a complicated guy. But then, Indian politics is a complicated game. It's always been that way."

That evening we had dinner at a Chinese restaurant in Ottawa's market square with Chief Manny Jules and Grand Chief Blaine Favel. Both were in their forties. Chief Jules, a friend and colleague of Wayne's, led the Kamloops band, the largest and wealthiest

Secwepemc (Shuswap) community, located across the South Thompson River from the city of Kamloops. Blaine Favel was the leader of the powerful Federation of Saskatchewan Indian Nations. He was also, I learned that evening, the great-grandson of Big Bear.

The dinner-table conversation was about business more than politics, although these two chiefs suggest there is little difference between the two. For them, the business of native politicians today lay in building economies for their nations. For that you had to be prepared to make the type of deals that Mercredi saw as a surrender. The economic engine that fuelled Favel's political dealings were the casinos that the Federation of Saskatchewan Indian Nations co-managed with the Saskatchewan government, bringing the federation millions of dollars a year which it distributed to the chiefs of the province. This wealth put the federation in a privileged position in relation to the impoverished organizations in the rest of the country. But Favel was unapologetic.

"The Saskatchewan chiefs are loyal to the federation," he said, "because it puts cheques in their hands." Later, when he spoke about applying to hold the Aboriginal Summer Games in Saskatchewan, he said that his chances of winning them were good because he'd "backstopped his bid with casino money."

We spoke for a while about his famous ancestor, Big Bear, Mercredi's personal hero and probably the greatest Indian leader of the nineteenth century. Big Bear refused to sign a treaty that surrendered his people's land to the Dominion government, and he was imprisoned for his part in the 1885 Northwest Rebellion.

Although it might not appear so at first glance, Favel said at the end of the evening, what they were doing — trying to create First Nations wealth — was simply carrying on Big Bear's work in a new era. "You can't have self-government if you are begging at someone else's table."

When the waiter came with the bill, we reached for our wallets. Chief Favel waved us off, tossing his American Express Gold Card into the tray.

After Iroquet and Ochasteguin left the Asticou, they passed through another series of rapids to Lac des Chênes, where they took a shortcut, leaving the Ottawa River as it swung in a large bend towards the north, and cutting across a series of twelve small lakes that emptied back into the Ottawa through Muskrat River. Allumette Island was just across the narrow channel. This was the land of Tessouat's Kichesipirini Algonquin. On his way to Ochasteguin's country the previous summer, Iroquet had spent many hours with Tessouat, the one-eyed chief, discussing the potential Algonquin/Wendat/French alliance. He was not surprised to find Tessouat, who was known for his fierce independence, reluctant to endorse the deal.

With their summer village on Morrison Island, at the head of a narrow set of rapids, Tessouat's people controlled much of the trade along the upper Ottawa. In most cases this meant charging tolls to traders who wanted to pass, but in some cases, when they suspected travellers were trying to cut into their own trade with northern peoples, they simply refused access. This is what they had traditionally done to the Wendat, who were heavily involved in northern trade through their dealings with the Nipissings.

Iroquet's argument that the great increase in river traffic between the French and the Wendat would pay handsome dividends to the Kichesipirini finally convinced Tessouat to give his reluctant approval to the alliance.

As Étienne Brûlé discovered when he arrived in their village that summer, the Kichesipirini Algonquins were already a prosperous people. They grew some of their own corn and tobacco despite the difficult climate, and they had at their disposal the fish stocks from the river and the rich hunting grounds to the north of the Ottawa, where they spent their winters. They carried on a considerable trade in manufactured goods with peoples farther north, and gained luxury goods from the travellers' toll. In addition, they were living far enough in the interior of Tenakìwin that Five Nations attacks on their villages were rare.

In his wanderings around the village, Brûlé was most impressed by the elaborate cemeteries. The gravesites were marked by large, decorated wooden crypts. In these ancient countries, honouring the dead and easing their passage to the other side remained one of the chief duties of the living. But among the Kichesipirini the death rites had sparked a flowering of artistry, with many of the larger crypts displaying finely carved wooden bas-reliefs of the faces of the deceased.

The travellers stayed around the village for several days, enjoying the break from paddling and portaging, and from the monotonous travel food. When they finally left the island, Tessouat was there to see them off. He watched as the paddlers took up the rhythm that was as natural to them as breathing. As they slipped into the predawn shadows, the one-eyed chief apparently still had misgivings about the new alliance. His future actions would show him to be a reluctant partner at best. But it was an indication of the balance of power at the time that Tessouat was concerned not with the handful of European traders he'd first encountered at Tadoussac seven years earlier, but with the growing power and influence of the Wendat, who had already built a lucrative trade network based on exporting their corn to the north and east. The Europeans were feared only because they might increase the power of the Wendat.

Journey to Lake Attignawantan

T HERE ARE DAYS when flying is perfect. When we arrived at the Gatineau airport, the sun was only half risen over the hills; the air was still, with not a breath of wind, and the sky was a deep, cloudless blue. We took time with the walk-around, checking ailerons, fins, rudder, cables, engine oil and fuel. These mandatory routine checks are important not only because you may spot something that could cause you grief in the air, but also because they put you in the right frame of mind for flying — one in which you absorb everything around you. You are continually checking altitude, pitch, speed through the air mass, ground-speed, engine RPMs, the shape and height of clouds and the ground below, where your charted track is being traced or, in aviation jargon, "made good." A pilot friend describes flying as a mind-emptying yogic absorption exercise, made more interesting by the fact that, if you lose your sense of equilibrium, you crash.

The temperature was rising quickly that morning, so we taxied to the end of the strip with the doors open, using the propeller as a cooling fan. We spun around to face the six thousand feet of runway, and moments later we were airborne. The air was as smooth as a northern lake at dawn, and it seemed as we climbed that we were the only ones in the sky.

Wayne glanced at our route map. "Only three thousand miles to go," he said. At that moment, as we began a shallow turn to the right to pick up our heading, I would have been happier if he had said thirty thousand.

We passed to the north of the city and followed the river over two slender lakes, Lac des Chênes and Lac des Chats. In just under three hours we would be landing for refuelling in North Bay, the city where I grew up. Then we would cross Lake Nipissing, pick up the French River and follow it to Georgian Bay, the site of the old Wendat empire.

I asked Wayne if he wanted to take over the controls. While he piloted, I lit a smoke and poured us a couple of cups of donut shop coffee from the thermos. We passed over Grand Calumet and Allumette islands, Tessouat's Kichesipirini territory, where people had been living for at least five thousand years. What we saw from the air was the gradual narrowing of the Ottawa Valley into a slender point, until the steep granite walls shouldered up to the edge of the river to form a canyon. We were back over the Canadian Shield, the same rocky, hummocky land mass we'd overflown on Quebec's north shore and left behind as we dipped into the Laurentian and Ottawa valleys.

When we reached the forks of the Ottawa and Mattawa, we were over country I knew from boyhood. Here the Ottawa swings northward to its source at Lake Timiskaming, while the thirty-five-mile Mattawa River connects travellers to its source at Trout Lake. As a child I had gone fishing for speckled trout in the Mattawa's swift waters with my father. When I was older, I camped at the river mouth and explored downstream with my friend Jack. Along its course the Mattawa tumbles over fourteen sets of small rapids, most of which can be mounted in a canoe by poling along the shallow shore.

That was how it was done in Iroquet's day. During the July 1610 trip, he told Étienne Brûlé about two special features of the river. One was at the midpoint, where the granite walls are cut by a series of deep caves. These caverns were said to be dangerous places inhabited by a particularly vicious beast with sharp teeth and razor-like claws that leapt out of the darkness and devoured anyone who approached the threshold. Prudent travellers, including the voyageurs who came later, always gave the caves a wide berth. It wasn't until the 1970s that archaeologists discovered that the mythical beasts had been protecting an ancient ochre mine.

The second feature was near the source of the Mattawa, on one of its broader sections; a curious alignment of stones across a shallow rapid allows you to virtually walk on the water. As a kid we called these the Stepping Stones. In Tenakìwin they were known by the same name, and were said to have appeared out of the waters to allow Nana'b'oozoo to cross when he was fleeing a pack of Weendigos.

Trout Lake, where I'd spent most of my early summers, passed beneath us. The steep hills ringing Four Mile Bay are formed by the mouth of an ancient volcano that is almost as old as the earth. When we were young, we believed its depths were unfathomable.

North Bay, on the shores of Lake Nipissing, was already in view, with the airport located on a steep ridge overlooking the city. Wayne handed over the controls and we began our descent.

While the Cessna was being refuelled, I took a walk to the end of the ramp. The city and the lake were spread out below. Looking east, I could see the section of Timiskaming highway, just outside of town, where my family used to live in a small yellow brick bungalow. Corpus Christi school was just over a mile away, and my sisters and I reached it by hiking along a trail through the bush. The school was over half native, with kids bused in from the Nipissing reserve in a rusty old schoolbus with broken windows. The advantage for us was that on the thirty-below-zero winter mornings, when the Indian bus wouldn't start, our school closed for the day.

When I mentioned the school to Wayne, he was curious about what we had thought of the native kids. I remembered only that, although we were far from wealthy, we considered them poor people, and that my mother occasionally gave our old clothes to the church, which distributed them to the kids on the reserve.

But there is something, I told him, that I always find strange about my childhood recollections of native people. When my friend Jack and I camped on the island at the mouth of the Mattawa, we knew this was the old canoe route and we spent many hours looking for arrowheads and romanticizing over the Indians who had once paddled these waters. Then I would go to school on Monday morning, to a class that was over half native, and I don't recall ever making the connection. The ancient peoples had long since disappeared, and all that was left were some brown people who often turned up at school wearing my old clothes. They seemed as out of place as gypsies. In our history lessons we studied the kings and queens of England, the plagues and wars of Europe and the discovery of North America by John Cabot. When the bell rang, the gypsies got back on their battered bus and trundled away.

Thirty years later, I had only one lingering connection to the city, or rather to a small piece of it. My father lies in the cemetery at the bottom of the airport hill. After his death, all of my family had left the city, scattering themselves between Montreal and Winnipeg. In the same way, the bones of my grandmothers and grandfathers were spread between Quebec and British Columbia. As I stood on the hillside it occurred to me that for the people of these lands, most of whom kept up an intimate and lifelong relationship with their dead, such a haphazard scattering of ancestral bones would have seemed frightening, would have robbed their lives of an important source of meaning. It wasn't until many years later that I realized the obvious: it was we who were the gypsies. The kids on the bus were living in their homeland. They not only knew of the stepping stones, they knew about Nana'b'oozoo. The story was one of many that marked and illuminated their ancestral land. For the people of the city, the land had no existence before the passage of the eighteen-year-old Brûlé in Iroquet's canoe. It had no history until the lumbermen cut their way up in the second half of the nineteenth century.

But by the time of Brûlé's arrival, this was already an ancient country. Lake Nipissing, below, had been lined with villages. It was reached by a long, muskeggy portage from Trout Lake that crosses a geographical divide. On the Trout Lake side, the waters flow towards the Ottawa and the St. Lawrence. On the Nipissing side, they flow southwest into Georgian Bay.

From the head of the Nipissing portage, it was only a short paddle across the bay to the main town of the Nipissing people. When the canoes were pulled up on the sandy beach, the Arendarhonon Wendat and Iroquet's Weskarin Algonquins were given a warm welcome by virtually all of the old town's eight hundred residents. The locals were eager to hear about the summer campaign against the Mohawk, who occasionally launched attacks as far inland as Nipissing country, and about the new alliance with the French. They listened carefully as Iroquet spoke of the joint military campaign with Champlain, and were somewhat startled when Iroquet then produced Étienne Brûlé, the first white man they had ever seen.

While the villagers examined him, with the usual combination of fascination and dismay at his strange colour and hairy face, Brûlé noted that Iroquet and the Nipissing leaders switched into the Wendat language when Ochasteguin was present, a sign of the relations among these countries. The Wendat were the regional power, so their language had become the language of trade and diplomacy.

The Nipissing were closely related to the Algonquin, but were distinct enough to be considered a separate people. Part of their difference came from the fact that they had adopted many of the Wendat customs. They wintered among the Attignawantan Wendat, and worked in close partnership with them in the northern trade. Like the Kichesipirini, they grew some of their own corn and tobacco, but they went further by holding Iroquoian-style Feasts of the Dead.

They also had some defining characteristics. Brûlé had been told by Iroquet that they had special powers in dealing with the spirit world. This belief was shared by all their neighbours, and for a time even the French referred to them as the Sorcerer Nation. (One missionary observed that, apart from their unfortunate habit of conversing with the Devil, they were a charming and courteous people.) As Wayne pointed out, their spiritual gifts could be a two-edged sword. Neighbouring peoples would sometimes pay the Nipissings to perform some sacred rite on their behalf. But at other times, when a string of bad luck hit and the neighbours were looking for a scapegoat, they could always turn around and accuse the Sorcerer Nation of performing black magic.

When they left the Nipissing village, the Wendat and Algonquin paddled across the wide, shallow lake to the western shore and the source of the seventy-mile French River, where it begins its rapid descent to Lake Attignawantan (Huron). The downstream trip, with a strong current pushing the canoes westward, was usually made in a day. Ochasteguin and his people were now just 175 miles from their home along the eastern shore of Georgian Bay. In the morning they pressed on, weaving among the bay's myriad islands from well before dawn to well after sunset. On the final day they broke camp just after two a.m. and paddled non-stop for twenty-three hours, arriving on the stony beach at the tip of the Penetanguishene peninsula in the moonlight of the following night. The exhausted travellers carried their canoes across the beach to the edge of the trees, tumped the trade goods to their foreheads and hauled them up the trail that wound along the sloping ridge to the walled city. Their arrival at Toanche was announced by the barking of dogs, then by excited voices. Fires were lit for a celebration. The Wendat traders and warriors had come home.

Étienne Brûlé was surprised to find himself in a bustling town of two or three thousand people. In the morning cooking and smoking fires burned under thatched rain shelters. Women ground corn into flour with stone pestles and stone wheels, tended char-coal fires beneath giant racks lined with curing fish, or crafted pot-tery and fired it in stone kilns. Old women and men whiled away their final summers in the shade while children occupied them-selves with a play version of life.

As Brûlé headed across the town square, he passed several dozen other longhouses and numerous outbuildings — guest houses, smokehouses, the steam-bath hut, the shaman's hut. In the middle of the square was a tall, decorated central pole, around which town assemblies were held and important announcements made. On the far end were drying racks for bear, beaver, deer and wolf pelts, a large storage area for spare longhouse and palisade poles and a special pit where the remains of slain animals could be given a respectful burial. Beyond this was an extensive garden with row on row of tobacco plants, which were too valuable to be grown out-side the town walls. If he had climbed the palisade's ramparts and looked out he would have seen hundreds of acres of cornfields, interspersed with beans and squash.

Toanche was one of the Wendat's main trading centres, but it was only one of more than a dozen towns on the peninsula, many of them considerably larger. They were linked by over two hundred miles of trails, and the total population of the peninsula has been es-timated at somewhere between thirty thousand and fifty thousand.

To the southwest of Huronia lay the Tionnontaté (Tobacco) Nation, an Iroquoian people allied with the Wendat. Between the Tionnontaté and the Five Nations were another Iroquoian people whom the Wendat called the Attiwandaronk, People Who Speak a Slightly Different Language. Europeans called the Attiwandaronk the Neutral Nation, because they avoided getting drawn into the battles between the Wendat and the Five Nations to the south. To the immediate north and west of Huronia lay the lands of the Anishnabe hunting peoples: the Algonquins, Ojibwa and Odawa.

What first struck Brûlé, as it did so many visitors to Iroquoian countries, was the abundance of naked human flesh. In summer the Wendat men wore only breechcloths, while the women wore skirts but were naked from the waist up. Europeans with a strong Christian background, like Champlain, generally professed to be offended by this practice, but many of the men found reason to spend an unusual amount of time visiting the villages.

Europeans also commented on the physical and social gracefulness of the people. Champlain described the Wendat as remarkably well proportioned, strong and robust. Father Gabriel Sagard, a Récollet missionary who arrived in Huronia in the early 1620s, marvelled at their good health and the almost complete absence of the crippling diseases that were common in Europe. Father Jean de Brébeuf, a Jesuit missionary who joined Brûlé in Toanche in the 1620s, described the Wendat as having "splendid," energetic bodies, but he was even more impressed by their manners.

"Among themselves," he reported, "the Indians are entirely courteous and polite. There is a genuine civility in their relations with one another. They never interrupt one another, never try to interject themselves into a conversation, never raise their voices, never show anger, never insult one another and always listen patiently to whoever is speaking." Another Jesuit visitor described the Wendat manner in terms of the nobility of the portraits of Roman emperors by classical painters. In their presence, the nervous, chattering Europeans often felt that they themselves were like noisy children — something the Wendat occasionally rebuked them for. Champlain described the Wendat as "happy," although he still found them "wretched" because of their nakedness.

Differences notwithstanding, the land of the Wendat was, like France, first and foremost agricultural. One modern horticulturist has estimated that the people grew fifteen to seventeen kinds of maize, sixty kinds of beans and eight kinds of squash. They also gathered thirty-four kinds of wild fruit, eleven kinds of nuts and fifty other wild foods.

But they were essentially a people of the corn. Around their towns and villages, in late summer, cornstalks waved in the breeze as far as the eye could see. As with the Maya three thousand miles to the south, corn festivals filled the social calendar and there was a complex system of rites and taboos to encourage the crop's health. A good corn harvest guaranteed a winter of ease; a bad one could mean a winter of hunger or even starvation.

It was the women who worked the land and gathered the wild foods. Land was passed down from mother to daughter, and women controlled everything to do with food — including the right to withhold it from any man who displeased them. This was accepted as only natural; in producing children and corn, women were the heart and soul of the community.

At some point soon after his arrival, Brûlé settled in with an adoptive family in Toanche. In midsummer he joined the men in the nearby forest for several weeks of cutting and burning, part of the continuous clearing operation to prepare the site of the next village. Because of soil depletion, the village and cropland were moved every ten to fifteen years. This required an enormous clearing and construction operation that began almost as soon as the people moved into the current village.

In the late summer, Brûlé accompanied the other young men on war parties into the lands of the Five Nations. In the early fall he went with his adoptive family to cabins on the islands on Lake Attignawantan (Georgian Bay) where fishing camps were located. Later in the fall he joined the deer hunt, when hundreds of people — men, women and children — headed to the deer fences in the Collingwood Hills. Animals were rounded up in narrowing enclosures for slaughter for their hides and winter meat. When the previous summer's crops had been good, winter was a time for games (including a version of ball hockey on ice), stories and social visits from town to town, or farther along the road, to friends and relatives living with the Tionnontaté or Attiwandaronk.

In spring the Wendat traded their remaining corn stocks for furs that northern peoples or middlemen traders brought down from their winter trapping. When the furs were amassed and bundled, it was again time to prepare for the journey east to trade them for axes, knives and kettles from Champlain and the other Europeans, who met them at the Lachine Rapids. The next time Champlain saw "his lad," as he called Brûlé, was at the rendezvous at Lachine in 1611. By this time the French teenager was naked too, except for breechcloth and moccasins, and seemed to have slipped comfortably into the Wendat rhythm of life.

Brûlé was not alone. To the surprise of Champlain and the leaders who followed, North America held a powerful attraction for Europeans. Father Sagard noted that Europeans were drawn to the native way of life far more often, and with more enthusiasm, than indigenous North Americans were to European ways. When Savignon returned from Paris for the 1611 rendezvous at Lachine, he described Europe as a strange and uncivilized land and, like almost every other North American who visited there, expressed no wish to return. Brûlé, on the other hand, had no hesitation in returning to Wendat country — as he would almost every year for the next quarter-century. In the end, when he was forced by the changing political and military threat to choose between Huronia and France, he didn't hesitate. He chose Huronia.

The tiny Huronia airport terminal shimmered in a heat mirage and the thermometer on the post outside read a hundred degrees. On the way up to Awenda Park at the tip of the peninsula, where we would be spending the night, we stopped near Midland at the Martyrs' Shrine, the main tourist attraction of the region. On the steep hill behind the shrine, the federal government has erected a large two-storey viewing platform. At the base is a map of the canoe route from Quebec to Huronia, showing the trip made by "the missionaries and Champlain." Again, no mention of the people who broke the trail and had been using it for thousands of years.

Champlain visited Huronia in 1615, five years after Brûlé's arrival. From the top of the platform it is easy to see why he described it as a jewel of a land. It's cut by seven short rivers, clad with oak and maple forests and ringed by white, sandy beaches. From the top of the platform you can gaze across the Wye River valley all the way to Lake Huron's shores. To the southeast the land rolls, gently at first and then more dramatically, into the Collingwood Hills. To the west the heavy forests begin, and somewhere along those dark trails lie Standing Rock and the road that the dead took to the spirit world. Looking down the valley, we could just make out the shore of the peninsula where it runs into Penetanguishene Bay. That was the site of Carhagouha, the main town of the Attignawantan Wendat and the place where the first missionary, Joseph Le Caron, a Récollet, settled in the summer of 1615, while Brûlé was still living in the port town of Toanche.

In contrast to Étienne Brûlé, Father Le Caron came from an upper-class family; in fact, he was said to have personally given instruction to the young Louis XIII. French court life was apparently not the best training for a North American missionary, because Le Caron proved to be an utter misfit in Wendat country. His troubles began on his journey into the country, when the Wendat identified him as something of a sissy. In his letters home Le Caron wrote that he could hardly express his suffering on the journey.

"I had to keep my paddle in hand all day long and row with all my strength with the Indians," he wrote. "More than a hundred times I walked in the rivers over sharp rocks, which cut my feet . . . and in the mud, in the woods to avoid the rapids and frightful waterfalls. And the hunger. We had only a little *sagmité*, which was dealt out to us morning and evening."

According to Le Caron, he bore it all bravely because of the rich harvest of souls he anticipated. "Alas! such a great number of infidels," he exclaimed, "and nothing but a drop of water is needed to make them children of God."

When he arrived at Carhagouha, Le Caron insisted on living outside the walls of the town, so the men were forced to build him a special hut. The people were surprised at his antisocial attitude, and they were even more surprised when they found out that he was fervently and inexplicably celibate. The women appear to have been particularly intrigued by this, and soon discovered that a little suggestive flirting could throw the black-robed stranger into a prolonged bout of blushing and stammering.

Even though they found Le Caron personally ridiculous, the Wendat understood that he was a holy man, and they were interested to hear what powers he had. They asked Brûlé about him, but Brûlé, who had little use for religion, suggested that they pay no attention to him. When Le Caron later asked Brûlé to teach him the Wendat language, Brûlé taught him — much to the amusement of the townsfolk — a collection of Wendat expletives as the names of commonplace objects. The people continued the amusing practice until Le Caron complained to Champlain that "you can never know when an Indian is making a joke, telling you with a straight face some horrible obscenity when you ask the word for, say, the sacred chalice." Le Caron blamed Brûlé for turning the people against him, and accused the young man of setting a terrible example for the infidels by adopting their way of life when Le Caron's goal was to convince them to adopt European ways. Like every priest who followed him, Le Caron urged Champlain to eject Brûlé from the country. But in this instance, it was Le Caron who fled, heading back to Kebek after less than a year without having won over a single infidel.

Brûlé ran into trouble of his own in 1615 when he travelled with a Wendat war party to Susquehannock country, south of Iroquoia. The plan was to enlist the Susquehannock in a joint campaign against the Five Nations, with the Wendat armies moving down from the north and the Susquehannock moving up from the south. The Susquehannock took too much time raising their army, however, and by the time they reached the meeting place it was too late; the Wendat forces had already moved on. On the way back to Huronia, Brûlé was captured by a group of Seneca. According to his own account, the Seneca tied him to the torture pole in their village and began ripping his fingernails off, while he recited the only Christian prayer he could remember — grace. Before his tormenters could move on to more serious tortures, a Seneca chief stopped them. Brûlé later said it was because a clap of thunder had frightened them, but the suspicion among a few Wendat was that Brûlé had been cut loose after making a deal with his captors to open up direct French trade with them. Whatever the cause, he was released and made his way back to Huronia alone.

At first, Wendat suspicions about his release seem not to have been widely held, since Brûlé was still free to travel to neighbouring countries whenever he wished — a privilege rarely extended to Europeans until well into the next century. During the early 1620s he became the first non-native to visit Lake Superior, when he travelled to Agawa Bay, to ancient copper mines that had been in more or less continuous operation for over five thousand years. Father Sagard mentions that Brûlé brought back an enormous piece of pure copper as a souvenir from this visit.

Sagard had arrived in Wendat country in 1623. Unlike Le Caron, he must have come to some kind of understanding with Brûlé, since the interpreter spent time teaching him the Wendat language. While scandalized by the fact that Brûlé had taken a Wendat wife and occasionally offered tobacco sacrifices to Nana'b'oozoo, Sagard seems eventually to have accepted Brûlé for what he was — a man of two cultures, who increasingly preferred the indigenous North American one.

Sagard's sympathy for Brûlé may have had something to do with the fact that by 1626 both men had a common enemy: the Jesuits. After several years of intense lobbying in Rome and at the French court, the Jesuits had succeeded in getting a virtual monopoly on North American missions. They wanted Sagard out because he was a Récollet. They wanted Brûlé out because he was a source of contradiction to their teachings. Sagard returned to France to write scathingly of the Jesuits, and the Jesuits responded by completely eradicating him and the other Récollets from their histories of the New World.

We spent the night at Awenda Park, at the tip of the peninsula, near where Toanche had been located. The park was full of young campers up from Toronto to escape the heat wave. At dusk, the beer parties began and the music and voices grew louder. Things quieted after midnight as one by one, the young revellers passed out. But the music played on.

I got up with the intention of turning it off myself, but Wayne was already on the way over. I sat on the picnic table under the brilliant starlit sky and lit a smoke. The Milky Way, which was said to be the cluster of the Wendat villages of the dead, was in the west. The trail that led there passed through the Collingwood Hills to Standing Rock, where the mythical Oscotarach, the Head Piercer, removed the brains of the Wendat dead. They then crossed the deep ravine and climbed the far slope into the sky. It was a journey that was made in the 1640s by virtually the entire Wendat nation.

CHAPTER NINE

The Fall of Huronia

A LARGE CROWD of Filipino tourists stood in the beating sun in the parking lot in front of the church at the Martyrs' Shrine, keeping an expectant watch on the darkened doorway. Wayne asked an elderly man what they were waiting for. "Two o'clock," he said. "We have the church for mass."

The shrine is booked almost continually during the summer by religious pilgrims from around the world, usually bringing their own priest to say mass in their language in the church dedicated to the Jesuit martyrs of Huronia. Inside, the altar is flanked by two glass cases with cassocked mannequins representing Brébeuf and Jérôme Lalemant, surrounded by banks of flickering candles. The sign said they cost two dollars each to light, and the wall was covered with little notes of thanks to the martyrs for indulgences granted.

We were early for our meeting with Father Farrell, the Jesuit rector of the shrine, so we headed over to the restaurant next to the gift shop. It's called the Champlain dining-room, but the walls are decorated with photos from Pope John Paul II's 1984 visit to the site. Wayne observed that they should have named the restaurant after Brébeuf, the main course of history, or Lalemant, the side dish. Wayne is nominally Catholic, but very nominally. On his first day of school, his mother had taken him to a Catholic school, but at the sight of the stern-looking nuns in black robes he had reacted so strongly, crying and clinging to his mother, that she had turned around and taken him down the street and enrolled him in the Protestant school. Nothing since that initial encounter, he said, had improved his opinion of Catholic religious orders, or the faith they represented.

At two o'clock we headed to the shrine office to meet Father Farrell. A young priest showed us into a cool, spacious library. The old Jesuit arrived a few minutes later. He was tall, grey-haired, slightly hunched with age, and had an angular, impassive face. He shook our hands. "Haimila," he said. "That doesn't sound Algonquin." Wayne told him he was from the west. "McFarlane doesn't sound Algonquin either," the priest added with a smile. "Although around Temagami there are some McGregors." That was Brenda's last name, but Wayne didn't volunteer the information.

The priest eased his old bones into a cushioned chair. He told us that he had been director of the shrine since 1962, and had seen it grow from the little church built on the hill in 1926 into the Catholic mecca of gift shops, restaurant and theme gardens that it is today. "We have over 300,000 visitors a year," he said. "Pope John Paul said mass on the field behind us."

When he spoke about the early missions, Father Farrell's story was similar to the one I had learned at Catholic schools more than thirty years earlier. He spoke about the missionaries' grit in travelling across the sea to spread the Word of God in a tough and unforgiving land. "They were not weaklings," he said. "Brébeuf was a big man, over six feet tall. The people admired his strength." Father Farrell went on to speak of Brébeuf's ability to match Huron paddlers stroke for stroke and to carry more than his share over portages.

Wayne nodded. "You can't help but admire men like Brébeuf," he said. "But one thing I've never really understood is why, exactly, he and the other missionaries came here in the first place."

Father Farrell, who had devoted most of his life to keeping the martyrs' memory alive, looked surprised by the question. "For love of the people," he said. His words hung in the air for a moment. "The people had spiritual needs. And they wanted to learn. Men like Father Brébeuf were teachers."

The learning process was a long and painful one for the Wendat, and the pace of the lessons increased in 1626, when the Jesuits arrived to assert their spiritual monopoly over the New World. Father Jean de Brébeuf settled in Toanche, the same town as Étienne Brûlé.

It was a time when the priests were coming under suspicion from many Wendat, who thought they were involved in sorcery designed to weaken their people so they could be taken advantage of in trade. Proof of this seemed to come in the summer of 1626, when reports filtered back to Huronia that a French Récollet, Father Joseph Daillon, had installed himself in Attiwandaronk (Neutral) territory around the western shore of Lake Ontario, and was promoting not only the Word of God but the need for expanding French trade into the south. The Wendat headman, Aenons, feared that the next step for the French would be to open up direct trade with the Five Nations, so he sent emissaries into Attiwandaronk territory to spread the rumour that Daillon was a sorcerer who had come to spread death among their people. When the Attiwandaronk council did not immediately evict the priest from their country, Aenons hired a couple of local men to give him a beating. Father Daillon barely escaped with his life.

In the spring of 1627, Brébeuf too found himself in trouble with the Wendat. The conflict began when he hung a crucifix over the door of his hut. When the peninsula went through a long dry spell at the beginning of the planting season, the townspeople began to question whether the lack of rain had something to do with the garish and disturbing talisman the priest had hung outside his door. They requested he take it down. Brébeuf refused. When the drought continued, people began to argue for the ejection of the Jesuits from their country. More delegations were sent to speak to Brébeuf about removing the cross. He continued to refuse. With the soil baking in the July sun and the corn shoots dying of thirst, an angry crowd gathered outside Brébeuf's hut, demanding that he remove the cross. When he once more refused, some of the young men wrestled him to the ground, beat him and tore down the cross themselves.

Brébeuf was unfazed. The Jesuit booklet on North American missions warned that "all the fine qualities which might make you loved and respected in France are like pearls trampled under the feet of swine." His mission had been set out in the papal *Sacra Congregatio de Propaganda Fide*, which had declared a worldwide war on demons, which were seen as embodied in manitous like Nana'b'oozoo and the lesser spirits of the lakes, rivers and mountains that the people of the ancient land paid their respects to.

The beating Brébeuf suffered at the hands of the young men was insignificant. He was prepared to go much further to propagate the faith. During this period, he recorded frequent dreams in which he saw himself either nailed to a cross or carrying one. In one of these, the cross was a hundred miles high and he was almost as tall. The top of the cross reached into heaven, and his agony could be seen throughout the land.

"Brébeuf always had a sense he was going to die here," Father Farrell told us. "That's one of the things that make him so special."

When we left the rectory, we took a quick tour around the grounds, which had a ten-foot wooden statue of Pope John Paul II, statues to all the martyrs and a special Brébeuf garden where the missionary was depicted on his knees gazing up at a twenty-foot cedar cross.

While Jean de Brébeuf was waiting for his expected martyrdom, Étienne Brûlé was struggling to remain in the country. The missionaries ordered him to leave North America in 1625 for "immorality," which apparently meant integrating into Wendat life. But after arriving at Kebek, he feigned illness until the last ship left the port in the fall. The following year, the Jesuits succeeded in having him evicted. Brûlé arrived at Le Havre and spent the winter in Paris, but he found himself lost in France. At thirty-five, he had spent over half his life in North America. His wife and friends were in Toanche, and all his skills were from that world. In the spring of 1627, he turned up at the docks in Le Havre. Ships were being loaded with trade goods and supplies for the small colony on the St. Lawrence and the interior trade, and Brûlé bought his way aboard. In defiance of the Jesuits, he was going home.

Brûlé spent two more years in Huronia before he found himself caught up in the old European tribal conflict between French and British. In the summer of 1629, he travelled to Kebek with the Wendat trade convoy and found that the French supply ship had still not arrived. Champlain sent him and Nicolas Marsolet, the interpreter with the Nipissing, to Tadoussac for news about the missing ship. When Brûlé and Marsolet arrived in Tadoussac they discovered three ships in port: the French supply ship, now flying a Union Jack, and two British ships belonging to the Kirke brothers, British privateers.

When the British learned that Brûlé and Marsolet were upcountry fur traders, they told them that they were taking over the fur business on the St. Lawrence and would be ejecting all French officials, including the Jesuits, from the region. The two interpreters, the British promised, would be free to stay as long as they agreed to trade with the British. News that the Jesuits were to be expelled greatly pleased Brûlé, and he certainly had no desire to return to France. Huronia was his home; Europe felt like exile. So when the Kirkes left Tadoussac to seize Kebek, Étienne Brûlé and Nicolas Marsolet were piloting the British ships. When Champlain surrendered, the Jesuits, who were being loaded on board for transport to England, recorded the dockside encounter between him and his former lads. The French commander heaped abuse on them and threatened them with the noose. Brûlé replied that he knew he would be hanged if he returned to France, but that it was too late; "the thing is done. We filled this cup and we will drink it."

The British period on the St. Lawrence would last three years, and during that time Brûlé and the Wendat would continue to trade at the post at Kebek. The people of the ancient lands were at first relieved to have gotten rid of the French priests, but they soon discovered that the British were troublesome in other ways. Among their trade goods was alcohol and, although the Wendat themselves refused to touch the stuff, they watched in alarm as their Algonquin allies experimented with the mysterious drink, and as trading festivals degenerated into drunken brawls. More disturbing was the fact that, unlike the French, the British refused to patrol the St. Lawrence to keep it free of Five Nations war parties, which began once again to slip up the Richelieu River and raid Algonquin and Wendat trade convoys.

When news travelled to Huronia in the fall of 1632, that the British were pulling out and the French would be returning to the St. Lawrence in the spring, the change was greeted with relief. The imposition of the priests seemed a minor irritation in comparison to the troubles the British had brought with them.

But the imminent return of Champlain left the Wendat with a thorny diplomatic problem. What should they do about Étienne Brûlé? The headman, Aenons, began to ponder this during the fall. He knew that Brûlé had been branded a traitor, and that Champlain had threatened to hang him. But by this time Brûlé had been living in Huronia for almost twenty-five years, and had been adopted into one of the clans. Aenons' would have to proceed cautiously. He dispatched an emissary to Kebek to sound out the French advance team on their feelings about Brûlé. The French interlocutor was blunt: Brûlé was guilty of treason under French law; if Champlain got hold of him he would hang him or have him drawn and quartered like Duval. When Aenons was told of this, he immediately called a council meeting to discuss the matter.

Aenons began by saying that he had a real affection for Étienne Brûlé. In the past, Brûlé had paddled with him to Kebek, matching his stroke on the water, shouldering his canoe on the portages. But no matter what he thought of him personally, Brûlé was French, not Wendat. It would be very difficult to protect him against his own people now that the French had returned. Brûlé would almost certainly be forced to flee Huronia, and the only place he could go was south, to work with the British in their Five Nations trade. The mention of Brûlé and the Five Nations recalled the old suspicion that the interpreter had made a deal with the Seneca in 1615 to save his life. Perhaps, to rehabilitate himself with Champlain, he might even try to divert the Five Nations trade from the British to the French, threatening the Wendat's position as a regional power. As the discussion progressed, Aenons said he could see only one course of action.

Many at the meeting were taken aback by his proposal, but by the time the council broke up a decision had been made. That same day, two young Wendat invited Brûlé to go hunting with them. A mile or two down the trail, one of the hunters dropped back to check a deer print. Brûlé was found later with his skull crushed by a single blow from a war club — the method of execution the Wendat used on their own people.

When news of the execution reached the village, a couple of councillors feigned surprise and suggested that he must have been caught by a Seneca war party. But everyone in Toanche, and soon everyone in Wendat territory and into Tenakìwin, knew the truth. The reaction caught Aenons off guard. He had known that some of his people would be upset by the execution, but it soon became clear that many saw it as a calculated murder of one of their own.

Feelings ran so high in Toanche that, a few months after Brûlé's death, the village literally split in two. Brûlé's family and friends left to set up the town of Wenrio, a couple of miles to the south, and those held responsible for the killing built the new town of Ihonatiria, a few miles to the north. Nor was it just a local matter. The southern Wendat blamed the northern Wendat for the killing, and the Algonquin, many of whom had counted Brûlé as a friend, blamed the entire Wendat nation. At one point the Algonquin even threatened war to avenge Brûlé's death.

Within Huronia, a gut-wrenching national debate continued over what the people were giving up in exchange for copper kettles and iron axes. Aenons, it was said, had ordered Brûlé's killing to appease Champlain for the fact that the Wendat had traded with the British. Had they reached the point where they would sacrifice one of their own to the whims of foreigners — people who were generally felt to be inferiors?

The political turmoil continued into 1634, when Jean de Brébeuf returned to the country. He arrived at midnight, with a group of Wendat traders who had not only avoided speaking to him about Brûlé, but had left him on the beach at midnight without telling him that Toanche had split into two villages. When Brébeuf struggled up the path with his baggage, he found only a deserted clearing where the village had once stood.

After stumbling around in the dark, he heard dogs barking in the distance and headed in that direction, arriving at the village of Ihonatiria, where the people who defended Brûlé's killing had settled.

Brébeuf followed the continuing debate over Brûlé with a mixture of concern and fascination. In 1635, when a mysterious epidemic swept through the northern towns, he recorded that people set fire to their infected houses to halt the spread of the disease. It was widely rumoured, he wrote, that a European woman emerged from the smoke and crackling flames and, speaking Wendat with an accent very much like Brûlé's, scolded them for murdering her brother.

The Brûlé question returned in 1636, during preparations for the Ossassané Feast of the Dead. As the date approached, Aenons was pressed to consult Brébeuf about reburying Brûlé's bones in the ossuary that held the rest of the northern nation's dead. But when the southern Wendat heard about the request, they argued that Brûlé should more properly be buried at *their* Feast of the Dead, since it was they who had originally brought him to the country.

During the 1636 national council, feelings ran high. At one point a southerner said, in a whisper loud enough for Aenons to hear, that of course Aenons and the northerners should have Brûlé's body, since it was they who had murdered him. Aenons said nothing but was furious at the remark. Later he and the southern leader quarrelled about it. Finally, to prevent the dispute from flaring into civil war, the idea of reburying Brûlé was quietly withdrawn, and the Feast of the Dead went on without him.

When we left the shrine, we drove to the hills above Nottawasaga Bay, on the south shore of the Penetanguishene peninsula, to the site of Ossassané. The road hugged the steep escarpment, giving us a dramatic view of the white sand beaches and blue waters of Lake Attignawantan. When we had Yarwood Point in sight we pulled over, and Wayne spread out the archaeological and field maps on the hood of the car. They showed Ossassané somewhere along the ridge northeast of the point. The ossuary where the 1636 Feast of the Dead had taken place was northwest of the town. Wayne pointed to a trail that led through the dry grass meadow towards a stand of maples, and compared the terrain to the archaeological map. He pointed at the meadow. "That would have been the cornfields," he said.

The ossuary site was about half a mile along an overgrown path. There were no markers, but we could see the overturned, baked clay soil of the old dig. The heat was building and even the birds had gone deep into the forest to find shade; the only sounds were the chirping of crickets and the buzz of a few lazy flies.

Three hundred and sixty years before, almost to the day, this clearing had been filled with thousands of people celebrating the Feast of the Dead. The occasion was marked every ten to fifteen years, in conjunction with the rotation of the corn crops and the moving of the towns. For the Wendat, the feasts and the accompanying rituals were a way to both honour the departed and release their souls for the difficult journey ahead.

The 1636 Ossassané feast was the largest and richest in Wendat history. As was the custom, the ten-day celebration began with the retrieval of bodies from forest scaffoldings where they had lain in burial shrouds since the last feast. While the women carefully cleansed the skeletons, the men dug a massive pit, nine feet deep and fifteen feet wide, over which they constructed a scaffold ten feet high and fifty feet wide. The grave pit was lined with a thick mattress of soft, prime beaver pelts and scores of gifts. In 1636 these included metal knives, axes, kettles and copper-tipped or brass-tipped arrows, scissors, iron bracelets, metal rings and decorative glass, as well as more traditional grave goods like corn-grinding wheels, snowshoes, finely carved amulets and pipes, tobacco pouches and medicine bundles. An even greater amount of wealth was exchanged among the living, with some of the richest traders giving virtually all they owned to their less well-off friends and neighbours.

Several days of mourning were followed by several more days of gift-giving, and on the final day of the feast the bones of the Wendat were mingled in the common grave. This had great symbolic importance, since it represented the unity of the nation. The Wendat were one people on earth and they would remain so for eternity — farming corn, beans and squash, hunting, fishing and trading together, in the village of the dead. When the final sacraments had been administered, the pit was filled in and a roofed structure was erected over it. At dawn of the tenth day people drifted home, physically and spiritually exhausted but at peace. The great passage of the spirits was under way, and their loved ones would be waiting for them when they themselves made the trek to the other world.

It was a journey the Wendat were making in ever-increasing numbers. The epidemic of 1635 was only a beginning. Over the next five years, the Wendat suffered a massive viral assault. The diseases included measles, mumps and influenza — invisible and unintended killers that arrived with the supply ships. The Innu of Nitassinan would be struck down first; then the plagues travelled up the St. Lawrence with the traders and priests, infecting the Algonquin of Tenakìwin and the Nipissings — who in turn brought the plagues north into the James Bay country, known as Eeyou Astchee, to infect people who had yet to lay eyes on a European. From Nipissing country the diseases also moved west to Huronia, and from there they were passed on to the Tionnontaté (Tobacco), Attiwandaronk (Neutral) and Erie nations to the south. From Huronia, the regional trading centre, the sickness spread to the northwest by way of the Odawa traders, who carried in Wendat and Attiwandaronk corn into Lake Superior country to exchange for furs and traditional trade goods. The ancient trade routes, the foundation of the Old Order, were turned into roads of death.

In the six-year period between 1634 and 1640 as much as one half of the Wendat nation died from European diseases, with a similar toll being taken in all the countries between Nitassinan and the farthest reaches of Danaiiwaad Ojibweg on the western shores of Lake Superior. For several years the people of Huronia were too sick and weak to harvest the corn, which rotted in the fields. The Jesuits sought to profit from this by using food from their own gardens to entice the sick and dying to the faith. It was during this period that they had their first breakthrough. In 1637 Chiawatenha, a thirty-five-year-old trader, went to Brébeuf in a weakened state to offer himself for baptism, in the hope that the foreign rite would cure him of the foreign disease. When he did in fact recover, he declared himself a Christian and began working to convert his family and friends.

The Jesuit *Relations* tell us that while the Wendat were still dying in droves, Chiawatenha stood in the village square preaching that, just as the axes and kettles of the Europeans were superior to the Wendat ones, so was their sorcery. He invited his countrymen to join him in the faith and have their bodies, as well as their spirits, healed.

Most Wendat deeply resented this trumpeting of the foreigners' message at a time when the nation was suffering the greatest tragedy in its history. Besides, most had a much different interpretation of the Jesuits' role in the epidemics. They had seen families and friends dying horrible deaths from hitherto unknown diseases while the "Black Robes" hovered in the doorways, unaffected. They suspected that Jesuits like Brébeuf were not the cure for the sickness but, through their sorcery, the cause of it. Twice in national councils the question of expelling the Jesuits or putting them to death was debated, and on two occasions Brébeuf himself was beaten up by gangs of young men for practising black magic.

To the dismay of the priests, Chiawatenha and his immediate family remained their only true converts, after more than a quarter-century of missionary work. And Chiawatenha was coming under increasing pressure from his people to abandon the European faith. He was repeatedly warned by headmen and elders to desist from European sorcery, but he refused to listen, instead announcing to all that he was working to convert the nation. While the people suffered, he visited the Jesuit mission in Kebek and returned with a sack of human bones that the priests said were relics of Christian saints. The bones proved Chiawatenha's intent to work witchcraft against his people, and his fate was sealed.

On August 2, 1640, Chiawatenha went into the field with his nieces to harvest the first squashes of the season. While bending down, he saw shadows moving in a nearby maple grove. He told the girls to hurry home, then turned back to face his executioners. Even though he was now a Christian, he was still a Wendat, so he didn't flee. He was found later that day, with his head crushed like a squash.

As it turned out, Chiawatenha's death was a godsend to the Jesuits. To protest the killing, his outraged family and a number of his clan members defiantly joined the foreign cult. Still, Christianity would likely have remained marginal among the Wendat if the Jesuits had not finally hit upon an ingenious scheme. To attract important trading families to the faith, they offered not just eternal life in the future, but rifles in the present.

By the early 1640s, the plagues had passed and the nation was struggling back to health. Children were being born, fields were being tended, good crops were once again offering surpluses for the northern trade. But a new shadow was being cast over the Wendat nation from the south, where the Five Nations were building up an alarming arsenal of weapons from their freewheeling trade in guns with the British and Dutch.

Wendat war parties in Five Nations country were suddenly facing barrages of musket-fire. They asked the French traders to sell them similar weapons, but French policy only allowed weapons to be sold to Christian Indians. A number of young Wendat lined up for religious instruction so they could get guns of their own, but the majority stayed away. As the arms race between the Wendat and the Five Nations continued throughout the decade, the Wendat fell further and further behind. The Five Nations, who had no priests to contend with, had unrestricted access to British arms.

Well-armed Iroquois war parties began creeping north with greater and greater frequency. By the fall of 1647 they were preparing a vast pincer movement into the northern lands that would sweep into enemy territories around both the eastern and western shores of Lake Ontario.

The Wendat found themselves not only vastly outgunned, but dangerously divided between the small but increasingly powerful Christian minority and the frustrated majority. Tensions between the two grew to a dangerous level when, on orders from the Jesuits, the Christian Wendat began to withdraw from traditional rituals, including vitally important gift-giving ceremonies. The Christian traders were observed to be hoarding their wealth, and the result was bitter feuds.

The final destruction of the once-powerful Wendat empire began on March 16, 1648, when winter snows were just beginning to recede from around Taenhatentaron. The southern Wendat town was thinly populated that winter, because many citizens had fled in the fall when a massive Five Nations army was rumoured to be approaching from the south. Those who had stayed kept constant watch from the palisade platforms, and regular patrols scouted the surrounding woods. When winter came, with frigid temperatures and deep snows, it was decided that the rumours had been false. No army could travel long distances in those conditions. If an attack came, it wouldn't be until April or May, when the bush was clear of ice and snow. So on March 16 most of the people of Taenhatentaron spent the day outside the palisade, tapping and boiling maple sap to produce the annual sugar supply.

Sometime after midnight they were roused by barking dogs, but most rolled over and buried themselves deeper in their bearskin robes. Then a cry went up from the Iroquois — part of an invading army of a thousand fighters who had slipped through Attiwandaronk country and spent the winter north of Lake Ontario in preparation for this unprecedented late-winter attack. The invaders breached the palisade before most of the villagers awoke. There was an explosion of musket-fire, and within minutes Taenhatentaron was a Five Nations town.

The main Iroquois force continued up the peninsula. Before dawn the nearby St. Louis mission, where Brébeuf and Lalemant were now living, was also under Five Nations control. The priests were hauled out into the early morning light of the square, where they were stripped naked and their fingernails were torn out. Then they were dragged through the snow to Taenhatentaron, to face torture and death.

The most ferocious attacks came from Wendat who had surrendered to the Iroquois. They blamed the Jesuits and their sorcery for sowing disunity in the nation, and expressed their hatred by repeatedly pouring boiling water over Brébeuf's head in a mocking re-enactment of baptism. The priest, who had been dreaming of martyrdom for almost twenty years, died in a few excruciating hours. Lalemant, a recent arrival who excited less hatred, was even less fortunate. He survived into the next morning.

During the spring, the northern Wendat gradually gathered their forces and halted the Five Nations advance halfway up the peninsula. But throughout the summer of 1648, and into the following winter, repeated attempts to drive the Five Nations out of southern Huronia failed. When spring came, Five Nations raids were stepped up around the peninsula, and the outgunned Wendat fled to the protection of the best-fortified towns and villages. When food supplies ran out, they were forced to disperse, burning their towns so they would not fall into the hands of the Five Nations armies.

Some headed for the islands of Lake Attignawantan to try to survive on fish while they made their way to Ojibwa and Odawa towns at the head of the lake. A large group went south and sought refuge among the Attiwandaronk. A group of about five thousand Wendat left with the Jesuits for Christian (Gahoendoe) Island, just off the end of the peninsula.

The largest number of Wendat decided the best course of action was simply to surrender to the Five Nations. As it turned out, these were the fortunate ones. The Five Nations had moved north to get access to the beaver lands and to build their confederacy. The Wendat who surrendered were treated well and escorted south to resettle in Five Nations territory. In some cases, whole Wendat villages were kept together and allowed to integrate gradually into their new country.

The remaining few, the defiant ones who broke into small bands and tried to remain free in the forests of their homeland, were hunted down and killed. Huronia would not be allowed to rise again.

CHAPTER TEN

Unceded
Indian Land

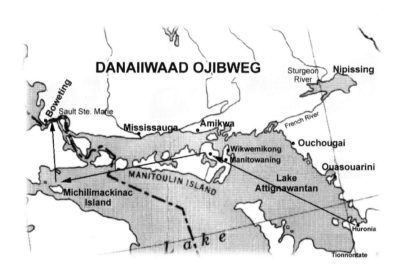

W E HAD BREAKFAST in a small café in downtown Midland, not far from the site of the old Wendat town of
Carhagouha. The heat wave was continuing. By nine
a.m. the temperature was already in the high eighties, and the entire peninsula was crowded with refugees from Toronto.

When Wayne had called Brenda the day before, she'd said
that they were having the same kind of weather in Kelowna. "Mid-
thirties every day for the past two weeks. Some kind of algae has
started growing in the reservoir, so the water out of the tap smells
like sewage. They're boiling it."

He lit a cigarette and the young waitress hurried over to tell us
we couldn't smoke. Breakfast was long in coming and the line of
people waiting for a table stretched into the street. Wayne recalled
Konrad Sioui telling us that the Wendake band council was arranging to send a group of Wendat here next year to hold a summer sol-
stice ceremony. "Some Wendat are even thinking of trying to move
back to the peninsula."

"It's pretty crowded here already," I said.

Wayne shrugged. "When you've lived in a place for thousands
of years, you don't easily give it up."

Especially when the actual leaving was a long, drawn-out agony.
In 1650 to 1651, the group of mainly Christian Wendat who had fled

to Christian Island with the Jesuits endured a hellish winter. The priests had brought enough mission corn to feed themselves but nothing for the people. At first the Wendat ate boiled acorns and roots to survive, but by early January starvation had set in. In desperation, a few small groups returned to the mainland to hunt. They were never heard of again. On the island, the deaths mounted. Many were forced to feed on the flesh of deceased family members. Only six hundred of the five thousand Wendat who had arrived on the island in the fall survived into spring. As soon as the ice left the lake, they began the long trek back to the St. Lawrence, to the old site of Stadacona, whence their grandparents and great-grandparents had departed seventy-five years earlier.

The Wendat were not the only people driven from their homeland in 1649 to 1650. The eastern pincer of the Iroquois attack had driven up the Ottawa River, causing the Algonquin to flee into the Gatineau Hills and northern Ontario bush. The invaders stopped to build a large fort on the Mattawa River, which they used as a forward base in their assault on Nipissing country. In the spring of 1650, the Mohawk swept across the La Vase Portage to Lake Nipissing to raze the villages that dotted the forty-mile shoreline. Those who survived the initial assaults fled up the Sturgeon River into the high country, where they remained exiled for two generations, aided by sympathetic Ojibwa and Cree. The Nipissing finally settled on the shores of Lake Nipigon, some six hundred miles to the west, and didn't filter back to their homeland until the end of the century. A Jesuit missionary who travelled east in the spring of 1651 with the six hundred Wendat refugees fleeing Christian Island wrote that Lake Nipissing, which had previously been lined with large villages, had become "nothing but a solitude."

The same fate befell the Wendat's Iroquoian neighbours. The Tionnontaté were overrun in the summer of 1649 by a second wave of attacks. Their fate was similar to that of the Wendat, with many killed in battle, many surrendering and being absorbed into the Five Nations and others scattering to seek shelter among allied peoples to the west. The same thing happened the following year to the Attiwandaronk to the south and the Erie to the southwest, with both nations suffering enormous losses before succumbing or fleeing. By 1651, virtually all the Iroquoian lands had been brought together under Five Nations control. The reach of Dekanawida's Great Law now stretched from just west of Kebek to the shores of Lake Erie, north to Georgian Bay and across southern Ontario to the St. Lawrence. This new, well-armed and organized land of Iroquoia, which was loosely aligned with the British to the south, was for the moment the greatest military and political force in North America.

We took a few minutes in the Midland café to look over the charts. That afternoon we would be flying to Manitoulin Island, where the Great Mystery — as the Ojibwa translate their word for the Creator (Kitchi-Manitou) — was still said to reside. The next day we would be heading to Sault Ste. Marie, where, in the late 1600s, the old Ojibwa capital of Boweting withstood the Five Nations attack and began to turn the tide of the war against the Iroquois.

When we arrived at the Huronia airport, Wayne noted that Charlie GUDD was listing oddly. "Looks like a flat," he said.

He was right. The beating sun had sweated the air from the port-side tire.

The terminal was new, built in the bright, functional style of Canadian government architecture, which made it indistinguishable from a passport or Revenue Canada office. The counterman asked what he could do for us. I asked him where we could get compressed air.

"Is that your plane?" He gestured to the lone, lopsided Cessna on the ramp. When I said it was, he reached under the counter and pulled out a bicycle pump. "You could try this," he said.

We took turns in the hundred-degree heat, one pumping while the other lifted up on the wing to lighten the load. As we worked, a man who looked to be in his early seventies appeared from nowhere to offer his help. Wayne glanced up, took a measure of his age and the fact that his face was already red and haggard from the heat and said tactfully, "We're almost done."

When the tire was reinflated, we headed for the shade of an overhanging tree to see if it would hold the air. The old fellow was waiting there with a woman of similar age. He told us that he was a pilot and, as old pilots do, went through a list of aircraft he had flown. The most notable was a DC-3 tail-dragger he'd flown in Africa in the 1950s. "It was still a wild place then," he said. "There were cannibals." He had worried about cannibals when he first landed at isolated jungle strips, he said, but he had soon learned that cannibals ate people for protein, not taste. There was enough protein in a human finger, he added, to sustain a man for a month.

While I took the pump back to the terminal, the old pilot continued telling Wayne about his African adventures. The cannibals had frightened him but he had been fond of the pygmies. When they wanted to leave the bush and go into a distant town, they would camp along one of the many old dirt airstrips and wait days, even weeks, until a plane landed. Then they'd climb on board, as confidently as if they'd bought a ticket for a holiday charter, and go wherever the plane took them. "Nobody minded because they were so tiny," he explained. "There was always room for another pygmy." His wife looked bored. She told Wayne that her husband came here every afternoon to watch the planes take off and land — and no doubt to tell his story about the pygmies and the cannibals.

While we were loading the plane, Wayne joked that this was how European history had always been written — through travellers' tales. An entire continent, the cradle of humankind, rich in peoples and cultures, had been reduced to the cannibals versus the pygmies. "He seems like a good guy," Wayne said. "But listening to him is like reading Cartier's journals."

In our climb out, we passed over Christian Island and flew west towards Manitoulin Island, where the Creator, the "Great Mystery," is said to have taken up residence. After only half an hour above the island-studded waters of old Lake Attignawantan, Manitoulin lay before us.

A hundred miles long and fifty miles wide, Manitoulin is the largest freshwater island in the world. From the distance we could see that it was riven by deep, narrow bays and mottled with oddly shaped lakes. In some places it seemed held together by the barest threads of land, like a giant, moth-eaten green blanket discarded in the waters.

When we were over Manitowaning Bay, we began our descent to the deserted airstrip. When we pulled up to the ramp, there was not a single plane parked on the grass tie-down area or a car in the parking lot. In the land of the Great Spirit, there wasn't a soul around. The small terminal was locked up tight but there was a pay phone on the outside wall. Wayne tried calling Roland Pangowish, an AFN staffer and old friend who came from the Wikwemikong reserve, on the eastern end of the island. But Rollie, it turned out, was back in Ottawa.

Someone had scratched "Tommy taxi" and a phone number on the wall. Wayne called the number and was told that Tommy had a few more pickups to make but that he'd get to the airport as soon as he could. We unloaded our gear and waited on the dusty roadside. A half-hour later, a thin cloud of dust appeared on the horizon. An old Chevy rattled into view and Tommy, whose face looked as beat-up as his Chevy, began speaking even before the car came to a full stop. "Hope you're not looking for a place to stay," he said.

It was powwow weekend. Everything was booked, even the campsites. If we liked, he would take us around to a few motels to see if they could squeeze us in, but first he had a few more calls to make. We could wait for him at the Schooner, the only restaurant in Manitowaning, the town just south of Wikwemikong. We passed by the road leading to the reserve. A large billboard announced *Wikwemikong: Unceded Indian Land.* "The government gave the

Indians the whole island," Tommy explained. "Ever since, they've been trying to make them give it back."

We drove into Manitowaning, which looked like a cowboy frontier town with its few, undecorated false storefronts, a collection of modest houses on unpaved roads running off the main street, and the folksy-looking Schooner restaurant. Small groups of young men and women, Odawa or Ojibwa, were gathered in the late-afternoon shade. This end of Manitoulin, as the billboard stated, was still Indian land. Archaeologists have unearthed evidence of continuous habitation on the island for almost ten thousand years, from a time when glaciers still rose from the shore of Georgian Bay. The young Odawa and Ojibwa kids hanging out in front of the Schooner restaurant traced their forebears back to those original people. It was also their ancestors who, in the latter half of the seventeenth century, drove the Iroquois from Danaiiwaad Ojibweg and Tenakìwin and back into their traditional lands south of the Great Lakes.

At the time of the Iroquois western march in the 1650s, the Odawa and Ojibwa were linked with the Potawatomi in the Council of the Three Fires. In this political and military alliance, the Potawatomi served as the Fire Keepers, the Odawa as the Trader Nation and the Ojibwa as the Faith Keepers.

The Ojibwa were by far the largest group in the council. Yet for Europeans they remained for many decades an invisible nation. Their country, Danaiiwaad Ojibweg, stretched from the village of Sagahanirini, just north of Huronia, to Outchibous, on the north shore of Lake Superior, where the ancient copper mines were located, but travellers didn't recognize them as a single people until the nineteenth century.

It was an understandable mistake. For most of the year, Ojibwa bands functioned like small autonomous nations, their leaders, or *ogimauh*, varying according to the task at hand. The best hunter would lead the hunt, the best speaker would take the lead in council, the best navigator would take charge on long journeys. If someone else began to show more talent for a task, people would simply follow the new man's lead. In Ojibwa life, leaders didn't seek out followers; the people sought out leaders.

All three nations had friendly relations with the Wendat, the Tionnontaté (Tobacco Nation) and the Attiwandaronk. As a trading nation, the Odawa — whose name comes from the Ojibwa *ottauwauh* ("to exchange") — had the closest relations with the northern Iroquoians. Long before the Europeans arrived, they were taking Wendat and Attiwandaronk corn into the northwest to exchange with the Cree for furs and northern manufactured goods. Like the Nipissings, who performed the same role in the James Bay region, they grew corn and tobacco for their own use; also, like the Nipissing, they had adopted some Iroquoian customs, such as the Feast of the Dead.

Like other peoples of the Great Lakes region, the nations of the Council of the Three Fires had been caught off guard by the swiftness and decisiveness of the Five Nations victory against the Wendat and their allies. During 1650 and 1651, small groups of Wendat, Neutral and Tobacco people sought refuge among the Ojibwa and Odawa, and large numbers of fleeing Nipissing passed through on their way to resettlement on the north shore of Lake Superior.

While the Council of the Three Fires was still trying to overcome the confusion caused by the collapse of the Wendat empire and the flow of refugees into their countries, they found themselves under attack. In 1652, bolstered by four summers of spectacular military successes, a hundred Five Nations fighters armed with rifles attacked the Ojibwa capital of Boweting, located on the St. Mary's River between Lake Huron and Lake Superior, where Sault Ste. Marie now stands. Most of the Ojibwa men were out hunting at the time, so the town was being defended by only fifty Ojibwa fighters backed by a few Wendat and Tionnontaté refugees.

Although outnumbered two to one and armed only with bows and arrows and war clubs, the defenders managed to drive off the attackers. But that battle was just the opening shot. The following year, 120 Iroquois warriors again marched across eastern Danaii-waad Ojibweg towards Boweting. This time they were met just north of Manitoulin by an equal number of Ojibwa and allies. In the fierce battle that followed, the Five Nations warriors discovered that while their muskets had given them a distinct advantage in attacking Wendat and other Iroquoian towns, they were much less useful in forest warfare against skilled hunters. The Iroquois war party was wiped out, except for one lone survivor who was set free to return to Iroquoia and warn his countrymen of the fate that awaited them if they ventured back into Danaiiwaad Ojibweg.

The Five Nations seem to have gotten the message, at least for the moment, because for most of the next decade they focused on consolidating their position in the captured Iroquoian territory by sending settlers to found a series of new towns in what is now Southern Ontario.

The Iroquois made a final assault on the Ojibwa heartland in 1662, entering the country undetected and planning a two-pronged attack. Their main army camped just east of Boweting, and from there they sent a force of a hundred men into the hills, to slip around west of the town. The Iroquoians arrived on the Superior shore in late afternoon and prepared for an early-morning attack.

In the evening, a keen-eyed Ojibwa sentry spotted smoke on a distant point. During the night, Ojibwa fighters crept through the hills to a steep ridge behind the Iroquois camp. When the dogs barked, they tossed them chunks of meat. The dogs settled down and the fighters waited until the sun — the war god — illuminated the sleeping bodies below. The Iroquois were awakened by a deadly downpour of sharpened-flint and copper-tipped arrows, and the blood shed that day washed away any hope that the Five Nations would conquer Danaiiwaad Ojibweg, or that a lasting peace would be struck between the two powerful military alliances of the northeast quarter of the continent.

The battle also marked the end of Five Nations expansion. From that day on it was the Iroquois who were on the defensive. The Ojibwa and Odawa marshalled a large army under the Odawa war chief Sahgimah, and led them to the Blue Mountain region northeast of old Huronia. Ojibwa intelligence had determined that an Iroquois battalion was heading north along the Lake Simcoe route. Sahgimah arranged his troops along both sides of a deep valley. When the Iroquois entered, he sprang the trap, closing off escape at both ends. Ojibwa and Odawa fighters, by this time armed with guns as well as traditional weapons, began what quickly became a slaughter of the Iroquois army. The only Iroquois who survived were those Sahgimah released so they could carry home news of their defeat.

From then on it was the Three Fires' forces who took the initiative, moving south to engage the Iroquois head-on. Over the next twenty years, ten new Iroquois towns, near modern-day Peterborough, Toronto and Burlington, were destroyed by advancing Ojibwa armies. By the turn of the century these armies had also driven the Five Nations from all of the conquered Wendat, Tionnontaté and Attiwandaronk lands. Today, most historians agree that it was the stunning defeat of the Five Nations in the Ojibwa war that ultimately forced the Iroquois to make peace with the French in 1701.

The Europeans did not discover the extent of the rout until more than half a century later. In 1755, official French maps of North America still showed southern Ontario as northern Iroquoia, dotted with Iroquois towns, even though the Ojibwa had evicted the Iroquois and had established hunting and gathering territories there. They called this territory Saguinan Land, after the great Odawa war chief who had led them to victory.

All that remained of the Iroquoian presence was the great quantity of bones that European settlers would later dig up when they were clearing the land. Even today, an Onondaga chant recalls the bitter sting of the greatest military disaster that had ever befallen the Iroquois people. What struck them most about the loss was the idea that the land they had laboured over, the precious cornfields, was now returning to bush. As the main refrain puts it, *Woh! Woh! The cleared land has become a thicket. The cleared places are deserted. They are in their graves — they who established it.*

While we ate supper on the terrace, Wayne spoke about the Odawa and the Ojibwa of Manitoulin. On his last visit to the island, he had been told by an Odawa friend that the Ojibwa living here were "refugees." According to his friend, the first small band of Ojibwa had moved onto the Manitoulin in about 1700 from the north shore of Georgian Bay after a winter of famine.

The snows had been too deep to hunt that year and the very young and very old were dying of starvation. The Ojibwa village was visited by a French priest who had only prayers to offer them. In desperation, to save the lives of their children, they killed the priest and fed their children his flesh. In the end, all survived but, fearing retribution, they fled their country in the spring for Manitoulin. The Odawa gave them refuge and the right to settle. But it was understood by both Odawa and Ojibwa that this was the Odawa's country. The Ojibwa remained, almost three hundred years later, still guests.

Tommy made an appearance, but he hadn't come for us. He went to the adjacent table where two attractive Odawa or Ojibwa women were nursing beers. One of them, who looked to be in her early thirties, greeted him warmly and stood, ready to leave. I caught Tommy's eye. "Should we wait here?" I asked.

He glanced at us in surprise, as if he'd forgotten about us. "Sure," he said. "I'm just going home to have some supper. I'll be back in an hour. You can meet me downstairs in the bar."

With its bare concrete decor, blaring jukebox and inebriated young men slumped over their beer, the bar reminded me of a Latin American cantina. Looking around, I noticed that I was the only non-native in the place. When the waiter brought us our

Cokes, Wayne asked if he knew Roland Pangowish. He nodded. "He's my cousin." When Wayne reached for his wallet to pay, he said, "It's on the house."

The drinkers were mainly young people who had spent the day at the powwow. We watched as one young guy who had been slumped over his beer was awakened by the waiter. The drinker tried to push him away, but in one fluid motion, reminiscent of a Wild West movie, he was jerked to his feet and sent sprawling through the open door.

Tommy came hurrying in a few minutes later. He said he was sorry again, but there was a guy outside with a bloody nose that he had to take home. He'd be right back. We waited for him outside the Schooner. The upstairs restaurant was just closing and the remaining customers, again almost all young natives, were filing out into the night. A few headed around the building to the bar entrance, but most disappeared along the darkened street. The sound of their voices faded under the strains of country-and-western music coming from the bar.

A half an hour later, a lone set of headlights approached along the deserted street. "It doesn't look good," Tommy admitted when we climbed back into his cab. "The island's just about booked, but we'll give it a try." We drove through miles of darkness before we came across a small motel. The *No Vacancy* sign was blinking red. "There's another a few miles up," Tommy said. We wheeled back out onto the highway and Tommy talked about Manitoulin. He had been born there and he'd lived off island for only a few years. "There's no place like it," he said. "This is Indian land." He didn't look Indian himself. Although he might have been Métis. But he spoke of the Indianness of the place with pride. If he had time in the morning, he said, he would take us to Sheguiandah, the ten-thousand-year-old habitation site.

After we'd stopped at one more no-vacancy motel, Wayne suggested that we head back to the airstrip. "It's a nice night," he said. "We could sleep under the wings."

"There's one more place," Tommy suggested. "But it's expensive." We hit the highway once again. By now it was after ten-thirty. After driving another twenty minutes without seeing so much as the lights of a passing car, we turned into a long driveway illuminated by coach lights. We were surprised to discover at the end a brightly lit manor that wouldn't have been out of place in Rosedale or Upper Westmount. When we stepped out of the car, we could hear one of Bach's sinfonias wafting through an open window. To complete the picture, the silver-haired woman at the reception desk spoke with a cultivated British accent. Two large rooms were open behind her. One was the dining-room, where a few late diners sat around linen-covered tables set with silver and crystal. The other was the lounge, where the sinfonia was playing and a dozen guests — among them a number of tanned, attractive women in evening dress — were having cocktails. In our dusty travelling clothes, with our duffel bags, we were obviously out of place. The receptionist eyed us coolly. She was sorry, she said, but there were no rooms available.

Tommy looked crestfallen. In a pleading voice he told her that we were flyers who'd had to put down for the night, and that all the motels on the island were full, making our plight sound much more dramatic than it was. Perhaps the reference to "flyers" roused in the British matron memories of flyboys of another era, because her demeanour changed. Two of the waiters had left for a couple of days, she suddenly recalled; the accommodations were poor, but she could let us use their room for the night.

The staff quarters were in the back of a spacious guest house near the lake. An American family was staying in the front, and looked at us askance as we entered. We headed into the back room — which was sparsely furnished, with a couple of beds stripped to the mattresses — and opened the window so we could smoke.

We went over the chart for the morning. Our plan was to fly first to the southwest corner of the lake, over Michilimackinac — the turtle-shaped island. According to most peoples from the

Great Lakes region, it was there that the world began, when Sky-woman fell from the heavens onto Michilimackinac, the turtle's back. Then we would head on to Sault Ste. Marie, old Boweting, once the capital of Danaiiwaad Ojibweg. From there we would follow the highway to the ancient copper mines.

We threw our sleeping bags on the unmade beds. There was no screen on the open window, and a swarm of mosquitoes had made it inside before we realized this and closed it. The cocktail-party music faded and we were left spending our night with the natural music of the country, the humming of hungry mosquitoes.

We took off from Manitoulin the next morning into a cloudy sky that continued to lower as we flew over Manitou Lake, the largest lake on the island, and over the open waters of Lake Huron. Michilimackinac Island, now known simply as Mackinac, lies on the American side of the lake, in the narrow strait separating Lake Huron from Lake Michigan.

By the time we had the island in sight, a light rain was falling, shrouding it in a filmy veil. An American tourist brochure advertised the island as a summer haven with vacation condos, restaurants and golf courses. No mention was made of the fact that, for millennia, the Great Lakes peoples viewed it as the birthplace of the earth. We considered landing at the small airstrip to look around, but Wayne said, "Let's keep going. The weather looks like it's coming down and, anyway, I'd rather think of this place as a great turtle-shaped island than as a low-rent American golf and country club." We banked back over the water and took our new heading to Boweting, another sacred site, at the rapids between Lake Huron and Lake Superior, where the Ojibwa people believe they were led after the original flood waters subsided.

CHAPTER ELEVEN

Ancient Mines

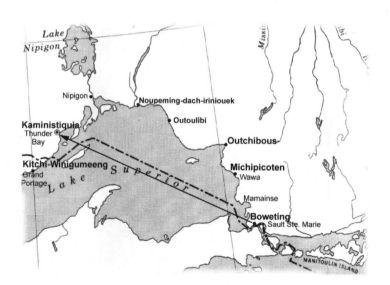

W HEN WE ARRIVED in Sault Ste. Marie, we headed west along the highway towards Gros Cap, the cliffs at the mouth of the St. Mary's River, where a giant bust of Nana'b'oozoo guards the entranceway to Lake Superior.

The tourist brochure described Gros Cap as having a scenic landscape, and advised travellers to bring their cameras. No mention was made of Nana'b'oozoo, but as soon as we stepped out of the car we saw the great hundred-foot rock angled over the surf. The rock face had been carved by time and by Lake Superior's winds into a striking profile of a human face, with crooked nose and strong cheekbones, gazing resolutely out over Ojibwa-Kitchi-Gummeeng, the Great Lake of the Ojibwa.

The open-armed stone figure of Nana'b'oozoo at the boiling kettles on the Ottawa River was only the first effigy on the Ancient trail. This was the second and, as at Asticou, travellers paused to make a tobacco offering before crossing the four-hundred-mile lake. The third Nana'b'oozoo effigy was on the far shore of the lake, where the twists and rolls of the Sibley Peninsula form the shape of a reclining figure, a sleeping giant. According to the old Ojibwa stories, that was where Nana'b'oozoo now lay. Before going to sleep, the great manitou had promised that he would waken after nine hundred years to restore the Old Order and the place of the people within it. Yet no one knew when that awakening would take place, because no one knew exactly when the manitou had lain down to rest.

We climbed the narrow trail up the rock face to the top of the massive stone head. The wind had come up, and the lake was now foaming with choppy waves. French voyageurs called that wind *la vieille*, the old woman. Over the centuries — indeed, over millennia — it had tossed countless travellers to their deaths. For paddlers it was not only fierce but stingy, keeping them on shore for an average of one day out of three during the crossing, and sometimes blowing up marathon storms that pinned them to shore for a week or more.

Wayne moved to the edge of the rock, where he found a surveyor's metal pin drilled into the granite. It was from the U.S. Army Corps of Engineers. America was just across the river, and the corps must have been surveying the midpoint of the river, where the international border runs. "Another settlers' claim post," he said. "It's one of those European miracles. Driving a stake or erecting a cross on someone else's land and, suddenly, it's yours." He smiled. "A kind of sorcery."

Boweting was an ancient meeting place in the Old Country, and these cliffs had their own power, with Ojibwa of surrounding communities still coming here for ceremonies. The stone effigy of Nana'b'oozoo, they say, is a reminder that this was, and will for ever be, the land of the manitous.

This is a message that the Ojibwa, more than any other people, have heeded through history. Nowhere would priests face more resistance than among the Faith Keepers of the Council of the Three Fires. The Ojibwa held firm to their spiritual heritage long after other nations had converted to Christianity, at least nominally. In fact, the Ojibwa moved aggressively to counter the priests' proselytizing. After the Jesuits set up their first mission, Ste. Marie, at Boweting in 1689, Ojibwa traditionalists established the Medaewaewin Society, which brought together medicine men and women "to preserve and advance the knowledge of plants and healing and to establish the relationship between health and upright living, known as walking the balance." Most of the sacred ceremonies associated with the Medaewaewin Society were soon practised by all Ojibwa, and, whenever possible, they were performed near the rapids and cliffs around Boweting, where the nation had been born. Even those who migrated east into old Iroquoian territory, or west onto the plains to become buffalo hunters, returned to this windswept rock for spiritual renewal.

From Gros Cap we drove farther along the highway as it arched to the north around Goulais Bay and Batchawana Bay. We were heading to the ancient copper mines at Mamainse, which had been in operation since before the time of the Egyptian pharaohs. We stopped at a tourist information booth near a small waterfall where a plaque identified the halfway point in the Trans-Canada Highway, between its beginning in St. John's and its terminus in Victoria.

In ancient times, too, there was a general awareness that this region was at the crossroads of North America. From here, goods went east along the French and Ottawa rivers to the St. Lawrence, and on to Nitassinan and Wabanaki; west across Lake Superior and into the Lake of the Woods and the Winnipeg River system to the plains; south through Lake Michigan and the Mississippi River to the Gulf of Mexico; and north up the Montreal and Michipicoten river systems to James Bay.

At a picnic table near the plaque, Wayne glanced over the map showing the Indian mines. He said he had known nothing about them until he was reading about the region in the months before we left. His first reaction on learning that they had existed for six thousand years, and that copper dug from the cliffs of Lake Superior had been found in burial mounds and village sites throughout North America, was to see it as part of a pattern. "Everything about the Old Order — medical knowledge, religious beliefs, artistic

achievements, industry, commercial relations — has been dis-
torted or dismissed," he said. "From Cartier's time to ours. Konrad
had it right. It's *twistory.*"

A gravel road led to an abandoned fishing pier. We headed north
along the narrow beach, around a jutting point, to the site of the
Indian mines. The cliff face rose dramatically, but it was cut by a
series of ledges. The Precambrian granite was laced with minerals:
thick veins of copper, oxidized green; narrow veins of glinting
pyrite — fool's gold; lacquered flecks of mica. When we moved
along the rock face, we could see where the miners had stood and
where they had painstakingly extracted the ore by pounding the
natural cracks and crevices to free it from the two-billion-year-old
granite. Men, and no doubt women, were working these open-
faced mines when the northern two-thirds of Canada were still
covered by the glacial cap.

Somewhere on the beach, the copper was heated in charcoal-
fired kilns. Craftsmen then worked it into jewellery, amulets, or
arrow or spear points, or simply hammered it into bars or rolled it
into pellets. The manufactures, bars or pellets were then shipped
in a two-thousand-mile radius. Archaeological excavations show
that, in return, the people of the region imported obsidian from
Wyoming mines more than a thousand miles away, Iroquoian pot-
tery from around Lake Erie and wampum shells from the Manitoba
lakes, as well as numerous wood and leather goods that have not
survived in the acid soil of the Canadian Shield.

The mines were not only ancient history; they were very much
part of historical times. On Mount Royal in 1535, Cartier noted
in his journal that one of the Mohawk had touched the metal
chain of Cartier's captain's whistle and pointed in the direction of
the Ottawa River to indicate where their supply of metal objects
came from. Later, the Mohawk drew a detailed map in the dirt,
showing the rivers and lakes, and even the major portages, to
be crossed on the nine-hundred-mile journey to the mines. This

was the land that Cartier would later refer to as the Kingdom of the Saguenay.

More evidence of the mines' existence came in 1611, when Champlain, on his way from Kebek to the Richelieu River, was presented with a foot-long bar of almost pure copper by an emissary from Iroquet, and was told it came from the mines on the Great Lake of the Ojibwa. Later that summer, when he sent Étienne Brûlé into the country with Iroquet, Champlain instructed him to search for the Indian mines. Brûlé finally made it onto Lake Superior in the summer of 1624, and he saw the mines and smelting operation in full production. Two years later, he brought a large copper ingot back to France with him. But memory of the mines, and the old order they were part of, faded during the nineteenth century when the ancient lands, its peoples, frontiers and history were brushed aside to make way for European industry.

The Ojibwa attachment to the territory and its ancient mines was expressed as late as 1846, when the Upper Canadian government awarded mineral rights in the Michipicoten region to the Quebec and Superior Mining Company. Chief Shinguacouse immediately travelled to Toronto to assert the Ojibwa right to the land, including their ancient mineral rights. After three years without government action, an armed Ojibwa party moved in to stop the foreign miners by force. Troops were then sent from Toronto, in what the press of the day dubbed the "Michipicoten War," to secure the Ojibwa copper for the mining company.

We'd brought sandwiches for lunch, and we sat on a couple of driftwood logs by the shore, where the waves broke on the sands. There was not a soul around, and nothing marked this beach as the country's most ancient industrial site.

Before we left, Wayne gathered a few small chunks of copper ore in his sack. He would keep them as a reminder, he said.

The old Indian Countries were not so much discovered by the Europeans, as revealed to them. In the classic sense of the term, there are virtually no explorers in Canadian history other than the mariners — Cabot, Hudson and Cook. Beyond the shoreline, the so-called explorers and discoverers were invariably men who had been granted entry by the people of the land. Newcomers almost always travelled in the company of local escorts, and often they were merely passengers — *supercargo*, one historian has called them — in the canoes of their hosts.

This was how Médard Chouart, Sieur Des Groseilliers, entered the Lake Superior region in the 1650s and continued the European westward push. With the collapse of the Wendat trade empire and the dispersal of their Algonquin allies, the French were pinned down on the St. Lawrence between the old Stadaconan and Hochelagan territories. The tiny colony was besieged by the powerful Five Nations army to the south, and near bankrupt because it was unable to send traders into the fur country. Its only lifeline was the large Odawa convoys that passed through the Five Nations territory on the Algonquin and Nipissing lands each year. It was under these desperate circumstances that, in 1654, Des Groseilliers wheedled his way on board an Odawa canoe in a convoy returning to the interior.

Des Groseilliers had arrived from France in 1640, and had served as a young lay worker with the Jesuits at a Huronia mission. When he joined the Odawa at Lachine in 1654, he was taken to the Ojibwa trading town at Michilimackinac, and from there he was given permission to visit the Ojibwa and Potawatomi villages on the shores of Lake Michigan. At the south end of the lake he encountered Dakota Sioux traders, who he said were well outfitted with copper ornaments and tools. In his travels around the lake, Des Groseilliers traded for a considerable quantity of furs. Returning to Michilimackinac, he picked up an eastbound Odawa convoy and travelled with it back to the St. Lawrence. In history books he is named as the "discoverer" of Lake Michigan, and he and his brother-in-law, Pierre-Esprit Radisson, are credited with numerous similar discoveries over the next two decades.

Neither Radisson nor Des Groseilliers had an official trading licence, so the following year, when they decided to try to repeat Des Groseilliers's western fur haul, they had to slip their canoes into the waters of Lake of Two Mountains in the dead of night to avoid arrest by colonial officials. The Ottawa/French River route was still largely empty of Algonquin, who had moved inland to escape the continuing threat of Iroquois war parties, so the two men spent most of the journey paddling and portaging at night and sleeping under the cover of the forest during the day. When they finally turned up at Boweting, they were welcomed by the local Ojibwa, who admired their courage in running the six-hundred-mile Iroquois gauntlet.

Radisson quickly became a popular figure around camp. At the age of sixteen he had been captured by the Mohawk and adopted by a Mohawk family that had lost a boy of its own in the war. Radisson lived with them for two years and then, while out hunting, killed three Mohawk in an escape attempt. He was recaptured and, surprisingly, forgiven for the killings. After three more years with the Mohawk, he succeeded in escaping back to New France. The story of his battles with the Iroquois were much appreciated by the local Ojibwa and visiting Cree traders, all of whom were veterans of the Iroquois war.

It was during the exchange of campfire stories that Radisson and Des Groseilliers were given what turned out to be an invaluable lesson in North American geography. A Cree trader told them about his homeland on a vast saltwater sea to the north. When the two Frenchmen inquired further, they were told that the Cree country, Eeyou Astchee, was reached through river systems that ran north to the saltwater sea from the height of land, the north/south watershed, above the Great Lake of the Ojibwa.

The general outlines of Hudson Bay had been charted in 1611 by Henry Hudson, but Europeans knew nothing of the rivers connecting the bay to the Great Lakes. The Cree trader at Boweting drew a map in the dirt, and the two Europeans quickly realized that if posts were opened at the mouths of the Hudson Bay rivers, goods could be brought in by ship directly from France, and the ships could return home with their holds full of furs from Cree territory.

Before leaving Boweting, Des Groseilliers and Radisson were permitted to trade around the shores of Lake Superior. The load of furs they amassed was so staggering that they had to scramble to find canoes to transport them. They ended up purchasing dozens of canoes from the local Ojibwa, and they struck various profit-sharing deals with local men to induce them to transport the cargo to New France under the protection of the annual Odawa/Ojibwa convoy.

The French at Lachine were astounded by the wealth of furs brought in that summer by the two men and their Ojibwa partners. But despite the fact that the furs probably saved the colony from economic collapse, Radisson and Des Groseilliers were arrested at the dockside for trading without a licence, and they were thrown into the stockade. When they were released, they asked the governor for a licence to pursue the northern trade via Hudson Bay. They were refused. Such a trade, they were told, would be in direct competition with the struggling colony. They responded the same way Brûlé had when working with his countrymen had become impossible: they went to the British. They travelled first to New England, to try to get backing to open up a Hudson Bay trading company. When they failed to find backers, they moved on to London, where they interested a group of powerful British investors. After a trial run brought back a shipload of furs in 1669, the Hudson's Bay Company was formally launched on May 2, 1670.

For the Ojibwa this was a time of unprecedented expansion. In the east, the Iroquois had been driven from southern Ontario, the new Saguinan Land. On the western frontier, the Dakota, who were also traditional enemies of the Ojibwa, were being pushed south by the Ojibwa and Cree alliance. The lands along the northwest shore of Lake Superior were claimed by both the Cree, as the southern limits of Eeyou Astchee, and the Ojibwa, as the western limits of Danaiiwaad Ojibweg. But the two peoples there had arrived at an arrangement not unlike the cantons of Switzerland: the land was shared between them in a patchwork of villages and hunting territories.

During this period, the distant countries and peoples beyond Boweting remained unknown to the Europeans. In 1660 the settled area of New France was still tiny, covering only 120 miles of old Iroquoian territory between Stadacona and Hochelaga. The main town, Quebec, had only 500 inhabitants, and the colony's theocratic nature was reflected in the fact that 130 of them were priests. By 1663, the struggling colony had been put under the direct control of Louis XIV and his court. Two years later, Louis dispatched a thousand soldiers from France and appointed Jean Talon as the first intendant of the new crown colony, with the mission of encouraging settlement. Shiploads of settlers were brought in to clear the land between Quebec and Montreal. By 1675 there were 7000 Europeans in New France, with Quebec City, Trois Rivières and Montreal emerging as busy little towns on the banks of the St. Lawrence. Considering the fact that in the first twenty-five years of the colony's life, from 1608 to 1633, barely two acres of Canadian forest had been cleared by Europeans, it was a remarkable period of growth. Yet the total population of New France in 1675 was only slightly larger than Cartier's estimation of the population of Hochelaga back in 1535.

The towns were far from secure. The inhabitants of New France were under constant threat of Iroquois attack when they left their fortified settlements. Several times, the Iroquois overran the villages as well. The most concerted attack came in 1689, when fifteen hundred Iroquois fighters landed on the island and slipped through the forest to surround the homes and public buildings. At dawn, they struck. In a matter of minutes, fifty-six of the seventy-five habitations were in flames. One hundred and twenty settlers were taken prisoner and between two dozen and two hundred were killed (French authorities gave the lower number, perhaps to minimize the loss).

More Iroquois raids followed, with thirty habitations on the east end of the island burned the following year. Most historians agree that the Iroquois could have driven the French from the St. Lawrence anytime during this period, if they had so chosen. But they always pulled back. They were confident that the Europeans, whom they thought of as inferiors, would never be able to overwhelm them. In the meantime, the French remained a useful source of iron goods in the form of war booty, and some Iroquois leaders hoped that at some point in the future they would be able to open up diplomatic and trade relations with them as a counterweight to their relations with the British to the south.

It was only after the Five Nations had been weakened by the Ojibwa war that the French were able to move back to the Great Lakes region in any significant numbers. Most of the returning French traders were stationed at the old Ojibwa towns of Michilimackinac or Boweting, but a few moved farther west to trade at the mouths of the rivers on Lake Superior. By 1725 small seasonal posts had opened to serve the Cree at Michipicoten, the Assiniboine at Nipigon, and the Cree and Ojibwa villages on the far shore at Kaministiquia and Kitchhi-Winigumeeng (Grand Portage). Not until after 1730 — almost 250 years after Cabot landed at Griquet — did Europeans make it past the river mouths to the western lands of the interior.

That first incursion was led by Pierre Gaultier de Varennes, Sieur de La Vérendrye, son of a whisky-post operator on the St. Maurice River and younger brother of the French official commissioned as commander of Lake Superior. While Pierre de La Vérendrye had been born in New France, he had been educated in France and commissioned in the French army, where he served in the War of the Spanish Succession. After serving with distinction and being wounded five times, he returned to Canada and arrived on Lake Superior in 1726 to administer a small post on Lake Nipigon. There he met a local Cree, called Pako, who described in general terms the complex trade route from the Great Lake of the

Ojibwa to Lake Ouinipigon (Winnipeg) and the three great rivers in the distant west: the Winnipeg, Red and Saskatchewan. When La Vérendrye inquired further, he was told of a bejewelled mountain in the land of the western spirits. Because he was certain that the Pacific lay near Lake Ouinipigon, he surmised that the three rivers Pako described must flow out of the lake and would carry him swiftly to the nearby western sea.

The following summer, La Vérendrye moved to the Kaministiquia post at the head of the lake, and the local Cree chief, Ochaga, drew him a detailed map of the route to Lake Ouinipigon that Pako had described the previous year. Using a sharpened piece of coal on birchbark, Ochaga plotted all the main rivers, lakes and portages that La Vérendrye would encounter on the five-hundred-mile journey.

La Vérendrye headed back to New France with the priceless birchbark map. He had been told that these previously uncharted regions had a rich storehouse of furs, and in his letters home he referred several times to a land near the source of one of the prairie rivers that was "held in great esteem by the savages." They had told him there was a mountain of precious stones there, "which sparkle night and day." But the savages, he noted, "call it the Dwelling of the Spirit" (Manitoba).

Back on the St. Lawrence, he spent his time trying to drum up official backing for a large-scale assault on this land of the spirit, where he would seek both new trading lands and the route to the western sea. In July 1731, armed with Ochaga's map, he set out from Fort Senneville — on the tip of Montreal Island — with fifty men, soldiers and traders. Among them were his three eldest sons and his nephew, La Jémeraye, who had some experience trading with the Dakota in southern Michigan, and who would serve as his second-in-command. La Vérendrye's plan was to use the expedition to set up a lucrative family business, opening with a string of trading posts through the rich fur territory, which would then finance his journey to the western sea.

In August 1731 the party arrived at Boweting, by then a booming town with local craftsmen busy manufacturing canoes and women harvesting and milling local *mahnnomin* (wild rice) for the native and the growing number of European traders. When La Vérendrye and his fifty men passed the towering rock gates at the mouth of St. Mary's River, where the giant stone bust of Nana'b'oozoo stares out over the Great Lake of the Ojibwa, they were heading into lands still described on European maps as *terra incognita*.

We intended to follow La Vérendrye's route across the lake, keeping to the northern shore. But when we went outside the next morning, the sky was overcast with a light drizzle. I called the airport weather office and was told there might be some clearing by noon; it was still wait-and-see.

We headed down to the site of the old rapids. The two other great rapids on the Ottawa, at Lachine and Asticou, had preserved at least some of their ancient thunder. But the Boweting rapids, starved by the upstream hydroelectric dams, showed only a few frothy patches where the waters had once roared.

The smoke and fire of a riverside steel mill formed a sombre backdrop. Travel weariness was setting in for both of us. The light rain continued, and the prospect of spending a day or more waiting in Sault Ste. Marie was dispiriting.

"I never liked this city," Wayne said. There was no particular reason why he didn't like it; he just felt that it was one of those closed-minded towns. "Maybe," he said, "it's because it's Irwin's hometown."

Ron Irwin, the Indian Affairs minister, was not a popular figure among native nationalists. Having begun his political career as the mayor of Sault Ste. Marie, he now represented the riding in Parliament. But he remained a small-town, glad-handing backslapper who, many native leaders said, acted as if he thought he himself were national chief. His bitter feuding with Ovide Mercredi was already the stuff of legend. It had begun on the day Irwin was sworn in as Indian Affairs minister, when Mercredi was quoted as describing him as "a nobody." Irwin had never forgiven him. Within months he had begun negotiating with Mercredi's main political rival, Chief Phil Fontaine, who was at that time head of the Assembly of Manitoba Chiefs, on a deal to transfer Indian Affairs administration in Manitoba to Fontaine's organization. It was something Mercredi fiercely opposed because the end result, he said, would lock native communities into municipal-style governments. But Chief Fontaine was in the camp of those leaders, like Chief Blaine Favel, who thought sovereignty had to be won back in small slices. Fontaine accepted Irwin's offer to negotiate the limited transfer of powers from the Department of Indian Affairs to the Assembly of Manitoba Chiefs and entered into an informal partnership with the minister. Irwin was effective in making deals with the chiefs he called the "big hitters," men like Phil Fontaine and Blaine Favel, who Mercredi would later refer to as "collaborators," for working too closely with the Indian Affairs Minister.

While we were walking back along the stony shore, we spotted a faint patch of blue in the northwest corner of the sky. We hurried back to the hotel, picked up our gear and went straight to the airport, stopping in at the flight service station for a quick weather briefing. The meteorologist showed us the weather radar and projection. The cloud cover would have a break of several hundred miles before the next front moved in. If we left right away, we would be flying towards the clearing.

There was still a light drizzle when we took off and climbed to 2000 feet, just under the cloud cover. But the blue was ahead, beckoning. When we reached it, we climbed to our cruise altitude of 6500 feet, passing over Iroquois Point, where the Five Nations army was wiped out in 1662. The Great Lake of the Ojibwa lay spread out below; a purple line of hills was visible to the north, but to the west and the south lay only water.

The break in the cloud was less than it had appeared on the radar at the Soo airport. A few puffy clouds passed beneath us, then a few more, until we were flying over a mackerel sky. On the radio, we heard that all the airstrips on the north shore — Wawa, Marathon, Terrace Bay — were back under cloud. But Thunder Bay, our destination, was still clear, so we continued west.

By the time we were in the middle of the lake, there was a solid bank of clouds below us, so technically we were no longer flying under visual flight rules. More worrying was that another layer was moving in above us. As we flew into this Cessna sandwich, towards what was still supposed to be open sky over Thunder Bay, Wayne leaned over and looked below. "Have we lost altitude?" he asked.

I glanced at the altitude indicator. "We're still at 6500," I said.

"Then the clouds are growing."

It was true. The tops of the cumulus clouds were growing as the clouds picked up moisture from the lake.

"I think there's a clearing ahead," he said.

We flew towards the patch of blue-grey for some time before realizing that it wasn't getting any closer. The blue-grey, it turned out, was only a trick of the light bouncing between the two layers of cloud. Glancing back and to the left, Wayne saw what he was sure was sunshine streaming through. We took a southern heading and ten minutes later we were able to head west again, flying on the edge of the front. Later, Wayne said he was particularly relieved when we found open sky. For some reason he had been thinking since we first plotted the course of our trip, that if we went down it would be into the fathomless waters of Lake Superior. He didn't know why. "Maybe," he said, "it's because I have ancestors, old Cree traders, still on the bottom."

The western shoreline of Lake Superior began to take shape. Thunder Bay lay ahead, straddling the Kaministiquia River. The airport was on the southern limits of the town, tucked behind Mount Mckay and a couple of towering paper-mill smokestacks.

Fifteen miles out, we passed over Nana'b'oozoo, reclining in his nine-hundred-year sleep.

Air traffic control told us to keep above two thousand feet for as long as possible, but even at that height the sulphur smell from the stacks filled the cockpit. Thunder Bay, a rough-and-tumble mill town and freighter-loading port, was where my father had grown up. It was also where La Vérendrye landed in August 1731, with his sons, his nephew and his company of fifty soldiers and traders.

Ochaga, who had drawn La Vérendrye the map of the western lands four years before, had heard of the French party's approach a week earlier, from a group of Assiniboine traders arriving from Boweting, and was waiting for them on shore.

The Cree celebrated the arrival of La Vérendrye's party at Kaministiquia with a welcoming feast. The Cree and Ojibwa were pleased that their French allies intended to set up a post in the interior lands for the same reason that Iroquet had been glad to have Champlain on the St. Lawrence. The French brought not only trade goods but their weapons, and as friends and trading partners they would be expected to fight alongside their hosts in the Dakota war.

After crossing the four-hundred-mile stretch of the Great Lake of the Ojibwa, La Vérendrye's men had arrived at Kaministiquia exhausted. They were not happy when, within days, their commander had them back on the water, paddling to Grand Portage to continue the journey into the interior under a Cree escort. The visitors were greeted warmly by the Ojibwa living at the base of the portage, but when they saw the steepness of the trail, and learned that it went on for nine punishing miles, their hearts sank.

CHAPTER TWELVE

Whitedog

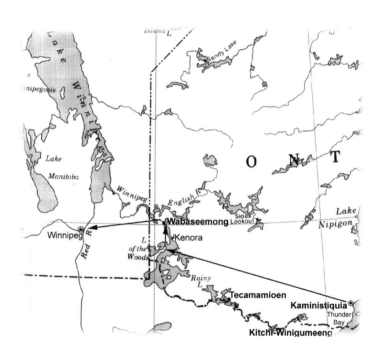

K AMINISTIQUIA is Cree for "the place where the river divides." It refers to the forks just past Thunder Bay, where
the river splits into three tributaries. When it comes
together again, it gains new vigour, to the point thirty miles up
where it crashes down 120 feet at Kakabeka, a waterfall higher than
Niagara. Native travellers occasionally took the Kaministiquia
west to Lake of the Woods and the Winnipeg River, but because
of the falls, and an equally daunting climb over the Dog Lake
portage, the preferred route was through the Kitchi-Winigumeeng
(Grand Portage), which begins on the Superior shore thirty miles
to the south.

Today Grand Portage is just over the international border, on
the American side. Even in La Vérendrye's day it was a border
town, at the southern limit of Danaiiwaad Ojibweg and the northern limit of Dakota country. The fact that the strategic portage was
then in Ojibwa hands is an indication of the momentum of the war
between the northern and southern peoples; the Ojibwa and their
allies were slowly pushing the Dakota not only from the shores of
Lake Superior, but from the Dakota's interior stronghold to the
west at Lake of the Woods. If they succeeded, they would greatly
expand their territory to the west, and gain control of the vital
transportation route to the plains.

We drove along the Superior shore, passed through the small border post and followed the signs to Grand Portage. When the road dipped down to the lakeshore, we came upon a U.S. Parks Service replica of the eighteenth-century fur trade fort. The Ojibwa, known as Chippewa in the U.S., now live in a village five miles to the south.

During the early years of the trade, the Grand Portage trail was famous, or perhaps infamous, for its length and punishing grade. At nine miles it was the longest carry on the whole cross-country route, rising sharply to a plateau, passing through a few weedy lakes, then steeply rising again before sloping back down to the Pigeon River, which flows into the Rainy River/Lake of the Woods system. We found the beginning of the well-beaten trail behind the fort and began to climb. Fifteen minutes along, we stopped to take in the view of Lake Superior. It was stunning, with the fort below at the head of Chapeau Bay and the waters of the immense lake stretching to the horizon. We turned back up the slope, expecting to see the top of the rise ahead. But instead the trail wound higher and higher. Ten minutes later we stopped again, completely winded, and headed back down to the fort.

After the first day at Grand Portage, La Vérendrye's men had moved only a tiny fraction of their supplies — thousands of pounds of foodstuffs, weapons, ammunition and trade goods — up the slope. When they considered that ahead lay many more days, perhaps weeks, of back-breaking labour, just so they could get into the interior in time to spend a miserable winter in makeshift shelters, they told their commander point-blank that they would go no farther that fall.

Ochaga — who, as a native leader, understood the difficulty of convincing people to do what they didn't want to do — watched the scene with interest. He was pleased when, after discussing the mutiny with his second-in-command, La Jémeraye, La Vérendrye came to ask Ochaga for a favour. He wanted to send La Jémeraye and his eldest son, Jean-Baptiste, into the interior for the winter, so that he could notify his backers in New France that his party had moved into *terra incognita*. He asked Ochaga to send a Cree party to accompany the pair to the lake shown as Tecamamioen (Rainy Lake) on the birchbark map, and to watch over them.

When this small advance party had been sent off, Ochaga invited La Vérendrye and the rest of his company to spend the winter back in Kaministiquia, as his guests. It turned out to be a pleasant interlude. The Cree and local Ojibwa and Assiniboine had a good supply of meat and wild rice, and the French had biscuits and brandy. When the snows weren't too deep, the men went hunting, and La Vérendrye took advantage of the opportunity to sound out Ochaga about the country ahead. Among the strangest stories he was told was one about a people far to the west who wore body armour and lived in large permanent houses. This could have been a reference to the people of the Pacific coast, who lived in plank houses and wore armour in war, but the Cree also said these people spoke a language not unlike French. The story intrigued La Vérendrye, and he looked forward to discovering this strange tribe in his western explorations. It now appears that the Cree, who were wide-ranging traders, were actually describing the new Spanish settlements in New Mexico. The fact that they were able to describe the Spanish language as similar to French suggests that, somewhere in their travels, they had come in contact with the Spanish — or at least with a people who had had direct contact with them, such as the Shoshoni.

La Vérendrye was also able to gain more immediate intelligence about the relations between the Cree and the Dakota. In many ways, the cultural and linguistic divide between the Algonkin-speaking Cree and Ojibwa and the Siouan-speaking Dakota mirrored that between the Iroquois and the Algonkin-speaking peoples of the east. The parallel even extended to the names used to describe their enemies. "Sioux" was a French abbreviation of the Ojibwa "Nadon'newsu," which means People Who Strike from behind the Rock, or Snake People.

While an informal ceasefire was in effect between the Dakota and the Cree and their allies, La Vérendrye was told that it was not expected to last. To ensure the safety of the French force in the interior, Ochaga said, he would send an armed party of Cree to escort them. While La Vérendrye welcomed the offer, he made it clear that he didn't want to become embroiled in local conflicts. Part of the reason was that the French were already trading with the Dakota south of Lake Michigan (something that Ochaga was aware of), but La Vérendrye also knew that any reignition of the war would immediately shut down the trade in the interior. Ochaga politely noted his concerns. But like Champlain and other European commanders, La Vérendrye would discover that political decisions, and especially decisions on war or peace, were made according to national needs. Foreign pedlars — even those with portable cannon — had no say in the matter.

When spring came, La Vérendrye appeared in no hurry to lead his men into the bush. At the end of May, when La Jémeraye returned from Tecamamioen with his Cree escort, his canoe laden with furs, the commander was still loitering on the shores of Lake Superior. It wasn't until July 14, at the end of the blackfly season, that he finally set out to conquer the Grand Portage.

After the tons of gear were finally hauled over the nine-mile trail to the Pigeon River shove-off point, it was a two-week paddle to Tecamamioen, where La Jémeraye and Jean-Baptiste had built Fort St. Pierre, which was little more than a square of felled logs. Halfway to the fort, La Vérendrye passed over the height of land where the rivers switched direction: waters on the southern side flowed into the Great Lakes, while waters to the north flowed towards Hudson Bay. At the watershed, La Vérendrye was convinced that he was now on his way to the fabled western sea, and expected to be camping on Pacific beaches within weeks.

When his party arrived at Tecamamioen at the end of July, a large gathering of local Cree and Ojibwa assembled to welcome him formally to their country. After a period of feasting and a joint council with his hosts, La Vérendrye pushed further west to Min-es-tic (Lake of the Woods) with about two dozen men. He was accompanied by an impressive flotilla of fifty Cree and Ojibwa canoes offering protection, they said, against Snake People attacks.

This allied escort led him through Min-es-tic's maze of islands and deposited him on the western shore of the lake, ten miles south of their main trade route to the west through Waszrush Onigum (Muskrat) Portage.

La Vérendrye's men immediately began building Fort St. Charles. It was a rough rectangle, a hundred feet long and sixty feet across, fortified with a double palisade fifteen feet high and protected by four bastions mounted with cannon. While construction was going on, the Cree and Ojibwa introduced La Vérendrye to the wonders of the local wild rice harvest, which was so plentiful that he was able to throw away the grain crop seeds he had brought from Montreal. During the winter his crew continued work on the fort, adding a powder magazine, commandant's house, chapel, missionary house and four barracks buildings for the soldiers and traders. In the spring of 1733, Fort St. Charles — then the westernmost post in this half of North America — was open for business.

The location of the fort had been chosen by the local Cree and Ojibwa for their own strategic reasons. It was situated on contested land, mid-lake between their side and the side of the Dakota. For the allies it provided a defensive position against Nadon'newsu raids on the northern half of the lake, and a staging area for their own attacks on Dakota villages on the southern half. By the time La Vérendrye realized this, it was too late. He had unwittingly built his trading post in a no-man's-land.

The establishment of the fort was celebrated by an Ojibwa rock painting on the northeast corner of the lake, showing the fort and a French flag flapping in the breeze. The painting marked not only the arrival of European traders in the western Cree and Ojibwa territory, but an important achievement in allied diplomacy. Europeans, with their cannons, had been positioned on the frontlines in the war with the Dakota for control of the interior waters.

The next morning, we flew La Vérendrye's route into the interior. We would be staying for a few days at my sister and brother-in-law's cottage north of Lake of the Woods. From there we would visit the nearby Whitedog reserve and the old canoe route along the Winnipeg River, which Ochaga had described to La Vérendrye as "the great river that flows towards the setting sun." We would be landing at Minaki Lodge, once a luxurious resort hotel that had been built in the bush along the main rail line as a way-stop for first-class train travellers. The lodge was closed, we had been told, but the airstrip was still usable.

The territory between Lake Superior and Lake of the Woods is still thinly populated. In our first two hours of flight we passed over only a handful of towns, flagged in the distance by trails of black smoke from pulp and paper mills. Interspersed between these towns along the ancient canoe routes there were still old Ojibwa settlements like Naicatchewenin, Stangecoming and Nicickousemenecaning.

But even with the small population, the region's forests were being intensely logged. The forest was latticed by a network of logging roads linking clearcut to clearcut, the recent ones jagged patches of brown and the older ones softened to a pale green as the brush fought to cover the wound.

As we flew west the land flattened, with the edge of the Shield shifting northward. The voyageurs wrote glowingly about this part of the trip because, for the first time since they had dipped their paddles in the Ottawa River, they were free of the hummocky granite of the Shield. The less rugged land reminded the European-born of home.

As we headed north from Tecamamioen, the shore of Lake of the Woods emerged into view. Like so many place-names in the country, it is a misnomer. The Cree called the lake Min-es-tic, Lake of the Islands, but French fur traders confused the name with the Cree word *mis-tic*: "lake of the woods." The name stuck, though one glance at the misty blue and green collage of the lake's fourteen thousand islands showed how much more fitting the Cree name was.

As we cut across it, the scattered clouds began to thicken and darken, and we dodged rain showers on our way to the western shore, the site of Fort St. Charles. Before a series of dams built in the 1960s raised the water level by nine feet, the fort was at the tip of a promontory at the head of a deep-gash bay. Now the site is on Magnuson's Island, separated from the mainland by a hundred-yard, four-foot-deep channel. It's a few hundred yards over the U.S. border, which follows the old canoe route from Lake Superior to the northwest angle of Lake of the Woods, where the border shifts northward to the forty-ninth parallel.

The skies continued to darken, so after a pass over Magnuson's we headed north towards Minaki. We flew over the crooked mouth of the Winnipeg River at Waszrush Onigum, now known as Rat (not Muskrat) Portage, into what the Cree called the *keeway-din* (northern regions). Kenora, seen first as a line of smoky mill stacks, was to our right. After a few minutes of scanning the bush, Wayne located the railway tracks that, according to our charts, would lead us to the Minaki airstrip.

My sister and brother-in-law's camp was on Rough Rock, a riverine lake on the Winnipeg River system about ten miles north of Minaki and ten miles south of Wabaseemong (Whitedog). There was no phone, not even a road into the cottage, so we had arranged to make a five-hundred-foot pass with waggling wings to let them know we'd arrived. We passed over the cottage twice and watched as my sister Mary and her husband, Terry, and more kids than I recalled them having, came out to wave, while Gomez, their slightly demented Portuguese water spaniel, raced wildly up and down the shore.

We continued for a few more minutes, until we saw the foamy waters coming from the turbines of the Whitedog dam. The village was hidden somewhere in the forest off to the right. As we swung back to the Minaki airstrip, Wayne said he knew of two old stories featuring white dogs. One took place at a time when all the peoples were living in two communities linked by a bridge over a mighty river. A white dog suddenly arrived in one village. The chief, a woman called Godaysiyo, was charmed by the beauty of the dog and claimed it as her own. This created jealousy among the people, which sparked a chain of events — Wayne couldn't recall just what they were — that ended with the bridge between the communities being destroyed and both Godaysiyo and the white dog drowning in the river. In the other story, a white dog suddenly appeared to a wandering nation to lead them to their appointed place in the world. The people followed the dog through the snows of a bitter winter until finally, in early spring, it led them to their allotted land, on the banks of the grandfather of all rivers, the Mississippi. At that time of year the waters were raging with winter runoff, and the exhausted dog approached too close. It was swept away and drowned. To reward the animal for its service, the Great Mystery lifted the dog's spirit from the waters and into the sky, where it became the Milky Way.

We spotted the airstrip and began our descent to what turned out to be a short, bumpy runway. After we tied the Cessna down to a set of cement-filled automobile tires on the frost-heaved ramp, we headed over to the "terminal," a tiny boarded-up shack with wires sticking out where someone had ripped the pay phone from the wall.

Minaki Lodge was out of sight, a mile or so away, on the lakeshore. For a time, it had been the jewel in the chain of resort hotels operated by Canadian National Railways. It was in the style of Château Montebello, and offered, along with excellent dining, luxurious rooms and a golf course, a genuine wilderness vacation with guided fly-out fishing trips. But it never made money. As railway traffic diminished, so did the lodge's clientele. Ownership changed hands several times, and three years previously the Whitedog band chief had been talked into buying it with the $4 million his band had been awarded for the flooding of their land in the 1960s. Then there had been a dispute over some huge repair bills, and the lodge was now shut down while the case went to the courts.

There were parallels, Wayne said, between the white dogs in the stories and the Whitedog reserve. In every story, through no fault of its own, the dog drowned.

That evening, while we were sitting in the screened-in porch at my sister's cottage, Mary said that, although the reserve was just ten miles up the bush road from the landing where they parked their car, they had visited it only once. She had been surprised by the poverty and the sense of isolation. The people were friendly enough, they smiled greetings, but she had a profound sense that she didn't belong, that she and Terry were interlopers. "We drove through it and then left," she said. "It's like a foreign country."

Archaeological evidence indicates that the land in this area has been occupied for over nine thousand years. By the mid-1700s, the region north of Lake of the Woods had the same mix of Ojibwa and Cree villages found around the northwest end of Lake Superior, although the Cree were increasingly shifting west towards the plains.

As late as the 1850s, this was still undisputed Indian land. It was then that a British survey crew was stopped by a party of two hundred armed Ojibwa and asked their intentions. When the survey boss said they were simply passing through on their way west, the Ojibwa were skeptical. The *ogimauh* told the surveyors that the country was Ojibwa territory and that it would be passed on to their children after they were gone. He asked the surveyors to take that message back to their queen, and he let them pass.

The Queen apparently never received the message, because in 1873 the people of the western half of Danaiiwaad Ojibweg were dispossessed of 55,000 square miles of their land for a $5 per person annuity. Twenty-three years earlier, the eastern half of Danaiiwaad Ojibweg had been expropriated under similar terms. On

Canadian maps, nothing was left of the ten-thousand-year-old nation but isolated settlements in the bush like Whitedog.

The first day at Rough Rock, we rose at dawn to go fishing. Terry was up first, making coffee. His son Peter headed down to the dock to fill the gas tank from the forty-five-gallon drum and fill the minnow pail from the minnow trap. Father and son worked together as a team, wordlessly, as men who fish together for a long time often do.

We headed first to the south channel. Terry explained that a strong set of rapids had once roared through there — one of twenty-six in the 120 miles of the Winnipeg River between Lake of the Woods and Lake Winnipeg — before the dams raised the water levels. Despite the changes brought about by the dams, the Winnipeg River remains among the most beautiful spots in the country. There is an eternal quality to the river that you find nowhere else, with flat stony beaches, and Group of Seven pines twisting out of granite crevices. Along the shoreline, flocks of white pelicans perch on smooth rock islands and herons feed in the shallows. As late as the start of the eighteenth century, travellers like Alexander Mackenzie noted that here "fish, venison and fowl, with wild rice are in great plenty." The land abounded, Mackenzie said, "in everything necessary to the wants of uncivilized man."

We caught half a dozen walleye before the sun rose in the sky and the heat caused the fish to stop biting. Then we headed up the lake to the still visible rapids in front of the dam, beaching our boat alongside the narrow channel once used by Ojibwa and Cree travellers to skirt the main body of the rapids. The channel had been partially blocked by rockfill to increase the flow to the dam, but we could still see the ancient trails around a couple of the *décharges*, where the travellers carried the loads above while canoes were dragged along the bucking waters below with root-twine ropes. Walking the trail, Wayne said it had occurred to him that his own Cree ancestors had likely passed along here at some point, as the people drifted into the west from their original homeland around James Bay. While he was entertaining these thoughts, Terry and Peter were ahead, speaking of the voyageurs tottering along the slippery trail with ninety-pound bundles of furs or trade goods tumped to their foreheads. "One trail," Wayne later remarked, "two countries."

It was 262 years since the first non-native had passed through the channel. In the summer of 1734, La Vérendrye once again sent La Jémeraye ahead with an armed Cree escort to establish a beach-head, this time at the edge of the plains at the great lake Ochaga had called Ouinipigon (Muddy Waters) — today's Lake Winnipeg.

La Vérendrye had hoped to reach the plains the previous year, but he had been bogged down by supply problems and by the threat of war around Lake of the Woods. In the fall of 1733, the Dakota had responded to what they saw as French provocation — the building of Fort St. Charles under Cree tutelage — by launching a series of harassing raids. The closest had killed four Cree traders just outside the walls of the fort. The Cree had asked La Vérendrye to join them in a retaliatory raid, but he had refused, and pleaded with the Cree and their allies to forgo revenge and make peace with the Dakota. His concern was financial. In his two years at Fort St. Charles, La Vérendrye had found that the enormous cost of shipping furs more than a thousand miles to the east was dramatically cutting into his profit. The situation was complicated by the difficulty in getting supplies and trade goods from Boweting. There were delays and missed shipments, and when he ran out of goods, the local Cree, Ojibwa and Assiniboine traders disappeared up the northern rivers to trade with the British. When he admonished them for disloyalty, the native traders were apologetic; they didn't like dealing with the British, they said, because the British treated them coolly and refused to advance them ammunition in the fall. But if La Vérendrye didn't have any goods to trade, what could they do? La Vérendrye, who'd left Fort Senneville with dreams of constructing great trading stations along his triumphal march to the sea, found himself isolated and near bankrupt on the boundary of two powerful nations that seemed to be edging towards all-out war.

In the winter of 1734–35, the Cree informed him that they were organizing a three-nation expeditionary force, with their Ojibwa and Assiniboine allies, for a spring attack on the Dakota. Once again La Vérendrye pleaded with them to maintain peaceful relations, but the Cree told him that the decision had already been made, and asked him to send some of his men to fight alongside them. La Vérendrye refused. When the ice left the lake, a force of seven hundred Cree, Ojibwa and Assiniboine fighters assembled near Fort St. Charles to begin the ceremonies of war. When the sounds of drumming reached the walls of the fort, La Vérendrye realized that continuing to refuse to participate would put his partnership with the Cree and Ojibwa in jeopardy. In this country, trade was based on friendship, and friends were expected to stand beside one another in times of war. When he saw that the war party was about to depart, he relented, and offered to send his oldest son, Jean-Baptiste, to join the allied force. With a Dakota slave as his porter and two Cree women to cook for him, Jean-Baptiste went off to fight alongside Ochaga's people.

As soon as they left, La Vérendrye put his men to work strengthening the fort's defences in preparation for the inevitable Dakota counterattack. While they were working, Cree travellers brought word from La Jémeraye that he had constructed a small fort up the mouth of the river that Ochaga had described as being the colour of vermilion — the Red River, ten miles south of Lake Ouinipigon. It was cause for celebration. Two hundred and thirty-eight years after Cabot's Griquet landing, the Europeans had finally arrived on the great plains.

We headed up to Whitedog the next morning, taking the boat across Rough Rock Lake, then driving along a gravel road. About four miles down, we reached the Whitedog dam, which remains an important landmark for the people of Wabaseemong. Their original community was upriver from here and now lies submerged under the dam's reservoir.

Six miles past the dam, we passed a hand-painted sign with the word "Wabaseemong" and a picture of a fierce-looking white husky. We turned a bend and saw a house, then another, and realized that we had arrived. There was no centre to the village; just a haphazard collection of Department of Indian Affairs frame houses strung out along the ridge above Whitedog Lake.

We stopped at a rundown gas station to ask where we could find Isaac Mandaminat, a former chief who, Wayne had been told, was the man to speak to. The interior of the station was dark and the shelves behind the counter were bare. When our eyes adjusted, we saw three young boys peering out at us from a corner. "Isaac lives in the house past the one with the 80 Merc in front," the oldest boy told us. Their eyes were empty saucers.

Whitedog, a native health worker in Ottawa had once told me, was a mess, plagued by alcoholism, gas-sniffing, unemployment and brief, despairing outbreaks of brother-shoots-brother violence. Recently that violence had turned inward, with a series of youth suicides.

We found Isaac in the band office, at the back of the darkened arena where the council offices were located. He was meeting with one of the councillors, a woman who looked to be in her early thirties. Isaac was in his late fifties. He was square-shouldered, his T-shirt revealing still muscular arms. He had a stern expression on his face and, when he spoke, he gave the impression of someone who was used to being listened to. The story he told us had many familiar elements, but its force lay in the number and intensity of the attacks the community had withstood over the past thirty years.

Before 1960, he said, Whitedog was still a good place to live. There was no road into the community, so the people travelled by boat to Minaki, twenty miles south, to work as fishing and hunting guides or to stock up on supplies at the store. While the fish and game were only a shadow of what they had been when Alexander Mackenzie described the natural riches of the land, they were still plentiful enough to sustain a small community like Whitedog.

But then, he said, bulldozers came crashing through the forest, without notice. The Indian agent came by and said the people had to move their village because the provincial power company was building a dam. The people of Whitedog said, "They can't do that, this is our land." The Indian agent said, "They're doing it. The land will be flooded."

"They didn't even warn us when they put the dam in operation," Isaac said. "They didn't tell us they were going to flood the old cemetery. People came out of the bush after the fall hunt to find their relatives' coffins floating down the river."

In some ways, the road had done more damage to the community than the dam. The road brought truckloads of white hunters onto their land, and brought Kenora to Whitedog's doorstep. Now only a ninety-minute drive along the bush road, the city had a reputation as one of Canada's unfriendliest towns for native people, with an informal Jim Crow keeping them out of all but the shabbiest restaurants and hotels into the late 1970s.

Ten years after the flood came the pestilence. In the early 1970s, the Indian Affairs agent turned up again to tell the people, "Stop eating the fish. They're full of poisons from the pulp mills upstream."

We told him, Isaac said, that we'd been eating the fish for hundreds, even thousands of years, and with the outsiders hunting our game, fish were all we had left.

"If you keep eating them," the Indian Affairs agent said, "you'll get sick. You could die." The health worker I'd spoken to in Ottawa had said that the people were still being tested for neurological disease caused by mercury poisoning.

Isaac went on to speak about the hydroelectric developments, the ongoing clearcutting and the litany of other crimes against the land since the bulldozers had arrived at his village. When he was called away to the phone, the rather shy councillor, who had listened respectfully while Isaac spoke, told us that, although she was on the band council, she was not a politician by choice. She had been a write-in candidate in the previous month's election, and had only found out about her new position late at night, after the votes were counted. "I never really wanted the job," she said, "but when it's handed to you, you have to take it."

One of the first problems facing the new council was what to do about Minaki. She told us that the former chief — not Isaac but the one after him — had gotten carried away by the idea of his people owning the lodge. When he had purchased it with the money the band had been awarded for the flooding of their lands, he'd ignored the fact that Minaki was a chronic money-loser, its glory days gone with the railways. Apparently he had dreams of turning it into a casino, she said, but he didn't consult the people about his plans. They were still hoping they would be able to either get a casino licence or unload it on someone else, but for now they could do nothing, because the contractor hired to make structural repairs said he was owed $3 million and had slapped a lien on the property.

But Minaki was only a money problem. The village's woes ran deeper. She spoke of the recent rash of youth suicides; within six weeks, four young men — all in their twenties, and two of them brothers — had hanged themselves. Three of the deaths had occurred on successive weekends. "It was like suicide was stalking Whitedog. On Friday night, we would wonder who would be gone by Sunday."

Isaac had returned and was standing by the door, listening. "The young people don't want to die," he said. "But what's the choice?"

Outside in the parking lot, a mangy dog was sleeping in the sun, and a young man, drunk, with the sugary smell of raw alcohol on his breath, asked us for a smoke. I gave him one and he lurched off towards the frame houses on the ridge above the lake.

Although Whitedog had problems shared by other communities, it was beyond typical. It had endured more than other villages, and it was still trapped in the turbulence created by outsiders coming to seize the land. "It's not the Book of Isaac," Wayne said. "It's the Book of Job."

In a Winnipeg newspaper the next day, Ron Irwin, the happy-go-lucky Indian Affairs minister, was quoted as saying that his government would be celebrating August 9, the International Day of Indigenous Peoples, with "an emphasis on trade and economic development initiatives involving indigenous people in Canada and abroad." In Whitedog, the past thirty years of "development initiatives" had left the forests stripped, the lands flooded, the fishery ruined, the people's health seriously damaged and young people placing shotguns in their mouths and blowing their brains out. "When I think of how those people have been treated," my sister said that evening, "it makes me ashamed to be a Canadian."

We took off from Minaki in the same kind of weather we had arrived in, with darkening skies and a few isolated showers. But this time the front cut the lake in two, with the western shore in sunshine and the eastern in a fine rain. We flew along the edge of the sunshine, with Wayne calling out landmarks on the map and identifying the larger islands in the maze below. He took us over Aulneau Island and past Falcon Island, where we banked left to pass low over the little island where, in June 1736, La Vérendrye had a painful reminder that he was still in someone else's country.

The winter of 1735–36 was a difficult one at Fort St. Charles. The wild rice harvest had been flooded out by heavy rains, and not only trade goods but food supplies were almost exhausted. In the spring, Cree traders returning from the west brought news that La Jémeraye had fallen ill and died over the winter at the Red River post. The plains were once again empty of Europeans.

When June came without any sign of the supply convoy from Kaministiquia, the commander decided to send a party east to find out what the holdup was. He chose Jean-Baptiste, his eldest son, to lead the expedition, and nineteen soldiers to accompany him. At the last minute Father Aulneau, the expedition priest, decided to join them, so on June 5, 1736, twenty-one men set out from Fort St. Charles.

They spent the first night on a small island only twenty miles east of the fort. The next morning they shoved off at first light, but they had paddled only a few strokes when twenty canoes — a hundred paddlers — rounded the crescent-shaped island to the north. They were Dakota. Judging from the amount of blood found in both sets of canoes, the fierce battle began on the lake. The French tried to blow the Dakota canoes out of the water with their portable cannon, but the big guns were cumbersome to reload and Jean-Baptiste's party was quickly driven back onto the island. They left their dead and wounded on the shore while they retreated to the wooded heights. The battle was ferocious, but the Europeans were outnumbered five to one. The outcome was never in doubt.

Three days later, a passing Cree trading party found all twenty-one French heads laid out on a beaver robe on a flat, exposed area of the island. Jean-Baptiste, who had gone to war against the Dakota the previous spring, was lying on his stomach, his back riddled with knife wounds and his torso decorated with garlands of porcupine quills. In another pointed message to the French commander, Father Aulneau's headless body was propped up by a spear shoved into his side. He was on one knee with his right hand raised over the bloody ground, as if he were giving absolution to his headless flock.

La Vérendrye took the news quietly. When the Cree and Ojibwa offered to mount a massive strike to avenge the deaths, he steadfastly refused. An escalation of the war would wipe out the trade entirely. And he needed the trade to reach the western sea.

The rain was beating heavily now, so after one pass over the site — still called Massacre Island — we banked left again and turned back towards the great river that flows straight for the setting sun.

Just past the reservoir created by the Whitedog dam, where the old village lies submerged, the land begins to flatten. Almost before realizing it, we were at the edge of the plains, with the muddy-looking waters of Lake Winnipeg in the distance. Beyond it lie the treeless lands where the people had been living for two hundred centuries or more when La Jémeraye arrived. We were approaching Wayne's homeland — his grandmother's country.

CHAPTER THIRTEEN

Muddy Waters

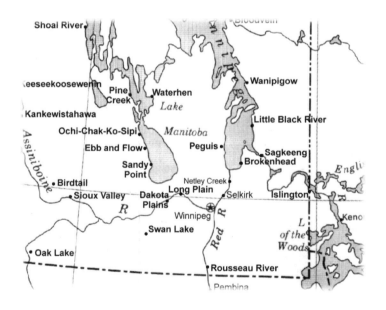

W ITHIN SIGHT of the main runway at Winnipeg International lies one of the few surviving sections of true prairie. In the late 1960s, someone noticed that only plants native to the area were growing on the unused thirty acres of land between the airport and Sturgeon Creek. When agronomists took a closer look, they discovered that somehow this broad meadow had never been put under the plough. It was a relic of the tall-grass prairie that in La Vérendrye's day stretched from Manitoba to Texas — a grassland larger than the African savannah or South American pampas, on the scale of the Russian steppes.

In tourist brochures the site is referred to as the "Living Prairie Museum." We visited it in late afternoon, when the information booth was closed and the field was empty. From a distance the waving two-foot-tall bluestem grasses gave the impression of uniformity, but when we walked along the path we spotted snowberry plants growing on the edge of gopher holes, brown-eyed Susans, goldenrod and thistles staking out their territory below the tall grasses. Farther along the trail, we came across a low plant that Wayne called prairie tumbleweed.

It is on the great plains, among the tall grasses of Manitoba and the mixed and shortgrass prairie to the west, that human habitation in what is now Canadian territory has been traced back the farthest.

Recent evidence suggests people were living here at least twenty thousand years ago. Over those millennia, the great, shifting countries built on this sea of grasses developed ways of life as unique and complex as the prairie itself. An ancient trading centre was located at the forks of the Red and Assiniboine rivers, now in downtown Winnipeg, almost ten thousand years ago. In ancient times there were also farming communities along the rich, flood-fed loam banks of the Red River. The farmers were likely Siouan-speakers, who dominated here until the early 1400s, when what climatologists refer to as the "Little Ice Age" began. The reduced growing season eventually made agriculture impossible, so the farmers drifted south and, according to some accounts, the region was taken over by the Siksika (Blackfoot), with other plains peoples: the Aaninena (the White Clay People known as Gros Ventre), Pikani (Peigan), Tsuu T'ina (Sarsi), Kainai (Blood) and Kutenai (Kootenay) occupying the lands to the west. In warmer periods these nations lived full-time on the plains. During the Little Ice Age they too were forced to retreat in winter to the shelter of the surrounding forests, to secure firewood and protection from the heavy snows and fierce prairie winds.

What kept them connected to this grassland were the sixty million buffalo that migrated north and south across the plains. The buffalo provided not only meat, which was eaten fresh and preserved as pemmican for year-round use, but clothing, bedding, housing material, covering for their travois (triangular sleds pulled by dogs) and bone and horn tools. Life was dominated by the buffalo hunt, and the people developed ingenious methods of tracking and intercepting migrating herds. Without horses, which only arrived with the Europeans, they had to do all this on foot.

Since buffalo did not take the same migration route each year, locating them in the prairie vastness took all the peoples' divination and tracking skills. And once a herd had been located, the work had only begun. If the hunters moved in and started to bring the animals down with spears and arrows, the herd would stampede and the hunters would be left in a cloud of dust, with only enough meat for their immediate needs.

The strategy adopted was a much larger and more complex version of the deer fences used in the east. Since the prairie was too immense for beasts to be captured with even the broadest network of fences, the hunters had to find some means of luring the buffalo into the V-shaped enclosures from many miles away. They accomplished this with a piece of animal theatre.

The main characters were the wolf and the calf. The actors were men; one would rub himself with the scent of the wolf and don a wolf's skin, while the other took the scent of a calf and donned a calf's hide. Together they would play and replay the same scenario. Calf-man would insinuate himself at the edge of the herd, on the side he wanted it to move away from. Wolf-man would move in and simulate an attack on calf-man. Seeing this, the herd would move in the desired direction. But knowing that the wolf would be occupied for some time with the kill, the animals would trot off in an orderly, unhurried fashion. Some time later, the lone wolf would appear again and take another stray calf, and the herd would trot off again in the direction of the fences. When the buffalo had been guided across the plains to the mouth of the V-shaped corral — often over many days — the people would emerge from the grasses, beating drums and shaking noise-makers to drive them into the enclosure or, in some cases, over a steep ridge to their deaths. Work would immediately begin on butchering carcasses, stretching hides and preparing pemmican: dried, ground meat mixed with berries and fat and sewn into pouches to preserve it through the winter.

When the summer hunt was over, the plains people gathered at trade fairs held by the corn-growing Mandan people or by the neighbouring Shoshoni, who were based in what is now the Montana foothills but spoke an Aztecan language. The fairs provided a wealth of exotic goods. Obsidian, which is still the sharpest substance known to man, was imported from northern British Columbia,

California and Wyoming. Knife River flint was imported from what is now North and South Dakota. Pottery was brought in all the way from Iroquois country. Spear points came from Hudson Bay and some copper goods came both from Lake Superior and down from Inuit and Dene lands on the shores of the Arctic Ocean. Decorative shells were imported from the Pacific, the Atlantic and as far south as the Gulf of Mexico.

In historical times the most prized trade items were Spanish horses, which came up through the trading network from the south. Horses were first acquired from the Spanish, through either trade or rustling, in the early 1600s, when Champlain was just arriving at Kebek. The Indian trade in horses had begun in the south by 1640, almost a century before La Jémeraye made it onto the plains. Horses transformed the lives of the people; they fit into their ancient cultures like a key into the lock of the Promised Land. Mounted villages of one or two thousand people began to replace the small bands. Buffalo herds were now far easier to locate, as mounted scouts could cover hundreds of square miles in a few days. Once the herd was found, the hunters could outrun even stampeding buffalo, and the hunt was described by European observers as breathtakingly exciting. Hunters galloped through clouds of dust while balancing precariously on their bareback mounts, firing arrows into the side of the buffalo's back, trying to pierce a lung. Like other native North Americans, the plains people worshipped at the altar of courage, and the buffalo hunt was looked forward to for its excitement as much as for its bounty.

Today, many of the descendents of those hunters are themselves corralled in Winnipeg's North End. When we walked along a downtown section of Main Street that evening, we passed a series of skid-row hotels and taverns, some boarded up, with Indian or Métis men — drunk or sick or both — slouched in the doorways. On one corner, two hard-looking young native women were waiting at the curb for customers.

The early evening air was scented with the bitter smell of burnt hops from a nearby brewery. This part of Winnipeg reminded him, Wayne said, of the flophouses, greasy spoons and skid-row hotels of 96th Street in Edmonton, a few blocks from where he had grown up. "In the first grade," he said, "I had to cross 96th Street to get to school. It used to scare me. But by the time I was seven or eight, I was hanging out a block away with the street kids. We used to meet in front of the Coffee Cup Inn, where the guys on the skids, mainly Indian and Métis, went for coffee."

Their main sport was shoplifting. "Me and the other kids used to hit Woodward department store, the W.W. Arcade hardware store and the Army/Navy store," he said. "But by the time I was twelve, I knew I wanted to get out of there. Everyone did. I was lucky to escape."

Places like Main and 96th streets often trap people not just for years but for lifetimes and generations. Some of the people there were grandchildren of men who'd lost their livelihood with the coming of the settlers, and had wandered in from reserves that had nothing — no jobs, no future, no hope. For these, Winnipeg provided no way out: no escape but the fleeting respite offered by booze or drugs, or by the spiritual inebriation of religious sects. Today increasing numbers of native people were moving into Winnipeg — people who had education, who found jobs in the city and lived more or less middle-class lives — but on the Main it was the forgotten refugees you saw.

Harold Two-Heart was one of these. We found him at the centre of a small crowd in front of a convenience store, standing over a native woman sprawled in a heap on the pavement with a halo of blood around her head. Wayne moved to the edge of the circle.

"This is what white people do to Indians," the man said, with a drunken slur but a matter-of-fact tone. He bent over the woman and gently lifted her head. "I can see her brains."

When the police and ambulance arrived, most of the crowd blended quietly into the night. One of the officers pulled the man aside and asked him who he was and what had happened. He told them his name and said that he and his girlfriend, Lorna, had been in a cab and had stopped to buy some potato chips. He had left her in the cab while he went to get the chips. When he'd come out, the taxi driver, a white man, had been pulling Lorna out of the car and throwing her down on the pavement. She had landed on her head. The cab had driven off. While Lorna, still looking lifeless, was loaded into the ambulance, Two-Heart added, "We were going to get married."

The police headed back to their squad car. Two-Heart glanced at Wayne. "Can I have a cigarette?"

Wayne handed him one. He told us that he and Lorna were from the Sagkeeng First Nation, the Ojibwa community at Fort Alexander, near the mouth of the Winnipeg River. They had spent the day at Lorna's cousins' flat nearby, apparently drinking, and he had gotten into a fight with one of the cousins. Two-Heart pointed to a gash above his eye and parted his hair to show another nasty wound. He and Lorna had been on their way to a friend's place in the taxi when they had decided to stop at the store. He was worried about Lorna.

"My sister died like that," he said.

The ambulance pulled away. Two-Heart stared after it, saying nothing.

"How are you going to find her?" Wayne asked.

He told us that the police had said they were taking her across the river to St. Boniface, but that he didn't have cab fare.

I wondered if the lack of cab fare had something to do with Harold and Lorna being evicted from the taxi.

"We'll get you a cab," Wayne said.

Several empty cabs passed us by before one stopped to take us across the Red River. When we arrived at the Hôpital Général St. Boniface, the emergency room was crowded with the sick and injured and those waiting for word. Two-Heart checked on Lorna's condition and was told that she still hadn't been seen by a doctor.

He told the nurse that she had cracked her head open, and that his sister had died that way, and the nurse hurried off. When she returned, she said that Lorna was in the examining room but it would be a while before she was looked at. At least an hour.

The three of us went out for a smoke in the park across the street, where streetlamps illuminated a large statue of a triumphant-looking European with an Indian in his shadow. We went over to take a look. It was a statue of Pierre Gaultier de Varennes et de La Vérendrye, erected in 1938, the plaque said, to celebrate the two-hundredth anniversary of the founding of Winnipeg. La Vérendrye was standing clutching a musket while a generic Indian crouched at his feet. The Latin inscription read, *Istas invenit terras easque humanitati et fidei apreuit* — "He found these lands and then he opened them to humanity and faith."

We sat on a nearby bench and smoked. Behind us were Montreal-style row houses, and calypso music issued from one of the open windows. Two-Heart assured us that the taxi driver would be sorry for what he'd done. Both his brothers, he said, were members of the Manitoba Warriors Society, and they didn't take kindly to white guys beating up Indian women. With that, he stood up, said he was going to get a beer, and disappeared into the darkness.

Two-Heart's Ojibwa people had arrived in the Red River Valley in historical times. They had come west after a series of upheavals that began in Nitassinan shook the foundations of the Tenakìwin and Danaiiwaad Ojibweg homelands. The initial cause of the turmoil was the Seven Years War, between France and England, which began in Europe in 1756 and quickly spread to the European holdings in North America.

For the people of Danaiiwaad Ojibweg, the war and its aftermath ended a brief, final golden age. By the mid-1750s their territory stretched almost a thousand miles, from Saguinan on Lake Ontario to the forests west of Lake Superior. From the northwest end of their territory, the Ojibwa travelled up to trade with the

British at Hudson Bay. The Boweting and Lake Huron Ojibwé continued to trade with the French along the old French/Mattawa/Ottawa route, and the Mississauga in Saguinan Land opened up trade, through Iroquoian territory, with the British to the south. When hostilities broke out between the French and English in the Lake Champlain region in the 1750s, the Boweting Ojibwa were confident enough of their position to send a contingent of peacekeeping troops to the St. Lawrence to defend the French colony against British attacks.

In the summer of 1757, Ojibwa expeditionary forces were accompanying French troops on a sweep through the Lake Champlain area when they crossed a smallpox-infected area. Some of the native fighters were infected and took the disease back to the Lake Superior region. With their heartland suddenly under attack from the devastating disease, the Ojibwa were forced to reduce their military force along the St. Lawrence.

It was around this time that the British began their final offensive against the French colonies in North America. In September 1759, General Wolfe and his British marines scaled the Quebec cliffs to the Plains of Abraham, and when the battle was over, the British were in control of the French bastion. After wintering in Quebec and fending off French counterattacks, they marched on Montreal, seizing it in September 1760. From there they moved inland to take over the remaining French forts and trading posts around the Great Lakes, and expelled French officials from the country.

In what is now southern Ontario, the disruptions caused by the British replacing the French were minimal, since the Mississauga Ojibwa had already developed trading relations with the British in New England. But in the rest of Danaiiwaad Ojibweg, the British arrival was cause for concern.

The Ojibwa had afforded certain privileges to the French because they were allies in the Iroquois war; they had established friendship, and in some cases kinship, with them. The Ojibwa had no such relations with the British, who were also suspect because they had been allied with their Iroquois enemies. Tension mounted throughout 1761, as British forces marched into Ojibwa territory to take over French forts and trading posts. By the spring of 1762, the Council of the Three Fires had decided to evict the uninvited guests from its territory.

The leader of the anti-British movement was Pontiac, an Odawa war chief living in southern Saguinan Land, near present-day Detroit. He was influenced by the Delaware Indian prophet Neolin, who was warning North American nations that if they "allowed the English among you, you are dead, maladies, smallpox and their poison will destroy you totally."

In mid-May 1762 the Pontiac uprising began, when the war chief's troops lay siege to Detroit. Within weeks, eight of the eleven remaining British forts fell into native hands.

The immediate effect of the uprising was to demonstrate to the British that they could not yet control territory in Indian country beyond the St. Lawrence. They would need to enter into some kind of formal alliance with the aboriginal peoples if they hoped to operate in their territory. This was reflected in the Royal Proclamation of 1763, which recognized the sovereignty of the indigenous nations of the Americas outside the narrow strip of land along the St. Lawrence that the British had taken from the French. Danaiiwaad Ojibweg and all the countries to the northwest were thereby recognized as self-governing nations. But there was a catch. Provisions were made for future surrender of Indian lands for European settlement, although this could only be accomplished through negotiations and treaties ratified by local or national indigenous assemblies.

As so often happened with indigenous peoples in the Americas, the Ojibwa won the war but, almost imperceptibly, lost the peace. Danaiiwaad Ojibweg continued to come under invasion by wave after wave of deadly European diseases, and its borders were being breached by settlements creeping west. Over the next century, Europe would slowly release into North America thirty million land-hungry settlers, a human tide that would swamp the ancient lands.

Harold Two-Heart's people began their trek west from Boweting in 1780, when the smallpox epidemics were at their most virulent. Once again, the disease had swept into Danaiiwaad Ojibweg from the east, and as the band moved west across Lake Superior, along the border lakes to the Winnipeg River, they discovered that the epidemic had preceded them. Throughout their journey they encountered villages where the dead outnumbered the living, and deserted villages where the survivors, overwhelmed by the deaths and fearing for their children's lives, had fled to the forests. When they reached the choppy waters of Lake Winnipeg and headed south to the river the colour of vermilion, they discovered that the sickness had also devastated the plains.

The first community they came to was a Cree village fifteen miles up the Red River, at the mouth of Netley Creek, near the place where La Jémeraye had set up the first European post forty-four years earlier. They found the village empty except for one small child, whom they took with them. Farther down the Red River they found an Assiniboine village with no survivors in sight. They pushed on to Pembina Mountain, south of Winnipeg, where they met a large body of Assiniboine and Cree who had abandoned the infected valley.

The Cree were pleased to see their Ojibwa cousins. "Your presence," the leading Cree chief told them, "will remove the cloud of sorrow that is in our minds." After the Ojibwa were feasted, they were formally invited to dwell on the edge of the plains with the Cree and Assiniboine, "to eat out of the same dish, to warm themselves at the same fire," and to make common cause against their enemies, the Dakota.

The new arrivals were given the land around the juncture of Netley Creek and the Red River as their hunting and fishing grounds. This is mild country with riverbanks covered in cattails and sandbar willows, and with a broad marsh rich in waterfowl. The Ojibwa moved into the abandoned Cree village and found the rivers still full of fish and the eastern forests well stocked with game. While the Cree and Assiniboine hunted buffalo and worked as middlemen bringing furs down from the north, the Ojibwa, with their woodland skills, slipped into the role of provisioners for the North West Company fur-trading post at the forks of the Red and Assiniboine rivers.

The Ojibwa named the creek Death River, but despite this sombre name they quickly made the land their home. Over time they acquired horses, and some families began spending part of the year on the plains, while the rest remained in the Red River Valley. Still, they kept their Anishnaubek culture, and most of the band still made pilgrimages back to Boweting to hold Medaewaewin ceremonies in the old heartland.

By the early 1800s, the Ojibwa were being led by Peguis, the son of the chief who had led them to the new country. He was known as Cutnose by his own people because he'd had the tip of his nose cut off during a "frolic" at Pembina, but his youthful escapades did not reflect his later leadership. He would use great caution in trying to steer through the turbulent times ahead, when rival fur companies went to war and the first settlers arrived on the plains.

The new fur trade rival to the HBC was the North West Company. It was based in Montreal and backed by largely Scottish capital. After the British conquest, it took over the old east-west French fur trade routes, employing Métis, French and native voyageurs to transport goods into the interior and bring out furs. By the end of the eighteenth century, the two companies were locked in a bitter battle for control of the Canadian trade. Tensions increased in the spring of 1812, when a small fleet of York boats arrived on the Red River from the north carrying an unexpected cargo: haggard-looking men, women and children. They stopped at Peguis's village at Netley Creek for provisions and were greeted warmly. The Ojibwa, long accustomed to seeing white men, and occasionally white women, were delighted to see the children. Fires were kicked to life and pots put on to boil as they prepared to feast their unexpected guests.

Although we didn't realize it, while we were waiting for Two-Heart to come back we were only a few hundred feet from the spot where, on September 4, 1812, Miles Macdonell formally took possession of Two-Heart's country by reading French and English versions of the letters of patent the Selkirk settlers had received from the Hudson's Bay Company.

These unannounced settlers were poor Scots who had been given 116,000 square miles of land that the Earl of Selkirk, a director of the Hudson's Bay Company, had purchased from the company for ten shillings. Seeing their sorry state, Peguis and his people helped them get established in the country and the settlers acknowledged their reliance on the Ojibwa by referring to Peguis as their "Colony Chief."

The local Métis employees of the North West Company were not nearly so sanguine about settlers moving into their midst. They sent representatives to warn Peguis that this was the thin edge of a wedge that would eventually drive the native people from their land.

Peguis listened to the Métis warning but kept silent. Later, in the village council, the Ojibwa decided that the handful of settlers could represent no threat to their nation, and some questioned the motivations of the Métis. When the Métis next came to Netley Creek, Peguis politely told them that he would have no part in any scheme to drive the settlers, whom he called his "children," from the country.

His decision to protect the settlers may have had something to do with the fact that, at the time, the Hudson's Bay Company was shamelessly courting him. In 1812, when the HBC opened up a post at Douglas Point — in what is now downtown Winnipeg, a few blocks from where we'd met Harold Two-Heart — Peguis was given a red serge captain's uniform in recognition of his importance to the company. The following year, he was taken north on a junket to visit the forts on Hudson Bay, and put up for a couple of nights in the captain's cabin of the HMS *Rosamond*. On his return to Netley Creek, he spoke glowingly of the treatment he had received, and of the new alliance that he had secured for his people.

In 1815, while Peguis was still being celebrated as colony chief, the Métis's worst fears about the settlers were confirmed. Officials at the Red River colony announced that pemmican could not be exported from the colony. At the time pemmican was the basic fuel of the western trade, and the North West Company was using its Red River post as a main pemmican provisioning depot. The proscription was thus viewed by the Métis as almost a declaration of war, designed to force them and the North West Company out of the region. Rumours began to circulate that the Métis were planning an all-out assault on the settlement and the Hudson's Bay post.

Officials of the colony and the Hudson's Bay Company turned to Peguis for help, asking that he intervene with the Métis to stave off the expected attack. When he met with them, Métis once again warned Peguis that the settlers had come to deprive the Ojibwa of their freedom and their land. They asked him to join them in their battle to drive the settlers out. Peguis refused. He could not believe that his "children" would ever be so ungrateful or presumptuous as to try to steal his land.

During the summer of 1815, heavily armed Métis traders and buffalo hunters began to gather on the banks of the Red River, across from the settlement. A frantic call went out to the colony chief to try to dissuade the Métis from an attack, and Peguis rode down to the Métis camp with a contingent of well-armed Ojibwa fighters. In the hope of winning him over, the Métis leaders put on a welcoming feast that included many kegs of brandy. While they drank, they pleaded with him to join them. But Peguis said he would never condone an attack on the settlers. Then he crossed the river to the colony to warn the settlers that the Métis "have no ears to listen to the words of Peace." He offered to give people refuge at Netley Creek, but warned them to stay low in their York boats when they headed upriver because he feared the Métis might start shooting from the shore.

The settlers were more than happy to take orders from their colony chief. "We know these lands are yours," local officials told Peguis. "If you tell us to leave, we will."

Because of Peguis's intervention, a confrontation was avoided that year. The following spring, however, word came that the Métis and North West traders were once again gathering for an attack. Peguis sent messengers to warn the new governor, Robert Semple, and to offer his assistance. Semple, who is described in the official record as "brave and obstinate," ignored both the warning and the offer. Instead, he instituted armed patrols around the territory. During one of these patrols, he and twenty-five of his men met a group of Métis at Seven Oaks, a farm on the flat riverbank known as Frog Plain. Semple launched into a long harangue, pointing out to the Métis that, given the power vested in him by the Hudson's Bay Company and the British Crown, he would no longer accept their threats and intimidation. The speech was cut short when a shot rang out. The Métis opened fire at once. In an instant, Semple and twenty of his men lay dead or dying on the plain. The Métis then moved on to attack and overrun the Hudson's Bay post.

Peguis was furious with the Métis for the attack. He dispatched his young men to retrieve the bodies of the slain, and moved his troops in to protect the settlers. The year after the Seven Oaks massacre, Hudson's Bay officials thanked Peguis for his assistance and Lord Selkirk himself travelled to the colony to award him a silver medal and an official letter saying that the Ojibwa chief was to be accorded "favour and respect" by all Company officials. Selkirk also presented Peguis with a "friendship treaty" between their two peoples that promised the people an annual gift of a hundred pounds of tobacco. Similar gifts were offered to the local Cree and Assiniboine.

The Seven Oaks massacre caused a scandal in Britain, as it was realized that the rival fur companies were literally at war with one another. Pressure to merge the two companies grew, and within five years the Hudson's Bay Company had swallowed its competitor.

The merger deprived the people of the ancient countries of an alternate market for their furs that they had been able to rely on since Radisson and Des Groseilliers had sailed into Hudson Bay in the late 1660s. As the posts of the North West Company closed down, hundreds of Métis and their families, suddenly out of work, drifted into the Red River colony from east and west. They were joined by a new influx of British settlers, and within a few years of the merger the colonists and Métis in the Red River Valley outnumbered the Ojibwa.

Peguis and his people were then brushed aside, and the Ojibwa leader found that his promised "favour and respect" quickly evaporated. In 1821 he tried to renew his alliance with the Hudson's Bay Company in the traditional way, by proposing the marriage of his daughter to the son of the new chief trader at the fort. The offer was dismissed out of hand, and Peguis, who six years before had been acclaimed as the saviour of the colony, found himself treated as something of a joke by the newcomers. During this period, he was informed that the land given to the Ojibwa by the Cree was no longer theirs. Selkirk's friendship treaty, they said, had been a purchase of the land, not a symbol of gratitude.

While we were waiting for Two-Heart to return, Wayne said that when he had read about Peguis many years before, he had viewed him as a kind of Hudson's Bay toady, parading around the settlement in his red serge uniform. But as he eased into middle age, his perspective was changing. "It's true that Peguis could have made common cause with the Métis and driven the settlers from the country," he said. "But that would only have been a temporary solution. Guys like Peguis were in an impossible position. Movable objects facing irresistible forces."

The continent was beginning to fill up in the east; the overflow was pushing west. European immigrants were moving en masse into the Saguinan Land around the Great Lakes. They were beginning to send armies of lumbermen into Tenakìwin to strip the country of its highly prized white pine, and prospectors into Danaiiwaad Ojibweg to search for precious metals. A tidal wave was breaking over the old countries; the people, weakened by disease and the disappearance of game, could not withstand its force.

Two-Heart appeared from the darkness with three bottles of beer. He offered us one but didn't seem displeased when we turned him down. We headed back to the emergency room. The nurse told us that Lorna was gone, but we found her sitting on a low cement wall outside, looking dazed. She had no bandage on her head, nothing to indicate that she had received any treatment at all. She told Harold that she'd woken in the emergency room and the nurse had said she could leave.

Two-Heart introduced us and handed her one of his beers. Lorna asked if she could borrow a cigarette, and told us her story. When Harold had gone into the store on Main Street, she said, the taxi driver had asked her if she had money to pay the fare. She had said she didn't. When he'd asked if Harold did, she'd said, "Ask him." She couldn't remember what had happened next, but apparently that was when he'd thrown her from the cab.

The four of us took a taxi back across the river to downtown Winnipeg. Harold asked to be let off on the Main, where they could try to find some friends before the taverns closed.

As he got out, he thanked us. He told us that nobody in Winnipeg had ever treated him like that. "People in Winnipeg aren't nice at all," he said. He asked for two more cigarettes, one for himself and another for Lorna, and they disappeared into the night.

Just three years before Confederation, Two-Heart's countryman, Peguis — still known as Cutnose to his people — published a manifesto denouncing the Hudson's Bay Company and the British. He regretted, he said, ever helping the swindlers who had accepted his aid and friendship and then stolen his land.

"Then he died," Wayne said. "Feeling like a fool for having given it all away."

"Selkirk did not tell us what was in the papers," Peguis had written during his final days, "and I regret to say we did not even ask."

CHAPTER FOURTEEN

Big Bear's Odyssey

F LYING OVER THE PLAINS in August was like flying over a vast quilt; wheat crops were drying to pale yellow, flax fields flowering to light blue and rapeseed fields ripening to bright orange. The pattern was broken only by the creases of the river valleys and an occasional pastel-green stain where a lake had evaporated in the heat of the prairie summer. As we flew west, the tableau changed while remaining essentially the same, like the moving dioramas of early picture shows.

In Peguis's time, the land from Winnipeg to Saskatoon was the homeland of great mounted nations: the peoples of the Blackfoot Confederacy — Siksika, Kainai, Pikani and Tsuu T'ina — as well as those who had moved out onto the plains with the arrival of the horse — the Cree, Ojibwa, Assiniboine and Métis.

The most numerous and powerful of these peoples were the Cree. They had been living in the woodlands at the northern limits of the grasslands for centuries, venturing onto the plains during seasonal hunts. By the mid-1700s, large numbers of Cree had moved permanently onto the grasslands and adopted the plains way of life. Eventually they began to distinguish themselves from their woodland brothers, referring to themselves as Nehiyawak (Cree) and to the woodland people as Saka:widhiniwak (Bush Cree). The Nehiyawak settled first in the northeast area of the plains, near the mouths of the great rivers flowing north into Hudson Bay, but gradually shifted south and west across the northern plains and parkland. Their Ojibwa and Assiniboine allies went through similar transformations, moving out to occupy the southeastern and south-central plains. In this great shifting of peoples, the Aaninena (Gros Ventre) were pushed south. The peoples of the Blackfoot Confederacy were pushed west, with the Kutenai, the westernmost people, forced to retreat back into the mountains.

With this continuous westward shift, the peoples of the Blackfoot Confederacy avoided contact with Europeans until the mid-eighteenth century. The first brief meeting came in 1754, when a Hudson's Bay Company agent, Anthony Henday, was sent down the Hayes River from York Factory to reconnoitre the plains. He travelled with Cree guides to the Saskatchewan River and paddled five days southwest of the village of W'Passkwayaw (The Pas), where they met a group of Cree buffalo hunters. Henday and his guides purchased a few pack horses from the hunters to carry their trade goods, then headed out onto the grasslands (which he called the Muskcuty Tuskee Plains) on foot. From mixed grasslands they moved to the shortgrass prairie and the land of the Siksika. Henday finally made contact with them northeast of modern-day Calgary, within sight of the Rocky Mountains. Or rather, the Siksika made contact with him.

In his journal, Henday wrote, "Then came to us four horse men on Horse-back; they told us they were sent from the main body to see whether we were Friends or Enemies." He convinced the horsemen that they were friends, and his party followed them on foot to a large camp of two hundred lodges, about 1,500 people. He and his guides were immediately taken to the council tent, where the headman, accompanied by twenty tribal elders, sat silently on a white buffalo skin. The headman motioned to Henday to sit at his right. Without a word spoken, welcome pipes were lit and passed around. When everyone had smoked, boiled buffalo meat was served in reed baskets. After he had eaten his fill, Henday was given an additional gift of ten buffalo tongues.

With the welcoming ceremony over, Henday told the headman that his Great Leader, who lived at the Great Waters, was inviting them "to see him and to bring him Beaver skins & Wolves skins: & they would get in return Powder, Shot, Guns, Cloth, Beads."

When the Cree interpreted his words, the headman was polite but evasive. It was an interesting proposition, he said, but the great waters of Hudson Bay were a long way off. After a few more minutes of pleasantries, Henday and his party were politely dismissed and escorted to guest lodges that had been set up a quarter-mile from the village. After passing the night, which was marked by steady movements of mounted parties arriving in the village, Henday was summoned back to the council tent. According to his journal, the headman told him that he didn't think the Siksika would be able to trade with Henday's people, because the great waters were too far away and his people

> could not live without buffalo flesh; and that they could not leave their horses &c: and many other obstacles, though they might be gotten over if they were acquainted with a Canoe, and could eat Fish, which they never do. The Chief further said they never wanted food, as they followed the Buffalo & killed them with Bows and Arrows; and he was informed the Natives that frequented the Settlements, were oftentimes starved on their journey.

The headman had a point. By the mid-1700s, nations dependent on trade were finding themselves in an increasingly precarious position. Because they spent their time and energy trapping or trading furs, the people found that a poor yield or a sudden drop in price could leave them unable to buy shot and powder for the winter. At times Indian traders would be given a welcoming rum, only to sober up three days later to discover that they had drunk away the whole value of their furs. Even Henday, a loyal company man, admitted that the headman's observations were "exceedingly true."

He stayed in the Siksika camp for another day, watching as new arrivals continued to ride in, swelling the gathering to 322 lodges, or 2,500 people. Before leaving, he watched them hunt buffalo on horseback with such skill that they were able to bring down a beast with one or two arrows. He noted that the finest rifle of the day could not have been more efficient. The Siksika made poor trade prospects, he reported, because they lacked for nothing.

During this period, the plains were a relatively peaceable place. The people of the Blackfoot Confederacy were closely allied with the Aaninena and had friendly relations with the Cree. The traditional enemies of the Blackfoot were the Shoshoni to the south, but warfare between them was sporadic. Tensions only began to mount in the late eighteenth century, when the Cree and Aaninena began to battle for control of the central plain. Outnumbered and outgunned, the Aaninena quickly retreated south to the Arapaho heartland. The Cree then moved into the old Aaninena territory, which brought them into direct contact with the Blackfoot peoples. At first relations remained friendly, but legend has it that around 1800 a dispute over the theft of some horses launched what would become a seventy-year war between the Cree and the Blackfoot.

One of the most intensive periods of fighting came in the 1820s. In 1824, a large Cree army came together for an attack on a Siksika camp near modern-day Edmonton. Four hundred Siksika were slain in a fierce battle. After celebrating the victory, the Cree broke up into smaller bands for the winter and rode back east to wait for Blackfoot retaliation.

The war with the Confederacy resumed in spring and continued for two more years, until both sides were exhausted by the fighting. When the Siksika chief, Old Swan, made an offer for peace in 1827, the Cree accepted. The two nations once again traded together and even camped together on the prairie.

The engine droned steadily and our airspeed showed ninety-five knots, but a stiff prairie wind on our nose was cutting our forward speed to closer to sixty miles an hour. Wayne pointed to the pencil-lines of dust billowing behind pickup trucks speeding along the concession roads below. Some of them were moving faster than we were.

The land below had been part of Mukatai's territory in the 1820s. An Ojibwa who led a mixed Cree and Ojibwa band, he had been one of the leading war chiefs during the flare-up in the Cree–Blackfoot war in 1824. After the battle, he led his people back to their winter camp at Jackfish Lake, near present-day North Battle-ford. During that winter his first son, Mistihai'muskwa (Big Bear), was born. Although he was born into war, Big Bear would grow up in peace on prairie that was still Indian land. His would be the last generation that could make that claim.

With his Cree ancestry, Wayne said, he viewed the story of Mistihai'muskwa as a great national epic, a story of Ulyssean pro-portions. A small man with a pockmarked face, Big Bear was far from a handsome Hollywood-style hero. But he was a man with a profound sense of justice who fought to preserve his people's in-dependence while he led them on an eight-year trek in search of the disappearing buffalo — and their own disappearing freedom.

We were on the way to Saskatoon to visit Big Bear's great-grandson by adoption, Blaine Favel. From the air, Saskatoon looked like an oasis. Before we saw the buildings, we saw the city's trees, a small forest on the plain that straddles the North Saskatchewan River.

We landed at mid-morning and took a cab to the Federation of Saskatchewan Indian Nations' office, in an industrial park on the edge of town. It seemed like an odd location for the office, but Wayne said that the industrial park had been built on Indian land. At the upstairs reception, the secretary told us that Grand Chief Favel was running late and asked if we would have a coffee in the cafeteria downstairs.

The cafeteria, like everything associated with the FSIN, was bright and efficient. It was late in the morning, and the only customers were a table of young staffers who looked like law students or MBAS. One of them was speaking on her cellphone; the others had their phones unholstered, lying on the table, ready for action. When Chief Favel appeared in the doorway, they greeted him respectfully.

Favel's office was spacious and, like Ovide Mercredi's, decorated with works of Indian art and traditional crafts. He apologized for being late, and for the fact that he could give us only a few minutes. It wasn't even noon yet, he said, and it had already been a hell of a day. But he was looking forward to his two o'clock — a meeting with the famous American country and western singer Garth Brooks, who was in town for a concert.

We chatted for a few minutes about his current project, a First Nations bank that he was working on with the Toronto-Dominion Bank and with the help of Indian Affairs Minister Ron Irwin. The bank, he said, would be capitalized in part by land claims money, and would take the risk of investing in native businesses.

Wayne pointed to the portrait of Big Bear on the wall. At the mention of his great-grandfather, Chief Favel's demeanour changed. He dropped the clipped banker's tone and became almost reverential. "Mistihai'muskwa," he said, "was the most misunderstood man in Canadian history.

Big Bear is said to be buried on Favel's Little Pine reserve, and when Favel was first elected band chief, in the early 1990s, a Government of Canada plaque marked the spot. It described Big Bear as a renegade, an insurrectionist who had been responsible for a dreadful massacre. "Nothing could be farther from the truth," Favel said. "Big Bear wanted peace."

Favel's first act as a young chief, he said, was to get rid of the government plaque and put up a memorial honouring the true spirit of Big Bear, a hero of Nelson Mandela proportions who showed the people the path to freedom and gave them a shining example to follow. He suggested, as he had in Ottawa, that he saw his own work as a continuation of Big Bear's.

He was interrupted by a series of phone calls. Some of them seemed important, but he apologized to us for the interruptions. Finally, after the third call, he said, "You should meet my mother. She lives just up in North Battleford. You're flying, so you can be there in less than an hour. She'll make you lunch." He put his mother on the speakerphone, told her we were on our way. When he put down the receiver, he apologized again for having so little time. An hour later we were back in the air, flying to North Battleford.

We were en route only twenty-five minutes before we began our descent. Wayne pointed to a large lake shaped a bit like Hudson and James Bay, twenty miles north of the airstrip.

"Jackfish Lake," he said. The place where Big Bear had been born.

On the way to meet with Chief Favel's mother, I pointed to the wide gap between Whitedog and the FSIN office. "There are poor communities in Saskatchewan too," Wayne said. "But the FSIN has casino money. It gives guys like Blaine the cash you need to make deals."

I asked about the communities without casinos.

"Ideally," he replied, "the rich would help the poor." His tone suggested that this ideal was rarely attained.

When Mistihai'muskwa was four years old, a strange death notice appeared in *The Times* of London. Shawnandithit, described as "an interesting female" and a woman of "extraordinary mental habits," was reported to have died of consumption at St. John's, Newfoundland, on June 29, 1829. With her death, the notice said, her "Red Indian or Beothick" people had "become extinct in their own orbit. They have been dislodged and disappeared from the earth." The notice in the St. John's parish register read: *Interred Nancy, Shanawditheaet. 23 South Side. (Very probably the last of the aborigines.)*

At Jackfish Lake in that era, the idea that the Nehiyawak would ever "become extinct in their own orbit," or would even lose control of their country, would have seemed absurd. Buffalo were still plentiful, and the people traded hides, fresh meat and pemmican at the Hudson's Bay post seventy miles to the east in exchange for rifles, shot and luxury goods. They bred their own horses and acquired more through raids on the Blackfoot, who were their only serious military rival. The European traders were isolated in small, scattered provisioning posts, and posed no discernible threat.

When he was growing up, Mistihai'muskwa was watched closely by the elders, who wanted to know whether he had the necessary traits — generosity, courage and cool-headedness — to inherit the chieftainship from his father. When the elders had determined that he had these qualities, they took him under their wing to school him in the old stories and spiritual practices. Mistihai'muskwa began to display his wisdom at the age of twelve. When he was recovering from a nearly fatal bout with smallpox he dreamed of "the coming of the white man, his purchase of the land, the bounteous presents from the Great Mother" and the poverty and loss of identity that would follow for his people. The elders listened to the boy's story respectfully, but were unable to comprehend such a thing. As his biographer, Hugh Dempsey, wrote, none of the plains peoples could imagine that "the white man would ever be anything more than a small, necessary evil in their lives."

But in the east the settler society was already working to create a new country — one that would extend over the ancient lands given to the native peoples by the Great Mystery. By the time of Big Bear's vision, a European-style state was beginning to grow from western Nitassinan, through northern Kanienke and through Tenakìwin, and in the Ojibwa heartland around the Great Lakes. In the 1840s, the former French lands on the St. Lawrence and the new British settlements in Saguinan were joined together into the Colony of Canada (Upper and Lower) and given a measure of self-government from the Colonial Office in London.

The leaders and financial backers of the new colony-nation were already envisioning a dominion stretching from the Atlantic to the Pacific. Their next conquest was Danaiiwaad Ojibweg, a country that had been brought to the brink of economic collapse over the previous fifty years by the winding down of the fur trade, by wave after wave of deadly epidemics, by the pressures on game brought about by the illegal incursion of settlers and lumbermen and by the scourge of alcoholism among people living near the trading posts. In September of 1850, the Ojibwa chiefs of the north shore of Lake Superior and Lake Huron were summoned to Boweting for a meeting with the Indian Commissioner, a former fur trader, William Robinson. Speaking through an interpreter, the commissioner said he wanted to make treaty with them.

The agreement, he said, would protect a portion of their lands from the settlers pushing north from Saguinan. It would also award each citizen of Danaiiwaad Ojibweg a small annuity as part of the quit rent. It would allow for shared usage of most of the vast territory, but would reserve to the Crown the right to dispense, sometime in the future, certain tracts to lumbermen, mining companies and settlers. The chiefs inquired about the alternatives. There were none. If they didn't sign, the lumbermen would still come, the miners would still come, and the settlers would come. And they would get nothing.

The meeting was held within earshot of the Boweting rapids, where the Ojibwa nation had been born; where, two hundred years earlier, they and their allies had halted and begun rolling back the advance of the Five Nations. But this new assault was like nothing they had encountered before. They could sign Robinson's documents and surrender control over much of their weakened country; they could refuse to sign and lose everything; or they could try to drive the Europeans from their lands. Eighty-five years earlier, at the time of Pontiac, that had been an option. But by 1850, wave after wave of epidemics had reduced the population of the Ojibwa and the Council of the Three Fires to tens of thousands, while the surge of immigration had swelled the settlers' numbers to a bewildering and unstoppable three million souls.

The lands the British were demanding covered all the territory north of Lake Superior and Lake Huron to the watershed where Rupert's Land, the Hudson Bay drainage area, began. The treaty terms had to be taken on faith, because none of the chiefs could read Robinson's documents. When they signed, they did so with totemic marks. Robinson pocketed the documents and headed back to Toronto, having just purchased an enormous country for a few thousand pounds and an annuity of about five dollars per person from a people who were widely believed to be headed for extinction. At some point, disease, despair and the forces of assimilation would, it was assumed, bring all the Indians to the same end as the Beothuk. And then the annuities would cease, the reserve lands would revert to the Crown and the European claim would be undisputed.

Although the colonial government congratulated itself for this quick annexation of Danaiiwaad Ojibweg, it would be another quarter-century before the treaty-makers made it past Wabeseemong to the grasslands. In fact, in the 1850s, when Big Bear was in his twenties, there was a flourishing of plains life and culture. While reduced in numbers, the buffalo were still plentiful enough to feed and clothe the people, and there were surplus hides and meat to trade. Relations among the plains nations, which by this time included the growing Métis people, were in a relatively peaceful period, and a long intermission between epidemics resulted in a steady increase in population. It was a time of prosperity and contentment, and the plains people thought — as all peoples do during such times — that the good times would continue forever.

Chief Favel's mother, Lucy, lived in a comfortable house on a pleasant tree-lined street in North Battleford. When we arrived, the small kitchen was full of people. One was her brother, Donald Chatsis; the others were local FSIN workers. One of them introduced herself as Vera Kasokeo and said she would take us to the Big Bear memorial after lunch.

As we sat around the table, we spoke of Blaine. He was obviously held in affectionate regard by everyone in the room. Wayne mentioned that Blaine was meeting Garth Brooks that afternoon and the response was one of amusement mixed with familial pride. "He's meeting Jean Chrétien next week," his mother said.

She had prepared a traditional meal of boiled meat and bannock. When we finished eating, I raised the subject of his connection to Big Bear. The table fell silent.

Lucy Favel said that she and her brother had been given up for adoption when they were young, and had been taken in by Horse Child, one of Big Bear's sons. "I grew up in Horse Child's house," she said softly, "but you have to understand my grandfather, Big Bear, was someone who was rarely mentioned. Some of his people had been hanged by the government. Others were put in jail. The rest had everything taken away from them. When I was growing up, people didn't talk about Big Bear, because they were afraid to."

It was a strangely awkward moment. We had come expecting to get family stories, anecdotes passed down from her adoptive father about her famous grandfather. But Horse Child had had few stories of his own youth that were fit for children. He had spent his childhood on the edge of starvation, as his father led his people in a search for the disappearing buffalo. He had survived the battles of the North-West Rebellion in 1885, and had been jailed with his father when he was only twelve years old. His people had then been scattered across the plains. It was not a life that led to fond family reminiscences. "They took everything," Lucy said. "Our land and even our horses. We were left with nothing."

After lunch, we left Lucy Favel's house with Vera Kasokeo, heading for the Big Bear monument that Blaine had erected when he was band chief. In minutes we were out of the city, driving across dusty concession roads in the direction of the adjacent Little Pine and Poundmaker reserves. The memorial had been erected in a low-lying fenced-in area on the roadside. It was a six-foot-high, two-stage sculpture with a granite block "representing

Mistihai'muskwa's unfinished struggle on behalf of the Cree people," Vera said. She pointed to the jagged column. "See? It shows we're still rebuilding."

"Big Bear stands tall in the memory of the Cree," the plaque read, "as a truly visionary leader who fought against the forces of Canadian colonialism and ultimately suffered for his Nation. The tragedy is that the remnants of Big Bear's tribe continue to be scattered."

Mistihai'muskwa (Big Bear) became band chief in 1861. As a young man he had distinguished himself in the Blackfoot wars as a warrior and a horse thief, and the Ojibwa half of his lineage was said to have given him spiritual powers, among them the ability to make himself disappear in battle. As band chief and eventually a national leader, his challenge would be to make sure that his people didn't disappear, as the Beothuk had, into the mists of time.

This suddenly became a possibility in the 1860s when the unthinkable occured. In 1863, the Cree travelled throughout the buffalo's usual range and found only empty grassland with a few packs of starving wolves. The buffalo were nowhere to be found. After the people suffered a long, hungry winter, the animals did return, but in dramatically reduced numbers. Fear spread throughout the Cree camps. The buffalo were not only their main food supply but a source of trade goods, clothing and shelter. What would happen if they disappeared?

The rapid decline in the herds is no mystery. Hide hunters and illegal settlers had been flowing into the buffalo's southern range, in the American west, for decades. They were slaughtering tens of thousands of buffalo a year, leaving mountains of meat, except for the prized tongues, to rot on the plains. In 1862 the flow of settlers became a flood when the U.S. government passed the Homestead Act and settlers washed over the southern plains to occupy the buffalo's winter range and intensify the slaughter.

At the same time that the buffalo were leaving the land, the Canadians were preparing to move in. In December of 1866, sixteen men from the Canadas and the colonies of Nova Scotia and New Brunswick were meeting at the Westminster Palace Hotel in London to put the finishing touches on a confederation that would join their colonies in a new "Dominion of Canada." The document they were working on, in consultation with British officials, would become known as the British North America Act. The constitution of the new confederation was largely silent on the subject of indigenous peoples. Their only mention was in Section 24, just before the section "Naturalization of Aliens." It gave the federal government power over "Indians and Lands reserved for the Indians."

Of more immediate importance for the people of the plains were the three-way discussions that had taken place in London between Sir John A. Macdonald, the British Colonial Office and the Hudson's Bay Company. Macdonald was given assurances by the other two that the HBC's vast holdings, which stretched from the western shore of Lake Superior to the Pacific Ocean, would be turned over to the new dominion to be administered as its Northwest Territory.

The deal was confirmed two years later, and for Big Bear and his people it came as an astounding piece of news: first, the idea that a company of foreign pedlars could imagine that it owned the land; secondly, that it had sold its bogus holdings to the Canadians.

As shock gradually turned to anger, government agents and listeners in the newly acquired territory warned Ottawa that there was a significant threat of armed resistance. Ottawa hurriedly sent emissaries to tell the people that it intended to respect their rights to the land and had no intention of interfering with their lives. Among the plains nations, the suspicion and outrage that had greeted the earlier news turned into confusion.

As in Peguis's day, the growing Métis population at Red River were the first to act. Under a young political leader, Louis Riel, and a tough war chief, Gabriel Dumont, the Métis took up arms. Realizing that an all-out war with the people of the plains would be inadvisable, the Canadians quickly granted the Métis a measure of self-government and admitted the Red River area into confederation with the Manitoba Act of 1870.

With the Métis pacified and the people of the plains in desperate straits because of the collapse of the buffalo herds, the new Dominion decided to move quickly to consolidate its claim on Indian lands. In 1871 a thousand Ojibwa and Cree gathered at Fort Garry to sign Treaty No. 1, in exchange for small annual payments and, more important, emergency rations to help their families survive the winter. The buffalo had completely disappeared on the eastern plains, and for the Canadian government the collapse had come as a godsend. For a mess of pottage, the government acquired rights to a territory larger than France and Germany combined — and it appeared that it would get it without a fight.

After a second treaty was signed, in southern Manitoba, the Dominion government moved to fill the gap between the Robinson treaty and Lake Winnipeg by signing Treaty No. 3 with the Ojibwa of western Danaiiwaad Ojibweg. The way to the west was now open, and the settlers' government was ready to move onto the central plains.

In 1874, Treaty No. 4 gave the settlers access to the lands of the Plains Cree, Plains Ojibwa and Assiniboine around Fort Qu'Appelle. With Treaty No. 5, in 1875, the Dominion acquired rights to the lands in an arc around Lake Winnipeg, north of the areas ceded in the previous four treaties.

As Big Bear watched the dizzying pace of treaty signings, he was revisited by the dream of his youth, of white men taking over his people's land. In the summer of 1875, George McDougall, a Protestant missionary working for the Dominion government, arrived in Big Bear's country bearing gifts, as was the custom, to give notice of a treaty meeting the following summer for the Cree of the central grasslands.

By this time, Big Bear was a senior chief with a following of more than a thousand people, and he met McDougall on the open plain. McDougall told him that the treaty meeting would be held the following August, at Fort Carlton and Fort Pitt. But instead of giving the expected quick acquiescence, Mistihai'muskwa stood and pointed to the carts with McDougall's gifts of tea, sugar, knives, ammunition and tobacco. "We want none of the Queen's presents," he said firmly. "When we set a fox trap we scatter pieces of meat all around but when the fox gets into the trap we knock him on the head. We want no baits! Let your chiefs come and talk like men with us."

Big Bear spent the next year meeting with other Cree chiefs and trying to build a common front. By the summer of 1876 he had won support from the majority of the chiefs of the central plain. In response, the government sought to isolate him and his followers by making separate deals with the more cooperative, and more desperate, leaders in the region. For the Fort Carlton and Fort Pitt meetings in August 1876, the government ensured that only the more accommodating chiefs — particularly the Christian chiefs, who were being strongly urged by local missionaries to accept the government's offer — were present.

When the provisions of Treaty No. 6 were announced to the assembled chiefs, they were similar to those of the previous five, but with a slight increase in the cash settlement. In exchange for the Plains Cree ceding 120,000 square miles, or more than twice the combined area of the three Maritime provinces, the government was offering twelve dollars per person as a signing bonus and an annuity of five dollars per head.

The chiefs knew that what was being offered promised a very bleak future for their people. Yet, with the devastation of the buffalo herd, they also knew that the choice was to accept the thin gruel of the government offer or have their people face starvation. After two days of painful discussions and vain attempts to have the terms of the treaty improved, they resigned themselves to their fate, and signed.

Big Bear heard about the meeting while he was out on the plains, and he rushed to Fort Pitt to try to take part in the negotiations. When he arrived, he discovered that he was too late — the totemic marks of the other chiefs were already on the document. When some of the chiefs tried to convince him to add his, he reacted angrily. "Stop, stop, my friends. I have never seen the Government before; I have seen [the government agent] many times. I heard the Government was to come and I said I shall see him. When I see him, I will make a request that he will save me from what I most dread; that is, a noose about my neck."

Big Bear continued to insist that Indian land wasn't "a piece of pemmican that can be cut off and given back to us in pieces," but he was acutely aware that he was walking a fine line. His fear was expressed in a vision he had after the Fort Pitt meeting.

"I saw a spring shooting up out of the ground," he told the people of his band. "I covered it with my hand, trying to smother it, but it spurted up between my fingers and ran over the back of my hand. It was a spring of blood." The unfair treaty, he feared, would lead to war. As with the Ojibwa chiefs at Boweting a quarter-century earlier, it was a war he believed his people could no longer win. Yet he couldn't bring himself to sign away his country, his children's birthright.

So he began his odyssey, leading his people across the plains, searching for the last small herds of buffalo and trying to find some way to preserve Cree independence from the encroaching Canadian state. When the Plains Cree heard about Big Bear's journey of refusal, they began to join him, until he was leading a camp of four hundred lodges, more than three thousand people.

At the outset, Big Bear had said that his wanderings would last four years; then he would return to see how those who had signed the treaty had fared. As it turned out, his quest lasted eight years, and represented the last painful march of freedom for the people of the ancient country. The great odyssey would end, finally, in sickness, hunger and — as Big Bear had feared — dispersal and death.

Vera Kasokeo suggested that we continue up the road to the Poundmaker Reserve, where the band and the FSIN had just opened a small historical museum on Cut Knife Hill, one of the battle sites of the 1885 rebellion. We stopped at the foot of the hill at a corral where fifteen buffalo were penned. A young Cree, Richard Tootoosis, wandered over to warn us not to get too close. All of them were bulls — the females wouldn't arrive until the fall — so the bulls were horny as hell and ready to charge at the slightest provocation. They edged towards us with enormous black-fleeced shoulders, strong, short legs and horns arcing around their massive lowered heads. We were close enough to smell their musk and hear their laboured breathing. It was humbling to consider that, during the time of our great-grandfathers, the plains were home to sixty million of these beasts. "We're going to build up the herd," Tootoosis said. "It will take time, but we're going to build it up."

He led us up to Cut Knife Hill to show us the site of Big Bear's Thirst Dance in 1884, and of his people's final battle the following spring.

During his travels in the late 1870s, Big Bear led his band south across the U.S. border. He spent several years avoiding the attempts of the U.S. Cavalry to chase him and his people back across the line, as well as ducking white thieves who made a living attacking weak and starving bands to steal their horses.

While Big Bear wandered, his following gradually diminished. The first to leave were the young warriors who had hoped he would lead them into battle; others left as hunger took its toll on the very young and the very old. Still, his camp remained more than a thousand strong in 1880, when he arrived at Fort Walsh and told the local North-West Mounted Police that his people needed rations. The police captain told him that he would have to sign the treaty first. Big Bear quietly refused, but the sight of hundreds of armed and hungry-looking Cree camping just outside the fort convinced the captain to begin dispensing rations anyway.

After resting near Fort Walsh, Big Bear headed one more time to the southern plains to look for buffalo, but this time he found only empty grasslands. The slaughter by hide hunters and settlers had been virtually complete. By the winter of 1881–82 his people were facing starvation. His youngest boy, Horse Child — Lucy Favel's adoptive father — was nine years old and was slowly dying, as so many children were, of malnutrition. As time went on, more and more of Big Bear's followers gathered their families and slipped away into the night, heading north to the Canadian fort in search of rations. Local officials would quickly designate one of the men in each breakaway group as "band chief." In exchange for life-saving rations, as well as reserve lands and treaty money, the newly appointed chief would offer his signature to Treaty No. 6 and renounce his people's right to their homeland.

By 1882, six years after the Fort Pitt treaty meeting, even members of Big Bear's own family were beginning to abandon him, so he led his remaining followers back to Fort Walsh. The sight of the chief and his hungry people in ragged clothes and rotting tepees was a surprise to the local Indian agent, but he was even more surprised when the famous holdout walked into his office and made a three-hour speech about the injustice of his people's treatment by the foreigners who'd come to steal their country. At the end, Big Bear said that he would sign the treaty, but only because he had been starved into it.

Big Bear's apparent capitulation was front-page news throughout Canada. But if Indian Department officials thought this was the end of his resistance, they were mistaken. He delayed his people's departure to their allotted reserve in the north as long as possible while his people fed on government rations. When he finally set out, he didn't go to the appointed land; he began wandering again, while he carried on a drawn-out, long-distance negotiation with the authorities over the location and size of his reserve.

In 1884, Big Bear made a final attempt to have the treaty provisions overturned. He called a mass meeting of all the Plains chiefs, to be held on Chief Poundmaker's reserve in the sloping Battle River valley below Cut Knife Hill. In accordance with Cree tradition, Big

Bear, as the spiritual as well as the political leader, sponsored a Thirst Dance, and the turnout of disaffected treaty Indians was remarkable. Thousands gathered for the ceremony, and for discussions about how they might work together to have the treaties revoked. Only fourteen years earlier, the Cree and Siksika had engaged in a brutal battle near Lethbridge that had left more than two hundred dead. It is a testament to Big Bear's power, and to the desperation of the people who had signed the treaties, that a Siksika delegation arrived to take part in the meeting.

"We have all been deceived in the same way," Big Bear told them. "The Government sent to us those who think themselves men. They bring everything crooked. They take our lands, they sell them and they buy themselves fine clothes. Then they clap their hands on their hips and call themselves men. They are not men. They have no honesty. They are an unsightly beast. Their faces are twisted from the appearance of honest men." Fired by Mistihai'-muskwa's words, the gathering decided to send him east to meet face to face with the Canadian government, to plead their case in the name of their centuries-long alliance with the Europeans. It was a crucial moment. Despite all the forces ranged against them, the prairie Indians appeared ready to make a last stand around a leader who had the strength and vision, and the oratorical skills, to present their case to the foreign powers.

But Big Bear would never get his chance to speak to the Canadian government. After the political discussions ended, the chiefs and thousands of Plains Indians held Thirst Dance ceremonies. While they were celebrating, a scuffle broke out between a Cree man and a white shopkeeper at a nearby post. A North-West Mounted Police contingent, which had been stationed in the vicinity, quickly moved in to arrest the Cree.

As soon as the men saw the red-coated officers approaching, they took to their mounts and began to circle the police, challenging them to fire the first shot. Greatly outnumbered, the police held their fire. But from the moment the warriors went into action, Big

Bear was no longer in control of the camp, or even of his own band. According to Cree tradition, when hostilities were imminent the war chief — in this case Kah-Paypamhchikwao (Wandering Spirit) — assumed authority. A political chief like Mistihai'muskwa faded to the background. When the police pulled back, Big Bear stepped forward again, but his followers had made their decision. His speech had momentarily filled them with hope that they could meet the foreign leaders and win back their political and land rights, but the sight of the police dragging one of their own out of the crowd reminded too many of them of the crushing reality of their lives, and the abyss of their loss. When his band left Poundmaker's reserve to head north to winter at the edge of the woodlands in the Fort Pitt area, only his wife and Horse Child, now eleven, were riding with Big Bear. The rest were riding with Kah-Paypamhchikwao.

CHAPTER FIFTEEN

The Last Stand

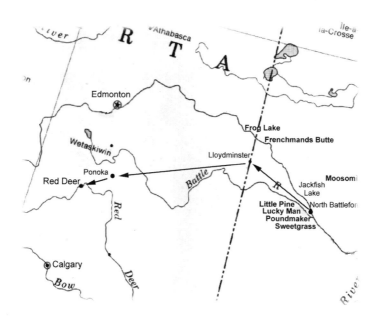

W E VISITED Jackfish Lake with Albert Angus. He was a lawer friend of Wayne's we'd run into the evening before, in the hotel bar in North Battleford. After law school, Angus had worked as a radio journalist and had briefly hosted a local television program. Now he was back practising law, but it wasn't paying much. He had taken seven local land-claim cases on contingency, and they were inching through the courts. To make ends meet, he was working on occasional contracts with the FSIN. The next day he would be overseeing a band referendum on traditional government in Moosomin. When we spoke about our trip, Angus said we should come with him, because Jackfish Lake — Black Powder's old campsite, where Big Bear was said to have been born — was just before the Moosomin turnoff.

The next morning, we drove north through rolling rangeland. Angus pulled off the highway just south of Cochin, beside a high hill overlooking the lake. We climbed to the top, where we could see most of the lake and dozens of miles of prairie in every direction. "There were more trees in those days," Angus said. "Big Bear's father, Mukatai, wintered here because of the firewood. And because of the view." During the winter of 1825, when the Ne-hiyawak Cree were at war with the Blackfoot, a sentry on this hill could spot either approaching Blackfoot or migrating buffalo a half-day's ride away. The actual camp, Angus said, was below us, on a flat section of land halfway between the hilltop and the lake.

While he was talking about Big Bear, Angus received a call on his cellphone. In the middle of the rangeland the ringing had a startling effect. He answered and spoke in Cree, and when he'd finished the call he said the Moosomin organizers were waiting for him so they could open the polls.

The referendum question, he explained, had to do with getting rid of the Department of Indian Affairs band council system and returning to a more traditional form of government. The present system, which made the chief answerable to the Department, had been put in place the year after the defeat of the Cree forces in the North-West Rebellion. Since then, Angus's people had been on a century-long journey to find their way back. "They used to use 'divide and conquer' against us," he said. "Now it's 'divide and ignore.'"

Albert Angus headed up the highway to Moosomin; we headed west along the back highways to Beardy.

The Beardy Reserve is two miles from Duck Lake. A roadside cairn marks the place where, on March 26, 1885, a group of Métis clashed with some North-West Mounted Police in the first battle of the rebellion. The encounter came only eight months after Big Bear called a chiefs' meeting at Beardy as a follow-up to the meeting at Poundmaker's Reserve. Twelve leading Cree chiefs attended, and together they drew up a list of eighteen grievances against the Canadians. From Beardy, Big Bear headed to nearby Fort Carlton to meet with Canadian officials. As he presented them with the grievances he said, "A year ago I stood alone in making these demands. Now the whole of the Indians are with me."

When J. M. Rae, the local Indian agent, looked over the list — which was a point-by-point indictment of the entire Canadian Indian policy — he reported to his superiors that the Indians meant business. "The thing has to be looked at seriously," he wrote, "& precautions taken ere it is too late."

After Fort Carlton, Big Bear made one more stop. He travelled to Prince Albert to meet with Louis Riel. The two men had met five years earlier, in Montana, during a period when Riel was holding meetings with a series of plains leaders. The great plains, Riel was telling native leaders, rightfully belonged to the Indians and the Métis people, and he urged them to make common cause in getting it back. During one of those meetings, Riel took a copy of Treaty No. 1, condemned it as a pack of lies and trampled it underfoot. In his first meeting with Big Bear, Riel had told him that he was held in high esteem for his refusal to sign the treaty, and had described him as "a man of good sense."

Big Bear and the other Nehiyawak were more ambivalent about the Métis. They shared part of the same lineage, and almost all the Métis spoke Cree, but as the Métis asserted their own nationhood they were doing it largely on Cree lands, and there was a concern that the Métis saw too much of the country as their own. But Big Bear understood that they had a common enemy in the Canadian government. At the Prince Albert meetings, which took place in a room above Jackson's drugstore, he sounded out Riel on his earlier promise to support Cree rights to the land. If the Métis won their rights, he asked Riel, "would they assist the Indians to win theirs?" The Métis leader said they certainly would. His plan was to throw out the Canadian imperialists and restore the land to all the peoples of the plains. According to Rev. Charles Quincy, the Anglican missionary at Fort Pitt, Big Bear and Riel formalized their alliance by signing a mutual assistance pact, although that document has never been found.

After the meeting, Big Bear slipped away to join his people on the trail to their wintering place on the shores of Frog Lake, and Riel added to the Métis manifesto the provision that "the Indians' rights should be respected as well as our own." During the winter he and Gabriel Dumont prepared for war.

The war of independence began on March 3, 1885, when Louis Riel proclaimed a Métis-led provisional government in the name of all the peoples of the plains. Two weeks later, the Métis seized the village of Batoche. Major Leif Crozier and a contingent of NWMP officers and volunteers were dispatched from Prince Albert to retake the village and arrest the insurgents. The Métis sent Gabriel Dumont and twenty-five soldiers towards Prince Albert from Batoche to turn back the approaching Canadians. The two sides met at Beardy's Reserve, two miles from Duck Lake, with the NWMP pulling their wagons around and the Métis digging a half-circle around them. The Beardy chief sent a respected Cree elder, Assiyiwin, to mediate. But when the old man met an NWMP officer in front of the police wagons, a scuffle broke out. Someone, apparently from the Canadian side, fired a shot. Assiyiwin was killed instantly. The Métis opened fire. By the time Crozier managed to make his retreat, eleven NWMP and one volunteer lay dead or dying. The Métis lost five men. The battle for control of the western half of the continent had begun.

Word of the outbreak of fighting reached the Cree camp at Frog Lake two days later. Big Bear was out moose-hunting at the time. When he returned to camp on April 1, he conferred with Wandering Spirit and his son Imasees, who was acknowledged as one of the leading warriors. That evening, the young men began to slip away to the west side of Frog Lake. The elders and women and children could hear the sound of songs and war dances wafting over the waters. After dark, Wandering Spirit crossed the lake to join them. During the night, the whole camp of more than a thousand Cree signalled their support for what was to come by joining Wandering Spirit and the warriors on the far shore.

The flight to Lloydminster took less than forty-five minutes. Frog Lake and the old site of Fort Pitt were another forty-five-minute drive north. Wayne had visited Beardy's Reserve, and Frog Lake and Batoche, with his granny, when he was eight or nine. They had travelled in an old panelled station wagon with a couple of his cousins, and he remembered that they camped on the roadsides.

It was a strange journey. His grandmother, who was born only twenty-five years after the death of Mistihai'muskwa, gave brief accounts of the events of 1885 at each stop along the way. They visited Beardy and they visited Frog Lake, where he had some cousins. He described the trip as a kind of Stations of the Cross of Cree and Métis history.

Driving north from Lloydminster, we were entering the limits of the parklands, where the prairie begins to merge with the northern bush. We passed abandoned houses and old collapsed homesteads. We crossed the North Saskatchewan River, then reached the fork where roads led to the east and west sides of the lake. We stopped at a small gas station and store where the clerk and all the customers were Cree. We were now on Frog Lake First Nation territory, near the northern limits of the Treaty No. 6 lands.

As we continued along the road to the west side of the lake, we passed a boarded-up chapel on a hill, and more Indian Affairs wood-frame houses, before reaching a rutted roadway. When we could drive no farther, we got out and took an overgrown path towards the water.

A hundred yards from shore, we came upon a clearing that had obviously had some recent ceremonial use, with fire pits, tepee rings and ceremonial bundles tied to the trees. In the centre was a mound of reddish stones eight feet long by about three feet wide, shaped like a funeral pyre.

From here, the path to the beach was narrow and reedy. As we reached the sandy shore a distant honking of geese grew louder and more insistent, until a flock flew over us towards the south. In that early spring when Wandering Spirit's young men made their war preparations along this beach, the geese would have been heading north.

When the sun broke over the hills behind them, Wandering Spirit stood and said again that it was time "to eat some two-legged meat," the warriors' expression for going into battle. He mounted his pinto pony and the young men followed, and the whole camp fell in behind as he rode off in the direction of the village of Frog Lake, the only white settlement for miles around.

The village had a chapel, a trading post, a ration post and a model farm where the Canadian government had installed an instructor to try to turn Cree horsemen into ploughmen. The dozen or so villagers, who included Métis as well as whites, were startled to see the Cree with black stripes under their eyes and their faces painted red or yellow. Wandering Spirit told his young men to herd the whites into the open. When they were assembled, he informed them that Frog Lake now belonged to his people, and that they were his prisoners. One of the two priests in the village told Wandering Spirit that they had just been on their way to mass. Wandering Spirit told them to go into the church and have their mass. When the service was under way, he joined them, striding to the front, still clutching his rifle, and genuflecting on one knee in mock solemnity. This amused some of his young men, who were standing watch at the back. When they laughed, the priest abruptly stopped the service.

Wandering Spirit ordered the prisoners outside once more, and told them to accompany the young men to the Cree camp. The women and some of the men began to obey, but Thomas Quinn, the Indian agent, refused.

"If you love your life, you will do as I say," the war chief warned him.

Quinn, a Métis working for the Canadian government, wasn't used to taking orders from Indians. He looked up and replied, with a touch of condescension, "Why should I go there?"

Those were his final words. Wandering Spirit lowered his rifle and blasted a hole in Quinn's head, and the others joined in. Within minutes, nine men lay dead in the muddy cart-tracks of Frog Lake's only street. In the confusion, Big Bear is said to have shouted for the men to stop firing; when the firing did stop, he immediately took possession of the rest of the prisoners to ensure their safety.

Big Bear's band stayed at Frog Lake for ten days, feasting on the stores and rations. Confused and wildly over-optimistic reports on the uprising filtered into his camp from other districts. Posts at Calgary, Edmonton, Fort Qu'Appelle and Carlton, they were told, had been taken by Métis and Cree insurgents, and Big Bear's good friend Poundmaker was said to be marching on Battleford.

On May 13, in a euphoric mood, Wandering Spirit led Big Bear's band in an attack on Fort Pitt, where HBC and NWMP officials were stationed. The small wooden fort lay exposed on the short grass prairie on the sloping bank of the North Saskatchewan River, and Wandering Spirit set up camp on the ridge above it. After a brief skirmish with a Canadian patrol, in which an NWMP officer was killed, the NWMP surrendered. Wandering Spirit permitted the remaining officers to leave on a scow, floating in the moonlight down the North Saskatchewan towards Battleford. The Cree then seized the fort and took forty-four more prisoners. Once again they liberated the stores of rations and firearms, and days of feasting followed. But the euphoria began to ebb as they heard more realistic accounts of the battles on other fronts. Both Riel's Métis and Poundmaker's Cree were pinned down by thousands of heavily armed Canadian soldiers and volunteers who had been rushed to the plains from the east on the almost completed railway.

By the end of May, a third Canadian battalion was said to be massing at Fort Edmonton, preparing to attack Big Bear's band from the west. Wandering Spirit kept his people at Fort Pitt, uncertain of which direction to take, until his scouts reported that, as they'd feared, a large military force armed with cannon was marching in their direction from the west. Wandering Spirit ordered the burning of Fort Pitt. With the fort in flames, he led his people into the cover of the forests north of the river.

After leaving the lake, we stopped alongside the oiled gravel road at the graveyard of those slain at Frog Lake. Nine iron crosses were set in three rows. On top of each was the word *massacred* and the name of one of the fallen. The graveyard was one of the stops on Wayne's childhood tour. He remembered visiting the spot, he said, but he couldn't recall what his grandmother had told him about Frog Lake. She had spoken a great deal about the history of Beardy and Batoche, but about Frog Lake she had said very little.

"As a kid I wasn't sure who exactly was buried here," Wayne said. "But from what I knew about the world, I just assumed they were Indians."

In Canadian newspapers the Frog Lake killings were front-page news, and Big Bear's name figured prominently in all accounts. He was the renegade chief who had refused to sign the treaty, and who had then refused to settle on the reserve, and he was now being blamed for single-handedly raising Cree resistance to Canadian expansion.

In the field, however, the ageing chief was still walking behind his people as they followed Wandering Spirit. The war chief led them to a wooded ridge near Red Deer Creek, five miles from Fort Pitt, at a place known locally as Frenchman's Butte. They carried everything they owned into a twisting, heavily wooded valley with marshland for a floor. Then they climbed the steep, eroded cliffs to the forested ridge above, where Wandering Spirit ordered the women and children to be hidden in the woods while the men dug firing pits along the edge.

General T. B. Strange arrived at the charred ruins of Fort Pitt with 225 soldiers, NWMP officers and volunteers dragging a nine-pound cannon. Big Bear's band was by then the last remaining prize in the war; the eight thousand Canadian troops in the field had already captured Poundmaker and Riel, and were ready to move north and west to link up with Strange's troops in a pincer movement against the remaining Cree holdouts. During the night, the general's camp was attacked by a small group of Wandering Spirit's rearguard scouts, and one of the scouts was killed in the firefight. In the morning Strange marched his men quickly along the trail north of the river, into the boggy valley below Frenchman's Butte.

General Strange had walked into Wandering Spirit's trap, and the battle turned into a rout. The Cree opened with a barrage of rifle fire from the heights. The general managed to fire a few rounds from his nine-pounder before realizing that he was in a hopeless position, and leading his men in a full retreat.

It was another victory for the Cree, but it would be their last. They now knew that the soldiers and militiamen would keep coming, from the west, the south and the east. Except for that small and shrinking northwest corner of the plains under Wandering Spirit's control, their country was under military occupation.

Mosquitoes buzzed in the shadows of the poplars at Frenchman's Butte, and Wayne and I lit cigarettes to keep them away. You can still see the Cree rifle pits dug into the ridge, and farther down, at the bottom of the slope behind the ridge, are the much larger depressions where the women and children and white prisoners were hidden.

Standing by the old firing pits, Wayne remarked that Big Bear seems to have known the war was unwinnable from the moment the band followed Wandering Spirit to the village of Frog Lake. "He hung back," Wayne said. "The white prisoners said he spent most of his time trying to keep the people calm and making sure the prisoners weren't harmed. He'd known this was coming all his life." At the age of twelve, Big Bear had foreseen the coming of the white man and the purchase of the lands. Later, he had seen the earth spouting springs of blood. Everything had come to pass. The Cree were seasoned fighters, and fearless, but they were fighting a war that had been lost when the buffalo disappeared from the plains.

When General Strange and his soldiers beat their hasty retreat, there were no whoops of joy or triumphal shots fired in the air. Three hundred and eighty-eight years after Cabot landed at Griquet, with his small band of European invaders, it was the Cree who stood alone in a land of strangers.

But they could not stand for long. Wandering Spirit urged his people to move quickly. They left the butte and travelled through the marshy valley. An old woman who could not keep up with the others slipped off the trail into the trees; when her family went back to look for her, they found she had quickly and quietly hanged herself. By nightfall it was clear that, with the hundreds of children and elders, they would never be able to outrun the Canadian soldiers. The camp began to split apart. A group of Bush Cree who had joined at Frog Lake were the first to leave, slipping away to head back to the fort to surrender. Wandering Spirit said that he was going after them to convince them to stay with the main group. Instead, he accompanied them to the fort that he himself had ordered burned to the ground only days before. When they arrived, the field had already been turned into a prison camp for 750 captured Cree. Wandering Spirit walked into the camp, still carrying his rifle. When the soldiers came to disarm him, he asked a woman for her buffalo-skinning knife, and plunged it into his own belly. The soldiers hurried to staunch the wound so that he wouldn't bleed to death.

Accompanied by his twelve-year-old son, Horse Child, Big Bear headed for Jackfish Lake and Fort Carlton, the land where he had been born, where he had grown up while the Cree were still a free people living in their own country. When father and son reached the North Saskatchewan, they built a rough raft, and when night came they floated downstream towards home. After midnight, five miles from Fort Carlton, which had been laid to ashes by Poundmaker a few weeks earlier, Big Bear spotted a tent on the shore. Thinking it was a Cree tent, he beached the raft and went up to ask for food. A startled trader saw the old Indian and recognized him, and fled across the river to the police post on the other side. Big Bear and Horse Child offered no resistance when the police came for them. The war was over.

On the morning of November 27, 1885, Wandering Spirit and five other Cree from Big Bear's band, as well as two Assiniboine, were put to death at Fort Battleford in a public hanging. All eight now lie buried in a small, overgrown cemetery in a bowl-shaped valley a mile from the fort.

The day after Wandering Spirit was hanged, Big Bear began serving his sentence in the bleak confines of Stony Mountain prison, on Peguis's old territory north of Winnipeg. He had been convicted as an accessory to murder, but the jury — after hearing testimony from the wife of one of the men slain at Frog Lake, and from the prisoners taken at Fort Pitt, who said Big Bear had tried to stop the killings and had treated them with a protective kindness throughout the ordeal — had recommended leniency. He was sentenced to three years. He had served only a year and a half when he was released because of his rapidly deteriorating health. A sick, tired old man, Big Bear went to live on Poundmaker's reserve, near Battleford, and died in his sleep on January 17, 1888.

Horse Child remained loyal to his father. There is a photo of him with Big Bear at the Regina jail, where the twelve-year-old was also imprisoned because he refused to leave his father's side. The photo shows young Horse Child's eyes downcast while Mistihai'-muskwa, son of Mukatai, sits wrapped in an old blanket, gazing into empty space. In later life, Horse Child remained silent about his father. Somewhere along the line, he even tried to bury the past. He changed his name to Joe Peemee and eked out a living on Little Pine Reserve, where he and his father now lie buried.

After the rebellion was put down in 1885, the Canadian government, confident that at last it had the ancient countries in hand, revised the Indian Act to ensure that chiefs would be responsible not to their people but to the occupying government. Henceforth, the Indian agents could remove chiefs from office and replace them with anyone in the band they felt would be more submissive. These measures pertained not just to the plains, but to all the Indian territories from Wee-soc-kadao (Newfoundland) to Nuu-chah-nulth (on the west coast of Vancouver Island). The system, with its Indian agents and with an Indian Affairs Department set up along the lines of the British Colonial Office, was old-fashioned imperialism. The stated goal was to absorb the Indian nations into the body politic until they disappeared. As new European diseases, like tuberculosis, took a rising annual toll on native populations, it was thought that their end was near. As late as 1930, MP Agnes Macphail speculated, in a House of Commons debate over allocating funds to fight tuberculosis among Indians, that "If the Indian race is a degenerated race, I am afraid that the whole effort is wasted. It may or may not be that a remnant of the race can be saved; I am not convinced one way or another."

While we were still on the ridge at Frenchman's Butte, Wayne said that this was the place he remembered most from his childhood travels with his grandmother. "I could imagine the clamour of rifle fire and the thunder of the general's cannon," he said. "I thought at the time that this was where everything had ended for the Indians. But this was just the end of the beginning."

CHAPTER SIXTEEN

The Plateau

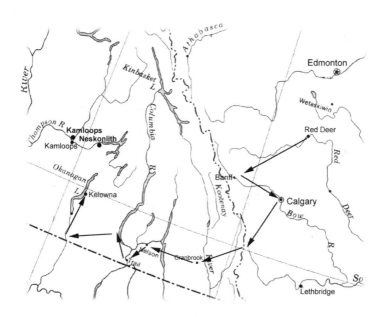

A T THE HOTEL in Lloydminster, Wayne had messages waiting from Arthur Manuel and Brenda. They wanted to know when he was coming back to work and coming home. Arthur said there was a mountain of work on his desk. Brenda reminded him that the baby was due in little more than a month.

So we flew to Red Deer that night, under a prairie sky lit by a late August moon and a sea of stars. We passed over a scattering of towns, small pools of light like fires on the plains. Most were settler towns, but some were villages where the Cree were still living on the land they had been rooted to for twenty thousand years or more.

We were up early the next morning to fly twenty minutes north of Red Deer to the Ponoka airstrip, where we'd arranged to have a fifty-hour check on the Cessna before heading through the mountains. This was Siksika country, but the owner of Triad Aviation, John Jefferies, was from Tyendinaga, a Mohawk community near Belleville on the Lake Ontario shore. Jefferies was the brother of one of Wayne's old girlfriends, and they had gone flying together a few times when Jefferies was a young pilot.

When we landed on the short runway — just three thousand feet — Jefferies was on the radio, guiding us to his hangar. We shut down in front of the open doors, and he came out with his two German shepherds to help us push the Cessna in. He was in his late thirties and had a clean-cut military look. Ten years ago he had been one of the first native guys in the country to get a commercial pilot's licence. He'd bought the maintenance hangar two years ago, with the hope of opening a flight school to teach young native people how to fly.

"I've been talking with some Cree bands in the north about sponsoring a program," he said. "The kids won't be able to afford it, so we'll need scholarships."

There was only one plane on the ramp, a twin-engine Cheyenne, and the hangar contained only one aircraft in for repairs, a two-seater Cessna 152. Evidence that Jefferies had time on his hands could be seen in the tools neatly lined up on the bench, and the floors swept clean of every speck of dust.

"But in the meantime," he admitted, "business is slow. My wife and I sold our house and we're living in a trailer out back."

The three of us did a walk-around. Jefferies obviously understood airplane owners as well as airplanes, because several times he paused to praise the old Cessna and to comment on how much better shape it was in than others of its age. When his mechanic wandered over and began to remove the cowling to get at the engine, we headed into the small office at the end of the hangar to have a coffee and check our charts for the best route through the Rockies.

Jefferies suggested we take Rogers Pass at Rocky Mountain House and follow the twists and turns of the Visual Flight Rules route marked on the map. "There're a couple of shortcuts if you know what you're doing," he said. "But you should probably stick to the chart. The main thing is to leave early when the air is calm. Try to be in the sky before the sun clears the horizon."

The Cheyenne pilot wandered in. He looked to be in his late fifties, and when he saw us looking over the charts he said, with that instant pilot-to-pilot familiarity, "Heading over the Rocks?" Wayne told him it would be our first time in the mountains. "You'll love it," he said. He had flown them dozens of times.

I asked if there was anything we should look for. He glanced down at our map and saw that we were using a VFR chart. "You're not going through the passes?" I told him that we were flying a 172 without oxygen, so we had no choice.

"I've never gone through the passes," he admitted. His pressurized twin-engine Cheyenne could fly over the mountains at 25,000 feet. He leaned over the desk and traced the twisting VFR route with his finger. "That'll be a hell of a ride," he said. His tone was not reassuring.

When the fifty-hour check was completed, we pushed the plane back onto the ramp. "Whatever you do," Jefferies repeated, "leave early in the morning."

We spent the night in Red Deer, getting ready for our assault on the mountains. After supper, I called the Calgary flight service station for the twenty-four-hour weather briefing. It didn't sound promising. There was a front-line north of Rogers Pass that would be creeping down during the morning, giving low visibilities and light showers by noon. But the weather briefer cautioned me that those times were approximate. "To be honest, anything can happen in the passes."

I asked him about the southern route, through Pincher Creek and the Crowsnest. Good visibility, he said, but a chance of CBS (thunderstorms) later in the day, and some strong winds. The problem was that the jetstream was winding over the Rockies east-northeast from Vancouver, which meant major turbulence. "I wouldn't recommend Crowsnest," he said.

I had originally intended to stop over a couple of days in Calgary to take a few mountain-flying lessons, but there was no time for that now. That evening, I took out the mountain-flying book Betsy had given me before I left and began flipping through it. It began with a chapter on mountain waves, which can create powerfully spinning rotor winds miles away from the peaks. To avoid them, the book warned, you had to keep an eye open for the "lennies" (lens-shaped clouds) that sat above the rotor winds. Pilots who learn to fly in the east skip over chapters like these during ground school. But now they were suddenly of great interest. There was a whole array of mountain conditions, the book warned, that could send little planes smacking into the side of a mountain or plummeting to the valley floor. On the subject of weather the book echoed the weather briefer. The mountains contained a patchwork of mini-systems that could change from good visibility to zero in a matter of minutes. You always had to be ready to make a quick escape.

It also warned of false altitude readings from pressure changes that made the instruments show you much higher than you actually were — a serious hazard when you were trying to thread your way between the peaks. Navigation instruments were of little use. The radio beacon instruments required line of sight and would be blocked by mountains ahead. Satellite instrument readings showed your destination airport, but they didn't show the mountains blocking your path. Wayne would have to guide us through the maze with the 1:500,000 scale charts as his only tool. Finally, there was a whole array of strange winds that danced around the passes, ricocheting off the walls and developing downdrafts and updrafts that could toss a little Cessna around like a cork on a stormy sea.

Wayne saw me underlining large sections of text. "So how's it look?" he asked.

"You don't want to know," I said.

Dawn was just beginning to glow in the eastern sky when we arrived at the Red Deer airstrip. By the time we took off on the north-facing runway and banked left, we could see the hulking shape of the mountains fifty miles to the west. As we approached Rogers Pass, we discovered that the weather briefer's prediction had been overly optimistic. It was 0700 hours and the pass was plugged up with fog and rain. I banked back towards Red Deer.

"Should we try the Crowsnest?" Wayne asked.

I reminded him of the jetstream and the briefer's warning. We flew in a large circle at the mouth of Rogers Pass while we went over our options. There were really only two: shut down for the day and hope tomorrow was better, or head south and try to make it through the Crowsnest. We finally decided to fly down to Calgary, have breakfast and then check with the flight service station to see if any change was expected.

We ate at the Spruce Goose, the pilots' restaurant on the edge of the tarmac at Calgary International. To the east there was perfect weather for flying, clear blue with unlimited visibility. But when we went upstairs to the FSS to check the weather radar, the briefer said that Rogers Pass would likely remain socked in all day, and that Crowsnest was still not recommended because of the winds. "But you never know," he added. "Sometimes, if you stay in the centre of the valley, it's not that bad. Just a little bumpy."

That was enough for Wayne. "Let's try it," he said. "If it's too bad, we can always head back out." I thought of the narrowness of some of the passes marked on the chart, and the fact that there was no reverse gear on a Cessna. But there was no guarantee that tomorrow or the next day would be better. We headed down to the ramp.

As we lifted off and began our turning climb towards the southwest, I couldn't help wondering if we were pushing our luck. I mentioned this to Wayne.

"I have complete confidence in your piloting," he said.

Those were the type of words, my ground-school instructor had once told me, that all light-plane pilots hear from too-eager passengers, just before they do something stupid.

With a tailwind out of the north, it took us just over an hour to reach Pincher Creek, near the meeting of the Crowsnest and Oldman rivers. The pass was now in sight, twenty miles ahead, standing silent and imposing between two jagged ten-thousand-foot towers of rock. I found myself swearing at the sight of it. From the distance, the opening appeared impossibly narrow. It looked as if our wingtips would scrape the rock if we tried to squeeze through. Wayne busied himself with the charts, identifying the points around us as best he could, and trying to determine what we should be looking for on the other side. It was important to get it right because in navigation, as in bookkeeping, mistakes quickly multiply. As the craggy towers approached, I was thinking about the wind warning, and the fact that it was now mid-morning, and about Jefferies' insistence that we start out at daybreak. Then the mountains, stunning pillars of Mesozoic rock, engulfed us.

The Rockies are large enough to create not only their own weather but their own history. Like virtually all of North America, they were peopled at least ten thousand years ago, after the ice retreated from the passes and the plateau. When we entered the Crowsnest, we were entering the interior country of the Kutenai.

It wasn't until the turn of the nineteenth century that Europeans penetrated the mysteries of the mountain countries. In 1800 two North West Company traders by the names of Lagrasse and Leblanc accompanied a Kutenai hunting party along the secret trails through the columns of rock to their mountain fortress of Akam. The traders passed the winter there, and the people named them K!sukinq!uku (Good Fire) and Sahaning!uku (Bad Fire), because of the preference of one for a crackling lodge fire, and of the other for a smaller blaze. But today no one can remember which was which.

After passing the winter in Akam, Good Fire and Bad Fire followed the Kutenai hunters out to the plains through the Crowsnest, and returned to the NWC post near Rocky Mountain House, which served the Siksika and Pikani peoples. During the summer, a Pikani war party slipped through the pass and travelled the Kutenai's secret trails to attack one of their hidden villages. The reason for the attack appears to be Pikani fears that the Kutenai, who had been supplied European goods by Pikani traders for decades, were opening independent trading relations with the Europeans. In the Kutenai councils that winter, it was decided that Good Fire and Bad Fire were in league with the Pikani and had betrayed the location of the hidden village. A death sentence was passed on the foreign pedlars. The following spring, when Good Fire and Bad Fire once again arrived at Crowsnest laden with trade goods, they were met by a group of Kutenai special forces, known as the Crazy Dogs, who escorted them on the road to Akam. The death sentences were carried out along the trail.

But the mountain kingdoms could not be closed off for ever. European traders were approaching from the south and the west as well as the east. The mountains would fall as Wee-soc-kadao had fallen, or Nitassinan and Tenakìwin had fallen, as Saguinan Land and Danaiiwaad Ojibweg and the plains had fallen. The first and most effective agent in bringing them down would, once again, be the deadly European diseases that clung to the newcomers and were silently passed to the people of the ancient lands.

The book on mountain flying had not exaggerated the force and weirdness of the mountain winds. At the moment we passed between the jagged towers, the Cessna was slapped into a downdraft that drove us towards the valley floor at a rate of seven hundred feet per minute. Realizing that I had made the mistake of entering the pass on the leeward side, I made a too-steep bank to windward. There was a strange whooshing sound. I glanced at the altimeter and saw that, even though we were in level flight, we were now climbing at a rate of seven hundred feet per minute. I pulled off the power. We kept climbing, with the powerful updraft turning our aircraft into a sailplane. To keep below the peaks, where the twisting rotor winds were found, I edged us back towards the centre, at last finding the corridor where the bumpy but flyable airstream was located. Almost as soon as we had settled in, we came upon the first sharp turn, of nearly 90 degrees. In the narrow pass we hit another updraft. I pulled off power and lowered our nose as we rode around the bend at a nose-down angle that should have put us in a steep dive — but the updraft maintained our altitude.

And so it went: hour after hour of picking our way through the canyons, dancing back and forth between updrafts and downdrafts in search of the flyable centre. A few times we flew into confusion, momentarily uncertain which way to turn in the maze of plunging valleys. But each time we squeezed through a narrow pass, we came upon a new opening and Wayne — who by this time had fifty hours as a navigator to his credit — found a way to return us to our route.

Almost three hours out of Calgary, we passed through Lizard Mountain Pass, which opened into the broad Kootenay River valley. We flew north up the valley for fifty miles, to our refuelling stop at Cranbrook. The ramp at the small airport was full of the parked planes of pilots with enough sense to stay out of the jet stream winds. But the weather briefer at the flight service station was just as ambiguous as the others. The route to Kelowna and Kamloops might be okay, he said, but it might not. The problem was that a northern front was moving south, bringing rain and frontal fog. They were forecasting that rain would begin in Kamloops in late afternoon or early evening, and then move south towards Kelowna.

We went downstairs for a coffee and a smoke. For the first time since we'd left Montreal in the wake of hurricane Bertha, I wasn't looking forward to getting back into the plane. I was going to suggest staying in Cranbrook and heading out early in the morning, when the winds were calm. But I heard Wayne call Brenda from the pay phone at the front. "We're going to try," he said.

I ordered another coffee. "So you want to continue?" I asked, when he came back to the table.

"It looks worse for tomorrow," he said. "We could get stuck for days."

As the pilot, I had the duty in situations like these — when we risked flying into frontal weather in mountain passes — to say, "No go." But Brenda, almost eight months pregnant, was waiting for Wayne in Kelowna.

"If visibility goes below ten miles," I said, "I'm turning back."

When we took off from Cranbrook, at the western edge of Akam, we had a half-hour of relatively easy flying down the Moyie Valley. We were heading for the lands of the Salishian peoples: the

Okanagan, Ntlakapamux (Thompson), Lillooet and Secwepemc (Shuswap) nations.

It had been nine hours since we left Red Deer, and a weariness was setting in. But the air was also starting to calm, and the mountain peaks were lowering to just under seven thousand feet as we approached the central plateau. Wayne suggested that we depart from the VFR route to take a few shortcuts but, having read the mountain-flying book, I decided against it. So we continued following the twists and turns on the map, heading north up Kootenay Lake and then southwest through the Columbia River system, where it empties into the Arrow Lakes. Midway up the lake, the route took a sharp left turn into a bowl-shaped valley. The chart showed the route passing above a small creek that flowed into Christina Lake, fifteen miles to the south. It also showed, at the south side of the bowl, two reversed brackets —)(— where the pass began.

"What are these?" Wayne asked.

I glanced over. "Never seen them before," I replied.

We found out a few moments later, when we flew towards the place where the opening was supposed to be.

"Do you see it?" I asked, as we approached the wall of rock. We were at 4000 feet, flying towards a solid-looking 8000-foot mountain.

"Not yet," he said.

I was within a minute or so of turning back when he spotted the opening to our left. It was disturbingly narrow. The winds inside the canyon were fierce. It was like riding a bucking horse or, as Wayne later observed, going through a rapid. We were batted up and down, pitching and yawing, for fifteen interminable minutes before we broke through into a small valley that swung around into Christina Lake.

"The reversed brackets," I pointed out, "must mean a narrow pass."

Wayne nodded. "Or, don't go there."

We flew south almost to the American border before the route headed west again, winding through a series of broad valleys and two more narrow passes. But by then it was late in the afternoon and the winds were dying down.

When we reached the Okanagan River at Osoyoos, we turned north for the long final stretch. But as we flew towards the south end of Lake Okanagan, we encountered clouds in the sequence you'd expect when flying into a front — cirrus, stratocirrus, stratus. By the time we reached the base of seventy-five-mile-long Lake Okanagan, a light rain was beginning to fall. I'd planned to drop Wayne off at Kelowna, where Brenda lived, and then fly on to Kamloops, where we'd meet in the morning. But the weather and weariness changed my mind. I called the flight service station at Penticton to change the flight plan to a full stop in Kelowna.

The radioman had a chatty tone. "Sounds like a good idea," he said. "You're already two hours over your flight plan. I called Creston, Nelson and Grand Forks looking for you."

I asked about the Kelowna weather. "A light rain now," he said, "but heavy rain is expected. If you hurry it up, you'll make it." I pushed the power up to 2500 rpms, and our airspeed edged towards 120 knots.

With the lateness of the day, and the cloud cover, the air was now still. As we flew up the lake in the rain, we relaxed and smoked. Wayne pointed ahead to the eastern shore, where evening lights were just beginning to flicker on. Then he took the controls as we glided up the lake in calm air. I stretched my hands, which were cramped from clutching the controls for most of the past thirteen hours. Kelowna tower cleared us for a downwind approach.

My landing wasn't pretty. There was a steep hill just beyond the runway, so we had to keep extra altitude even after our turn on final approach. Then, tired and overly mindful of the hill, I was slow on pulling off the power. We were almost over the runway and we still had seven hundred feet of altitude to lose. I should have aborted and gone around to make a proper approach.

We touched down on the second third of the slippery runway, with a heavy thud. As we taxied to the ramp, I could feel a wobble on the left tire of the main landing gear. We were hobbled, but we were down.

I had dinner with Wayne and Brenda at her townhouse on the Westbank reserve, across the narrow lake from Kelowna. The rain had stopped and the sky had cleared, so Wayne barbecued some steaks on the deck.

Westbank is far from what most Canadians think of as a reserve. It has the look and feel of a west coast suburban development and it sits on what is becoming some of the most expensive real estate in the country. While places like Whitedog struggle to keep their heads above water, places like Westbank have the luxury of worrying about losing their souls.

I was invited to stay the night, but it was a long time since Wayne and Brenda had seen one another, and Wayne and I had spent more than enough time together, so I headed for a Kelowna hotel. He drove me across the bridge. "It's like I can still see the whole country in my mind's eye," he said. "Every inch of it."

We had arranged to meet Arthur the next day at the Secwepemc powwow on the Kamloops reserve. But we were late getting started after we stopped by the airport to have a mechanic look at our damaged landing gear. It was a two-hour drive to Kamloops and along the way, Wayne pointed out a spot where, a few years ago, archaeologists dug up an old grave from this valley floor. It contained the skeleton of a tall, slender young man, probably a runner because of his physique. The skeleton was judged to be about eight thousand years old.

A runner was a highly respected man in Secwepemcul'ecw. Before horses arrived in the interior in the early nineteenth century, canoes were used on the lakes and on the slow-moving sections of some rivers, but the frequent rapids, roaring through narrow canyons, made extended river travel almost impossible. The people did much of their travelling on foot, along a vast network of trails that connected the thirty towns and villages of Secwepem-cul'ecw with the four neighbouring countries. Since quick commu-nication was sometimes necessary, each village had long-distance runners to carry messages to the next one, like runners in a relay race. To keep in shape, and to prove their skill, these athletic young men used to race the sunlight up the mountain.

The flats beside the powwow grounds stretch back a half-mile from the river before the land rises into a steep, dry ridge. The old Kamloops Industrial Residential School, the large red-brick Vic-torian building where three generations of Salishian kids served time under the military-style discipline of Catholic Christian Brothers and nuns, stands at the base of the hill. Today the school houses the offices of the Shuswap Nation Tribal Council, and the sign at the entrance reads *Est'il'* — "Stop" in Secwepemc. The schoolyard parking lot was jammed, so we parked on the grass and joined a great stream of people — probably two-thirds native, one-third non-native — heading past the school, past the stands selling bannock and salmon and hamburgers, to a large, open-air arena formed by a roofed circle of giant cedar beams.

A Navajo group was in the centre ring, performing a Round Dance. There were a couple of thousand people in the stands and the atmosphere was circus-like. These powwows were part of a year-round circuit that travelled through North America with pro-fessional dancers and drummers.

A few drops of rain fell from a passing cloud. When the Navajo finished, the announcer said, in the slightly smarmy tone of an-nouncers everywhere, that they should be careful with their Indian power, because they had caused the rain to fall.

Wayne spotted a council member from the Neskonlith band and asked him if he'd seen Arthur. "Arthur's gone back home," he replied. "But he said to tell you that you have a mountain of work on your desk."

CHAPTER SEVENTEEN

Sea unto Sea

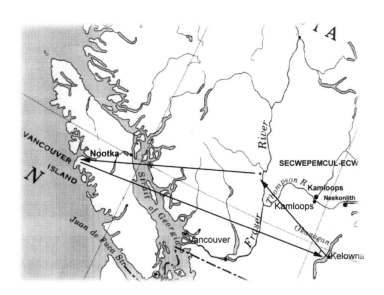

E VENTS THAT TOOK CENTURIES to unfold in the east — the arrival of European merchants, priests, soldiers and settlers, and then the seizure of the land — were telescoped into decades in the interior plateau.

The first white man to reach the area was Alexander Ross, a Scot working for the Americans. In 1812, while Canadians were at war with Americans in the east, he rode north with a trading party from an American post at the juncture of the Okanagan and Columbia rivers. He took the old Indian trail along the east side of the Okanagan, and met Indian travellers who told him to stay on that side of the river until he reached Osoyoos Lake, and then switch to the west side. The trail would take him to Lake Okanagan. When he reached the lake, Ross's party stopped to trade with the local people. Then they rode farther north into Nlak'pamux (Thompson Indian) country, where they spent the winter trading in the local villages. By spring Ross had amassed 2500 furs, and he sent half his party back to the Columbia River with the haul.

Encouraged by his success, Ross asked the Nlak'pamux about the country to the north. They told him that it was the homeland of their Secwepemc friends and allies, the largest nation on the interior plateau. They offered to take Ross to visit Secwepemcul'ecw, the country of the Secwepemc, and he readily agreed to go.

After several days of riding the trail through dry hills and broad sweeping valleys, the party reached the high ridge above the Thompson River, where it divides into the North and South Thompson. Ross says that his guides called it Cum Cloops (the Fork in the River), a mispronounciation of the Secwepemc "Kamloops." As luck would have it, they had arrived in the middle of a local trade fair; two thousand Secwepemc and allied people were gathered on the flats where the powwow grounds are now located.

Ross stayed at Kamloops for ten days, trading all his goods for another large haul of furs, and then returned to the small post at the Columbia and Okanagan rivers and shipped the furs down the Columbia to the coast. It would be the last summer without whites in Secwepemcul'ecw.

In the fall, while the whole nation was busy preparing for the start of the main salmon run, word came that the traders were back. They had returned to the spring meeting-place and were building a permanent post on the Kamloops flats.

When the local headmen asked what the pedlars were doing, the Americans asked permission to camp over the winter. They had brought trade goods, they said, and they would be resupplied in the spring. The Secwepemc gave the foreigners permission to stay as long as they kept themselves within the traditional limits imposed on guests in someone else's country — they were to take nothing without asking.

The trade brought the Secwepemc new wealth. They now had their own source of ironwares and rifles, which they could use in battles with the coastal peoples to the west and the Siksika to the east. Yet they were not greatly dependent on the trade, since their main economic resource remained the rich fall salmon run, which ensured them a year-round food supply. Because of this independence, the European traders complained that "the Indians are very insolent to the whites." When foreign traders were seen overstepping their bounds, retribution could be swift. In 1841, when Samuel Black, the chief Hudson's Bay Company factor in the interior, was seen to be interfering in local affairs, he was killed on the spot. The fur company accepted his death as a cost of doing business in the region. Their only concession was to move their post across the river and fortify it with a fifteen-foot palisade.

Arthur Manuel's great-grandfather, who in later life was given the Christian name Dick Andrew, was born shortly after the execution of Black. When he was growing to manhood, in the 1840s and 1850s, the rhythm of life continued almost unchanged from ancient times. As a boy, he too practised running by racing the sunlight up the mountainside. When he reached puberty, he was sent into the hills on a vision quest, a ritual in which a young man fasted alone in the hope of finding a direction for his life. Arthur's great-grandfather must have had a powerful vision, because he became what is popularly known as a medicine man, but what his grandson referred to as an Indian doctor.

While Dick Andrew was learning about natural medicines and the psychological care that accompanied them, the first wave of disturbances passed through the country. A stream of whites began to move up from the south, using the ancient trails to cross Secwepemcul'ecw en route to rumoured goldfields in the Cariboo Mountains. This was in 1858, and many of the travellers were the same lawless miners and prospectors who had flooded California ten years earlier.

The people reacted to this sudden invasion with alarm. Neskonlith, the ranking chief of the Shuswap Lakes region, began to police his territory with a phalanx of mounted fighters. Colonial agents warned of the possibility of an Indian war breaking out if the whites tried to establish themselves in the territory. During this period another trader at Kamloops was killed. But as tensions increased and armed conflict became a real threat, the miners and pedlars moving through Secwepemcul'ecw were suddenly saved by an unseen ally: smallpox.

By 1861 smallpox was devastating the coastal peoples, and by spring the following year it had arrived in Secwepemcul'ecw. The disease, as always, struck quickly. It arrived with a burning fever that laid the victim low. On the third day a rash appeared on the head, arms, legs, hands and feet. The rash blistered and became pustular, with ulcerations developing all over the body, even inside the mouth. The terrifying scourge swept through Secwepemc villages from west to east, slaying two-thirds of the nation in a single year.

Chief Neskonlith tried to escape its wrath by leading his people, including twenty-year-old Dick Andrew, into the hills. Still, half the band was wiped out, and the whole nation was stunned by the loss. They would have no time for recovery. Miners were still flowing into the country; even before the gold rush had ended, the land rush would begin.

The last time I'd visited the B.C. interior, Bob Manuel, Arthur's elder brother, had shown me the remains of Dick Andrew's *kekuli*, or pithouse. All that was left was a large, round, caved-in pit along the riverbank, but at one time it had been a substantial home, about forty feet in diameter and dug four feet into the earth. Large cedar beams formed the above-ground conical top, with woven reed and bark matting covering the frame. For extra insulation, sod was laid over the matting, giving the structure the look of a Viking house.

"The women entered through a small door in the side," Bob explained. "The men entered through a hole in the roof and climbed down a ladder. In the spring, or during mild spells in winter, families would spend the day sitting on their roofs, talking with their neighbours."

The old *kekuli* was just across the road from the Neskonlith Community Hall, where Arthur was holding one of the regular meetings of the three Shuswap Lake bands involved in the land claim. I'd arranged to meet him and Wayne there at lunch. When I arrived, the chiefs and councillors were having a smoke outside. Wayne handed me a copy of the claim to look through that afternoon. "Pure Trutchery," he said. When I read through the document, I learned that Joseph Trutch, the B.C. land commissioner in the 1860s (and later a B.C. lieutenant-governor), was the villain of the piece.

Neskonlith led his people back down from the hills in the summer of 1862. Not only was his country reeling from the loss of two-thirds of its population, but it suddenly faced a blanket land claim from the most powerful empire on earth. The British had established a colony on Vancouver Island in 1849. In 1858, when American gold-seekers began to pour into the old countries of the interior plateau, colonial authorities moved to establish the colony of British Columbia on the mainland — even though the only British subjects in the vast, mountainous territory between the coast and the plains were a handful of Hudson's Bay Company employees living in isolated and heavily fortified posts.

To make way for settlement, the governor of the territory, James Douglas, would first have to make peace with the local peoples. On Vancouver Island, which was heavily garrisoned with British marines, Douglas had followed the usual treaty process of awarding small land grants per family, and small annual payments. But by the time he became governor of the great mainland territory, he no longer had the funds to pay even the small land-use annuities he'd offered the coastal people, and in the interior he had no military forces to intimidate the smallpox-ravaged nations. So he was forced to negotiate with the interior people without a great deal of leverage.

In the spring of 1861, Douglas sent his agents into the country to explain that at some point settlers would be coming, and to ask the people of each band what lands they required for their own use. The agent William Cox first visited the Secwepemc bands at Bonaparte and Kamloops in the late summer of 1862, and the Shuswap Lakes band in the fall.

Neskonlith listened attentively as Cox explained the situation. People were coming to settle, Cox said, but the British understood that the Shuswap Lake bands also had to ensure their future. So Cox asked Neskonlith to point out to him the territory they needed for their livelihood. With half his people dying from small-pox over the previous year, and thousands of miners passing through his territory, Neskonlith knew he couldn't drive the newcomers off by force, so he described the land his band used most intensely. The territory began up at Adams Lake, where the salmon-spawning streams were located, took in the heavy forests above Little Shuswap Lake and swung west for almost fifty miles along the valley and the forests beyond, almost all the way to Kamloops. Cox, who had neither cash inducements nor immediate military resources to use as negotiating tools, agreed to recognize these lands as belonging to Neskonlith's band. He handed Neskonlith a brief written acknowledgement of title; then the two men rode off together to drive in survey posts marking the limits of the territory.

Neskonlith and his people had surrendered a great deal simply by agreeing to let the settlers come into Secwepemcul'ecw. But the area they were left with took in hundreds of square miles and would allow them to continue to live a traditional life. It included hunting territories, grazing lands, a large forest rich in the people's history and, most important, the vital salmon-spawning creeks.

As soon as James Douglas resigned as governor in 1864, the settlers began to exert pressure on his successor, Frederick Seymour, to reduce the Indian lands. Amor De Cosmos, who would later become a B.C. premier, had berated Douglas for even bothering to consult with "the red vagrants" in allotting reserve lands. He demanded Seymour overturn the Douglas deal. The new governor gave the job to his land commissioner, Joseph Trutch, who sent another agent, Walter Moberly, into the interior with the mission of slashing back the so-called Douglas reserves. Moberly arrived in Secwepemcul'ecw in July 1865; by the time he returned to Victoria, he had hacked off more than ninety percent of the land Cox had allotted in the name of the Crown three years earlier.

Moberly left two widely different accounts of how he accomplished this.

In his published memoirs, he says that he first got rid of Neskonlith by sending him on what amounted to a wild goose chase. He gave the respected chief a packet of papers so important, he said, that he could trust only Neskonlith to deliver them personally to Lytton, sixty miles up the Thompson River. Neskonlith, who had had fair dealings with the previous Douglas regime, agreed to make the delivery. The papers were addressed to a friend of Moberly's and the cover note instructed the friend to keep Neskonlith occupied at Lytton for as long as possible. Moberly says that, with Neskonlith out of the way, he was able to get quick agreement to his revised proposal from the lesser leaders.

In his report to the land commissioner, Moberly gives a far different version. He describes what amounts to bribing Neskonlith to accept the slashing of his people's territory.

"I had a big talk with Indians," he writes, "and gave them a good blow-out. Then I conferred with their chief, old Nesquinalt [*sic*], who was a cunning old beggar. We were camped 200 or 300 feet from the beach, and while the Indians were sitting round the fire at supper I asked Nesquinalt to take a little walk with me down the beach. He did so, and I told him when we sat down, that we wanted the Indian reserve matter settled, and I showed him where the boundary should go. I then took out of my pocket $200, which I had with me in $20 pieces. I put $100 on each knee. The money shone in the moonlight, and I told him I would put that in his pocket the following morning if he would agree. Next morning all was settled."

That afternoon, I borrowed Wayne's truck to take a drive in the hills above the large section of Neskonlith territory on the north side of the river. The houses below were scattered along the strip of hayfields on the valley floor. The top of the ridge was dry, open land with short grasses, a few late August wildflowers and the occasional stand of ponderosa pine.

The old graveyard is located on flat tableland on top of the highest ridge. It has been in use since the nineteenth century, when Big Bear's people were making their last stand at Frenchman's Butte. Wayne had read somewhere that the Cree of Rocky Mountain House had sent emissaries through Rogers Pass and along the South Thompson in the summer of 1885 to inform their Secwepemc allies that war had broken out. The news filled the interior with excitement. If the European tide could be reversed on the plains, they believed it could be reversed on the interior plateau as well. It was a fleeting hope. As soon as Mistihai'muskwa was in custody, the government restrictions placed on the plains peoples were placed on indigenous peoples across the land. Not only were chiefs made employees of the Canadian government, but a pass system was instituted, requiring Indians on reserves to get permission from the Indian agent to leave the community, even to cross the river to town. Potlatch, the elaborate west coast gift-giving ceremony, as well as the Sun Dance and the Thirst Dance, were made illegal. In fact, Indian gatherings of any kind, on or off the reserve, required permission from the local Indian agent. By the 1890s, the Department of Indian Affairs had set up, in partnership with the churches, a mandatory residential school system designed to separate the young from their families and culture, and to assimilate them into Canadian life.

Surprisingly, even these draconian measures were not enough to "settle" things. The B.C. interior nations came together in 1910 at Spence's Bridge to launch a political action movement that came to be known as the Allied Tribes, devoted to getting their countries back. A petition to that effect was drafted at the end of the meeting, and sent to Prime Minister Laurier and to the British Crown. The people of the interior then used money collected from selling hay and firewood to hire lawyers to fight their claim in court. In 1923, band members of Neskonlith sent Chief William Pierrish to London with another petition to the Privy Council, asking for the return of the land seized under British colonial rule. The same year, the Mohawk leader Deskeheh was in Geneva, requesting that the Iroquois Nation be accepted as a full member in the League of Nations. The old countries were refusing to die. In fact, they seemed to be struggling back. In 1927 the Dominion government moved to close the door once and for all. It passed an order-in-council that had the effect of making Indian land claims illegal. That law remained on the books, and was strictly enforced, until the 1950s. Canada was, in effect, holding the fifty-some original nations of the land under strict house arrest, and it did so for more than two generations.

The cemetary was surrounded by a small, ungated fence. The grave of Dick Andrew was at the edge of the ridge, overlooking the village and the river and, to the west, the blue waters of Little Shuswap Lake. Andrew had been born into freedom in 1840, and had died in 1941, after a century-long life in an occupied country. Like many grandparents during those times, he and his wife, Macreet, had raised several of their grandchildren. At the turn of the century he raised the Pierrish children, including William, after their mother died in a drowning accident. In the 1920s he raised Arthur's father, George Manuel, after George's father collapsed one day in his hayfield. George Manuel followed in William Pierrish's footsteps, with his grandfather's encouragement. Beginning as an activist hitchhiking around the B.C. interior in the 1950s, Manuel became the founding president of the National Indian Brotherhood and the World Council of Indigenous Peoples in the 1970s. His vision took in indigenous nations of North and South America, Africa and Eurasia that had been swamped by European expansion in the eighteenth and nineteenth centuries. He called these nations the Fourth World, and he was convinced that the ancient countries, along with Secwepemcul'ecw, would someday, somehow, rise again.

I stopped by Arthur Manuel's place on the way out. His home is on the pine-covered slopes overlooking the river. Arthur had been elected chief only two years before, but his father had held the job almost forty years earlier, and his uncle Joe in the 1970s, and his older brother Bob in the 1980s.

In a relatively poor community like Neskonlith, the chief's job brings low pay and long hours. You are called on to battle the Department of Indian Affairs and other government departments, and to oversee the band's complex social welfare system, still a lifeline for many on the reserve, while trying to create or find a few jobs for the people. You have to ensure funding for the education and general care of the young. You have to perform dozens of other duties: attending funerals, making sure the water is potable, and keeping sanitary landfills sanitary, stop signs in place and roads ploughed in winter. The chiefs are also called on to console grieving families and to find care for infants left on the doorstep of the band office because their teenaged mothers can't cope. On top of this, they are expected to lead the larger battles for the land and future of a small but ancient nation. In these battles, Arthur once told me, justice is always pitted against power. "And justice always has a hard row to hoe."

If you took the job of chief seriously, Wayne had said, it was an impossible job. "And Arthur takes it seriously."

We sat in Arthur's kitchen and I asked him what he thought of the upcoming Cabot celebrations, I expected he would have a ready answer, similar to Konrad's reply that celebrating the arrival was shameful because of what it meant: the beginning of the long and painful destruction of the Old Order. But Arthur thought about it for a while. "Canadians have something to celebrate over their five hundred years here," he said. "The problem begins when they refuse to make room for others."

He said he had been sent to provincial schools and had spent a short time at residential school, and that he had learned about John Cabot when he was young. He knew about Cabot, he said, long before he knew about Chief Neskonlith, though he had grown up on the Neskonlith reserve. "They wanted to get rid of Indians so they tried to get rid of our culture, our language, our traditions and our history," he said. "They didn't quite succeed, and now we're trying to rebuild. The land claim is only part of it."

The three bands around the Shuswap Lakes were launching a detailed study of the traditional use of the lands in their territory. Arthur referred to it as "a kind of cultural mapping." They were trying to give the Secwepemc name for every mountain and hill, every lake and stream, every valley and tableland. After interviewing elders and combing through historical documents, they would locate the sites of the old *kekuli* villages, where up to a thousand Secwepemc spent their winters in permanent houses, separating into smaller bands in the spring to hunt in the hills for elk, mountain goats, bighorn sheep and deer. The individual hunting areas would be identified, as would the places along the river where weirs and spearing platforms were built for the fall salmon run that saw the river turn red with millions of chinook heading up to the gravelly creek beds above Adams Lake.

When the idea of the study was first introduced around the three communities, it ran into unexpected resistance from some of the elders. They liked the idea in principle, but they were afraid the information would be stolen and misused, just as the land had been stolen and misused. They did not want the location of certain medicinal plants to be widely known, lest outsiders move in and seize them. The same applied to the areas where people had always gone for spiritual respite. Some of these sites had become accessible already, and significant rock paintings had been vandalized.

Arthur's kitchen window framed the South Thompson River and the dry hills that rise steeply to the west. The cemetery where his father, grandfather and great-grandfather lie buried, is on the top of the first ridge. The stand of ponderosa pines slightly to the north once shaded his grandfather's hut. The site of his great-grandfather's *kekuli* is on the riverbank, only a few hundred feet from where we were sitting. "When we were kids," Arthur said, "we didn't have running water, so we had to haul it up from the river. A couple of times a day we would pass by the site of the *kekuli*. All that was left is a hole in the ground, but it connected us to that world." He thought for a moment. "We're still connected. It's our land."

The following year, Arthur's views would get support from an unexpected source. The Supreme Court rendered its so-called Delgamuukw Decision, which recognized, for the first time, that Aboriginal title to the land existed, and that it was equal to Crown title. The case was a major legal breakthrough and the Supreme Court justices called on both the federal government and native nations to get together to reconcile the legal deadlock.

Arthur called me the night the judgment was released. He had recently been elected the head of the Shuswap Nation Tribal Council, the national Secwepemc government, and he'd spent the day going over the judgment. "Now we have something to build on," he said. "If there are any treaties to be signed, they will not have to deal with our right to the land. They'll have to deal with the right of Canadians to stay here."

A short time later Arthur was also elected the head of a new group of the seven nations in the B.C. interior with a mandate to fight for the implementation of the historic Supreme Court decision. "All we have to do," he said, "is to force the government to obey its own laws." He added, "But it's something Canada always has trouble doing when it comes to Indians."

Wayne and I left Kelowna for our brief flight to the coast on Saturday morning. Our plan was to fly through the passes to Whistler, then cut across the Strait of Georgia to Vancouver Island and across the island to Nootka. There was no airstrip there — in fact, our chart didn't even show a road to Captain Cook's landing site, so this would be a day of pure flying.

The jetstream had moved to the south a few days earlier, and the morning was calm. We took off just before dawn and swung out over Lake Okanagan. As the sun rose behind us and began heating the valley floor, the air became bumpier, but it was nothing like the jolts we'd encountered on the way in from Crowsnest. On this flight we had time to enjoy the sheer beauty of the mountains. As we approached Mount Currie, we could see the icefields off to the northwest, the massive coastal range that remained snow-covered year-round.

Just before Whistler, we turned to a heading of almost 270, flying over a range of much smaller mountains, about seven thousand feet high. In the distance we could already see the maze of islands in the Strait of Georgia. We began a long descent towards Campbell River, on the east coast of Vancouver Island, where we refuelled.

A few minutes after we were back in the air, we saw the Pacific shore of the island. We flew towards the radio beacon on Hesquiat Peninsula, near the natural harbour where Captain James Cook first met Chief Maquinna of the Nuu-chah-nulth, which means "all along the coast." Wayne called out the scattered towns in the rain forest, which is now mottled by clearcuts.

The meeting between Maquinna and Cook took place in 1778. It was the Nuu-chah-nulth's second sighting of a European ship. A Spanish frigate had anchored at the same spot four years earlier, but the crew had been unable to land because of rough seas. When Cook's *Resolution* anchored in much calmer waters, Chief Maquinna told his young men to "go out and try to understand what these people want and what they are after."

It was late afternoon when the Nuu-chah-nulth gathered together a welcoming flotilla of sea-going canoes. They shoved off the beach with three shouts that a crewman on the *Resolution* reported sounded like *Halloo! Halloo! Halloo!* The young men paddled with a ceremonial three strokes in the water, then a flourish with the paddles and another shout of *Halloo!*

The Nuu-chah-nulth ringed the ship. As the sun set, they began to sing a song of welcome, which a crewman described as "by no means unpleasant to the Ear." When the song ended, the

Resolution gave reply with a fife and drum. The Nuu-chah-nulth listened with interest. They sang another song and the ship replied with a tune on the French horn. With the impromptu battle of the bands over, the main party of the Nuu-chah-nulth retired to the shore, leaving a small guard that spent the chilly March night slowly circling the ship.

The Nuu-chah-nulth were not intimidated by the British. They and the other coastal peoples were wealthy and powerful nations in their own right. They were seafarers who travelled the coast in large dugouts, and the coastal countries of the Tlingit, Nishg'a, Gitksan, Tsimshian, Haida, Haisla, Heiltsuk, Bella Coola, Nuu-chah-nulth and Coastal Salish were the most densely populated on Canadian territory. Europeans were surprised to find people living in cedar-plank houses in large, permanent villages dotting the coast. They were amazed at their artistic achievements in their house murals, carvings and theatrical arts. But what brought the two cultures together was trade.

When Maquinna's people paddled out to the *Resolution* the next morning to begin trading with the newcomers, they are said to have called out, "*Nootka itcheme. Nootka itcheme,*" which means "Go around to the harbour," and pointed around the promontory. Hearing only *Nootka*, and seeing the people pointing to the land, Cook assumed that Nootka was the name of the country. In his log he recorded the name of the people as "Nootka Indians."

When trading finally commenced, Cook was very pleased by the wealth of furs the "Nootka" brought to the ship's side. The sea otter, called sea beaver in Cook's day, were especially numerous. These were also highly prized by the Europeans, and Cook quickly filled his hold with them. When he arrived back in Hawaii that fall, the load of sea beaver pelts attracted instant interest and a high price. Word of the rich fur harvest spread quickly from port to port, sparking a mad sea-beaver rush along the west coast of the island and mainland. The history of the eastern seaboard of the continent was about to be played out in the west.

Wayne had the map folded in his lap. He pointed out Tlupana Inlet below and, just ahead, Cook Channel and Maquinna Point, at the mouth of Nootka Sound. Cook's landing place was off a small tidal island that Wayne spotted by the red roof of the lighthouse that marked it. We circled out over the sea, where the mountains rose from the waters, then banked towards the land. We passed over Nuu-chah-nulth villages that still line the isolated coast. The people get their livelihood from the sea even today, but in recent years — like the buffalo on the plains and the cod on the Atlantic coast — the salmon have begun to disappear, as great Canadian, American and international fleets vacuum the sea, and logging companies destroy the interior spawning beds.

The evening before the flight back, I had dinner near my hotel with Wayne and Brenda. The conversation was light and amusing. Brenda said she had told Wayne several times over the summer, particularly on those hundred-degree days, that this might be his first child, but it was her last. They were both living in the future now, counting the weeks and days to the birth of their child; which they now knew would be a son.

After dinner, we walked to the parking lot. I was going to head off to my hotel when Wayne called me over to his truck. He pulled a long grey feather from his glove compartment. "It's the pilot feather from an eagle," he said. "For luck, when you head back across the country." I gave him two sets of pilot wings — one for himself, the other for his unborn son. We shook hands, and he and Brenda headed across the lake to the Westbank Reserve.

I flew out through Rogers Pass in the calm of first light the next morning. With no wind, I was able to climb to 9500 feet — just below the level where oxygen is required I was in Calgary in four hours. I stopped at the Spruce Goose for breakfast, then spent the rest of the day over the plains, which were now different shades of gold. Flying alone in good weather is a special kind of pleasure.

You keep watch, you scan your instruments, but alone in the cockpit, with the drone of the engine, you feel part of the sky.

The land below, once wild grassland stretching down to Texas, was now a ploughed and fenced-in granary. But the country has gone through many changes, from cold and barren tundra, to subtropical rainforest, to renewed cold. The constant, for twenty thousand years and more, has been the people. On the approach to Regina, where I spent the first night, I passed by the Day Star, Muskowekwan, Standing Buffalo, Muscowpetung, Piapot, Pasqua and Poorman reserves. The next morning I took off over the Carry-the-Kettle, Cowessess, Sakimay, Ochapowace, Waywayseecappo, Birdtail and Rolling River reserves — ancient towns from an ancient country fighting to regain its place in history.

I spent the second night in Thunder Bay, where Nana'b'oozoo lies in his nine-hundred-year sleep. I arrived over Kawennote Tiohtià:ke — "the place where the peoples divide" — at twilight the next day. St-Hubert tower cleared me for a straight-in approach, and I landed to the south of the island, on the broad Kentaké plain.

Brenda and Wayne's son, Terrance Dana, was born on October 1. When he was old enough to travel, Wayne told me on the phone, they would take him to see his granny in Edmonton, and then east to visit Tenakìwin, his mother's country.

CHAPTER EIGHTEEN

Bonavista

I T WAS A BUSY FALL AND WINTER, Wayne said, with the new
child and the increasing work load. He was still commuting
between Kamloops and Kelowna, as band manager at Neskonlith and as a consultant at the Secwepemc Nation Tribal Council. In the spring of 1997, he had become a First Nations delegate to
an AFN–federal government committee responsible for setting up a
new land-claims commission.

We had planned to complete our own journey by flying back to
Newfoundland for the official Cabot quincentenary celebrations
at Bonavista on June 24, 1997. There was some doubt at first about
whether he could make it, but in early June he called to say that he
would be in Quebec City on June 20, at a claims committee meeting. He could take a few days off so we could make a run for it. If
the weather turned bad, though, he couldn't wait around. He had
to be back in Kamloops by June 27.

We agreed to meet at noon on the twenty-first at L'Aviatrice, a
pilots' café across from the Aviation Esso on the edge of Quebec
City's Jean Lesage airport ramp. I was there when Wayne pulled
up in a cab. We only planned to fly to Cape Breton that afternoon,
so we took our time over lunch. Wayne said he'd heard that the
AFN advance party, which included Russell Diabo and Roland Pangowish (the guy we'd tried to meet up with on Manitoulin), were

already in Bonavista, trying to arrange a meeting between Ovide Mercredi and the Queen when she arrived on the twenty-third. They were also planning to hold a small native ceremony on the shore with a group of Labrador Innu. "If Ovide is kept away from the official party," he added, "the Innu will be there to protest."

The five-hundred-year celebrations had been part of Canadian and British media hype for months. In May a replica of John Cabot's ship, the *Matthew*, had set sail from Bristol with a British and Canadian crew dressed in period costumes. The national news in both countries had been following the progress of the ship through remote satellite broadcasts. Even though no one really believed that Cabot had landed at Bonavista, the re-enactment of the landing would take place there because, as the local MP had explained, "that's where the Cabot statue is."

The Newfoundland tourism ministry had announced that it was expecting sixty thousand people to flood the village to watch Queen Elizabeth welcome the *Matthew*'s arrival. To the surprise of Ovide Mercredi and the AFN staffers, none of the official welcomers would be native people. As in the original landfall five hundred years earlier, the people of the country would be expected to watch from the trees.

The flight to Sydney took us over Quebec's Beauce region, through the heart of Wabanaki — over the dark green Appalachian Mountains of northern Maine to the flatlands of the Acadian shore, not far from the spot where Donnacona and his people had met Cartier. While we flew, Wayne filled me in on the AFN national chief election that would be taking place in July in Vancouver. It looked like an uninspiring choice as far as the front-runners went, he said. After announcing that he wouldn't run again, Ovide had changed his mind and said he would. But after six years in the job, with little to show for it in concrete gains, his supporters had dwindled to those who saw him as a better alternative than the other two leading candidates. One of these was Wendy Grant, a B.C. coastal leader who was suspect, Wayne said, because she had close political ties to the federal government. Arthur was also concerned because she was working with a group of B.C. chiefs who had entered into negotiations with the government that put their aboriginal rights to the land on the table.

The other front-runner was Phil Fontaine, Mercredi's old nemesis from Manitoba. "Phil can do the job," Wayne said. "But a lot of chiefs are looking for someone who can lead the fight for the land. Phil tends to focus on social battles."

The surprise was that there would also be a Manuel in the race. At the last minute — the deadline for nominations was midnight that night, June 21 — Arthur's older brother, Bob, had thrown his hat into the ring, and old Manuel supporters around the country were spending the day trying to ensure that he had his nomination papers signed by the necessary fifteen chiefs so that he could become an official candidate.

"Can he win?" I asked.

Wayne shrugged. "Probably not. But he can talk about some issues. He's going to talk about the land and nothing else." He smiled. "I think Arthur talked him into it."

Bob Manuel had run for national chief once before, in 1978, when he was just thirty years old. It was the time when George Manuel was head of the World Council of Indigenous Peoples, Arthur was head of the National Indian Youth Association and Bob was head of the Union of B.C. Indian Chiefs. In the national chiefs election, Bob lost by only two votes.

"But he's been away from it for a while," Wayne said. "There's no time to mount a proper campaign. And he has to get those fifteen nominations in."

When we landed in Moncton to fuel up, we were surprised to see two U.S. Marines F-18s and an RAF Harrier jet, all fully armed with air-to-air missiles, parked at the edge of the tarmac. We asked the fueller what was up. "NATO's got planes all over the Maritimes," he said. "They're here to protect the Queen."

As we walked away, Wayne asked, "From who? From Ovide?"

By the time we finished our climb out at Moncton we were over the Northumberland Strait, between New Brunswick and Prince Edward Island. As we flew over the calm waters towards the folded green hills of Cape Breton, the radio began to crackle with traffic. Approaching Sydney, we learned that the airstrip was buzzing with Harriers, Hornets and F-18s. On our final approach we could see two black Hornets pulling onto the runway in front of us. I radioed our position from two miles out. Suddenly, in a puff of smoke, the runway was cleared and the jets were streaking over the ocean.

We headed across the tarmac to the terminal, past a row of parked fighter planes. The crowd of locals who had gathered at the fence to watch the impromptu air show welcomed us and our awkward-looking Charlie GUDD with mock applause.

"We're going to see the Queen," Wayne said as we passed the fence. There was a ripple of laughter.

We checked into the Sydney Holiday Inn and Wayne called Arthur. Bob was still one nomination short, but Joanna — the wife of Russell Diabo, the AFN staffer in Newfoundland — had just left Ottawa to drive to Golden Lake, a reserve on the edge of Algonquin Park, to see if she could get the chief there to sign the final nomination paper.

We were up at dawn the next morning. While we were checking out, the receptionist handed Wayne a phone message that had come in during the night. It was from Arthur. "We have the fifteenth," it said.

To reach Newfoundland from Sydney we had to cross 150 miles of the North Atlantic, a stretch that the Mi'kmaq canoes travelled in the old days to fish along the coast. To make the flight over the open sea, we were supposed to carry gas-inflatable life preservers and a two-man gas-inflatable raft. But I had been unable to locate either in Montreal. I had tracked down a place in Halifax that rented rafts, but discovered that they were too heavy to carry in the Cessna. So we ended up flying with only a couple of foam life preservers I'd picked up at Canadian Tire. Given the small size of the Cessna doors, we wouldn't be able to put them on until we were outside the plane, treading water. Still, as we climbed 7500 feet above the ocean, we saw that we had chosen a good time to cross the strait without survival gear. Cabot Strait (named when it was still believed that Cabot had landed off Cape Breton) was littered with NATO warships and what looked, from a mile and a half up, to be one or two aircraft carriers. "If we have to ditch," I said, "we can aim for one of those."

After we passed over the small French islands of St. Pierre and Miquelon, Newfoundland's Burin Peninsula loomed into view. The terrain is made up largely of convoluted bare grey rock that looks vaguely like exposed brain matter. As we entered St. John's airspace, we encountered another heavy military presence. The Queen was scheduled to land the following morning. When we rolled to a stop in front of the Esso fuel truck, a couple of young linemen came out and said they had to pull all the planes off the ramp and put them in hangars, so there would be no place to conceal a bomb.

We drove to Bonavista that afternoon. The village wasn't much to look at. There were a few stores and rundown restaurants along a recently paved main street. Clapboard houses were scattered in no apparent pattern along dirt roads that wound through the bare rounded hills overlooking the sea.

When we pulled up in front of the bed and breakfast where Russell Diabo and Roland Pangowish were staying, they were standing in the driveway, just getting into their rental car. Both Diabo, a Mohawk, and Pangowish, an Odawa, were hefty guys, built like barroom bouncers, but at the AFN they worked as political organizers and advisers. Diabo was also a very shrewd political strategist. I had met him briefly many years ago in Montreal, and recently I'd run into him in Ottawa a few times while I was freelancing for the *Globe and Mail*, and I was impressed by his ability to map out the political terrain in detail. He understood the journalists' need for background material, especially when we were writing about the Byzantine world of Indian politics, and was always prepared to load down reporters with a wheelbarrowful of clippings, faxes, reports and policy papers that, put together, neatly backed up his case.

Diabo and Pangowish were still negotiating with the event organizers to get Ovide Mercredi a role in the official ceremonies, and arranging for a campsite for two busloads of Innu who would be arriving the next day for the Indian ceremony. When we met them in the driveway, the conversation quickly turned to Bob's candidacy.

"Keeping all the bases covered, eh, Russ?" Wayne joked. He was referring to the fact that, while his wife had been driving through the night to get Bob's fifteenth nomination, Russell, as an AFN staffer, was working for Ovide.

He smiled. "Don't start," he said. He was a friend of Bob's, and the last-minute candidacy had caught him by surprise. He changed the subject. "The government guys don't seem to want anything to do with Ovide." The attempts to have him included in the ceremony were going nowhere. The local organizers were friendly, but the political protocol officers from Ottawa looked as if they just wanted the two Indians to go away. It was unnecessary to add the national chief to the official delegation, they told Diabo and Pangowish, because native people would be represented by the chief of the tiny Mi'kmaq community on the southern coast. "But Ovide's the national chief," Diabo said, "and he's going to be here anyway. Why not include him?" The officials said they would see, but Russell said that meant no.

Diabo and Pangowish were heading up to the campsite they'd arranged for the busloads of Innu protesters, and they offered to show us around.

The area around the village pier, where the *Matthew* was to arrive and the ceremonies were to take place, had been roped off by security men. Inside, construction workers were erecting a protected platform from which the Queen would make her speech. The grey skies buzzed with military and RCMP helicopters.

A few tourists had already gathered, many of them wearing red-and-white Cabot souvenir caps that resembled chef's hats, and they were wandering around aimlessly. There wasn't even a restaurant open around the harbour, so, like us, they stared off at the workers and up at the circling helicopters. A large CBC satellite truck arrived and was waved through security to the camera towers in front of the Queen's platform. The only preparation for the tens of thousands of people expected to come to see the Queen in person were a few red-and-white streamers on the lampposts and a long bank of portable toilets at the back of the parking lot. While we were watching the work progress, a local fisherman in big boots and coveralls walked over to us. Diabo asked him what he thought of the celebration. "Waste of time," he said, and pointed at the newly resurfaced main street. "All we get out of this is a bit of fuckin' pavement." When he left, Pangowish said this was typical of the response of the local people they'd spoken to. The official government celebration of five hundred years of Europeans in North America seemed to have taken on the weight, importance and style of Groundhog Day.

Wayne and I headed back to St. John's for the night. "This could have been a great moment of people coming together," he said during the drive along the foggy highway. "Canadians could have planned this anniversary with the people and we could have looked at our history together. Instead it's the same old story. They're still trying to keep us a crossbow-shot away from the ship."

The Queen was scheduled to arrive at eleven the next morning, at the same hangar where we'd parked the Cessna. When we went for breakfast, the city was being drenched by a downpour that continued as we drove out to the airport an hour later. It was only nine a.m., but the avenues were already decorated with Union Jacks and maple-leaf flags for the Queen's cavalcade, and artillery pieces had been moved in front of the legislature for the twenty-one-gun salute.

Officials were just beginning to put up the security net around the airport when we arrived. I told the RCMP officer that our plane was in the hangar and we needed to get to it. He waved us in. When we pulled into the Aviation Esso lot, an overdressed couple were unloading wheelchair kids from a large van into the rain. The girls were wearing party dresses, the boys miniature salesmen suits. These children would be among the props waiting to greet the Queen. In a scene that might have been lifted from a bad Disney movie, the woman was frantically pushing and pulling them out of the van, in a hurry to get them out of the rain and into the Aviation Esso waiting area. The kids, in wheelchairs and on crutches, had harried and haunted looks on their faces. A few of them looked as though they were about to cry.

The Queen finally arrived, in the middle of another torrential downpour, and was met by the Governor General, a crowd of dignitaries and the still anxious-looking crippled children. Umbrellas were thrust over Her Majesty, but it was too late. She headed for cover, looking soggy, uncomfortable and unregal.

"She didn't see her shadow," Wayne said while we were driving back to Bonavista. "That must mean five hundred more years of Europeans." Then he thought for a moment. "Or is it the other way around?"

We stood with Diabo and Pangowish, watching the two busloads of Innu set up their bush tents on the wet and windy hillside. Ovide Mercredi had just arrived and he was conferring with his team. When he spotted Wayne, he headed in our direction. By this time he had heard that Bob Manuel was in the race for his job, so his demeanour was, if anything, friendlier than usual. At some point he might be interested in doing a deal with the Manuel camp. After a few pleasantries, he told us that he too would be camping out in the rain that evening. Then he left to check out the location on the point where he would be holding the native ceremony to mark the anniversary of the landing.

An old lighthouse, freshly painted white with red trim, stood at the end of the jutting point. The John Cabot statue was a hundred yards back, on the high, bare rock. The native ceremony began at eight p.m., on the flat, scrubby shoulder of land below the statue. At that moment, five hundred years earlier, Giovanni Caboto, his son and fifteen Bristolmen had been somewhere out on the sea when the scent of land came to them. They believed that they had come at last to the almost mythical lands of the Grand Khan. Ahead lay the riches of the Orient.

Now a hundred people stood on the dark, windy shore, more than half of them Innu, the rest curious tourists, huddling in a circle around Ovide in near freezing temperatures brought by a cold front out of Labrador. A tiny old Innu woman cleansed Mercredi's spirit with burning sweetgrass. He and Innu Nation president Katie Rich made speeches.

Mercredi spoke about the struggle in general terms, describing Cabot's arrival as a black day for indigenous people everywhere in the country, since it led to the gradual usurpation of their land and liberty. Today, he said, they were fighting back from that darkness, and they would let nothing stand in their way.

Katie Rich spoke about the genocide of the Innu's Beothuk cousins. She called for a moment of silence in their memory, and ended by saying that the Innu had to struggle with every fibre of their being to ensure that they did not suffer the same fate.

As the rains beat harder, Ovide asked everyone to bring a stone and place it in the middle of the circle. Within a few minutes a small cairn had been erected. The crowd lingered for a moment, as if expecting something more, then quietly dispersed into the damp, chilly night.

The Queen arrived in Bonavista by helicopter the next morning, in time to greet the *Matthew* as it sailed into the bay in a ceremony that was broadcast live in Canada and Britain. When she finished her speech, she made a brief walkabout. The Innu and AFN delegation had been given a spot down the road from the harbour, across from the seniors' home, which the Queen was scheduled to visit. On her way, she spotted them and moved towards them. The Deputy Prime Minister, Sheila Copps, who was at the Queen's side, tried to steer her away. But the melancholy monarch went over to shake a few Innu hands. And then she was gone. The television cameras caught the national chief, dressed in buckskins, staring blankly at the royal procession as it passed him by.

Two days later, the Queen flew to the Labrador village of Sheshatshui at the invitation of the local Innu. Tents were set up along the inlet, where the Nitassinan welcoming ceremonies took place. The Queen was given flowers and a letter by two children. The letter said that the people's homeland was not Canada but the ten-thousand-year-old country of Nitassinan. As Innu, it said, "we believe we are entitled as a People to full ownership rights over the lands which we have lived upon since the glaciers retreated from this peninsula." The Queen handed the letter to an aide and walked on.

The chief, Paul Rich, introduced her to his councillors and the village elders. As they walked along the shore, Rich told her simply that "the Innu did not choose to live under someone else's laws."

Her Majesty Queen Elizabeth II, the successor to Henry VII who handed Giovanni Caboto the patent to discover and exploit new lands in the name of the British Crown, nodded politely and walked on.

KEY TO
ABORIGINAL NATIONS

Naming always presents problems in dealing with the history of aboriginal nations. Most were known by several names: those they called themselves; names their neighbours (both friends and enemies) gave them; and those the newly arrived Europeans called them, which were often mispronunciations or mistranslations. The brief glossary below provides a quick reference for some of the more confusing ones.

Algonkian Peoples This is a large language group that includes Mi'kmaq, Innu, Cree, Algonquin, Ojibwa, and Odawa of the eastern woodlands, as well as the Blackfoot peoples (Blackfoot, Blood and Peigans) of the western plains.

Algonquin The Algonquins called themselves the Màmìwininì, which means simply, "the people." The name Algonquin is believed to have been given them by their Algonkian-speaking friends and it is said to mean "ally."

Anishnabe Peoples This is the name now commonly given to the allied Algonkian-speaking peoples of the Laurentian Shield. It means "the good beings," and refers to the Algonquin, Ojibwa and Odawa peoples. Increasingly, it is being extended to include the neighbouring Cree and Innu as well.

Assiniboine The people we know as the Assiniboine were Siouan speakers and part of the Yanktonai tribe of the Dakota nation. They broke away from the Dakota in the late 1500s and sought refuge with the Cree and Ojibwa in the Lake of the Woods region. The name Assiniboine was said to be given them by the Cree and means "people who still cook with stones," in reference to the fact that the Assiniboine had not yet to come into contact with the Europeans and gained access to copper kettles.

Blackfoot The people we know today as the Blackfoot call themselves the Siksika, and are closely aligned with the Blood, who call themselves the Kainai people, and the Peigans, who call themselves the Pikani people. Collectively, these three allied nations referred to themselves as the Soyitapi, which means "the true people of the plains."

Blackfoot Confederacy This refers to a military alliance that included the Blackfoot peoples, the Siksika, Kainai and Pikani, as well as the Sarsi (Tsuu T'ina). The Aaninena (Gros Ventre) were an informal part of the Confederacy until the early 19th century, when they were driven south by the Cree.

Cree Cree and the French *Cris* are now the accepted identification of the people who began as the Kenistenaag people, living around James Bay. In the 19th century, they split into two branches, the Nehiyawak (Plains Cree) and the Saka:widhiniwak (Bush Cree).

Huron The origin of the word is uncertain, but it is believed to come from a French word for *boar*, and was used to denote wildness. The people called themselves Wendat (Peninsula Dwellers), and at the time of the European arrival in the interior, they were divided into four tribal groups: the Attignawantan (Bear Nation), Attigneenongnahac (Barking Dog Nation), Arendarhonon (Rock Nation) and Tahontaenrat (Deer Nation), located on the Penetanguishene Peninsula.

Iroquoian Peoples This refers to the related peoples living around the Great Lakes and along the St. Lawrence River when the Europeans arrived. Along with the Five Nations Iroquois, they included the Wendat, the Tionnontaté (Tobacco), Attiwandaronk (Neutral) and Erie peoples. Some historians have also identified the Stadaconans and Hochelagans as a separate "Laurentian Iroquois" nation that disappeared in the late 17th century.

Iroquois (Five Nations) The Iroquois living to the south of the Great Lakes at the time of contact, the Mohawk, Seneca, Oneida, Onondaga and Cayuga, were known as the Five Nations. The Five Nations referred to themselves the Rotinohshonni, the People of the Longhouse.

Montagnais The Montagnais, or the Mountaineers, received their name from the early French explorers who named them after their homeland in the Laurentian mountains. The people call themselves Innu, which means "the people" in their language.

Shuswap/Interior Salish The name Shuswap is a mistranslation of Secwepemc. They are the largest nation of four interior Salish peoples [the others are the Thompson (Ntlakapamux), Lillooet and Okanagan] living on British Columbia's central plateau.

NOTES

This is a summary of some of the most important historical sources for this book, as well as notes on the direct quotes that we have used.

The quote on p.20 about Cabot's approach to the Newfoundland coast comes from Morison, Samuel, *The European Discovery of America* (Oxford University Press, 1993) p.172. The description of Cabot's landing and of the early encounters between the Beothuk and Europeans come from *The Beothuks Or Red Indians* (Cambridge University Press, 1915), a compilation of primary sources on the Beothuk. All of the quotes in chapters three and four came from Cartier's journals.

The quotes from Champlain's journals in chapters five to eight were cited in Morris Bishop's *Champlain: The Life of Fortitude* (first published by Alfred A. Knopf in 1948 and republished by McClelland and Stewart in 1971). The quotations from the Great Law of Peace and the account of Dekanawida's youth in chapter six came from *The Constitution of the Five Nations or The Iroquois Book of the Great Law* (University of the State of New York, 1916). Additional information, and many of the Mohawk terms, came from Gerald Taiaiake Alfred and his excellent book on Kahnawake history, *Heeding the Voices of Our Ancestors* (Oxford University Press, 1995).

Much of the background information on 17th century life in Tenakìwin and Huronia comes from Bruce Trigger's *The Children of Aataentsic: A History of the Huron People to 1660* (McGill Queens, 1987), Morris Bishop's *Champlain,* Gabriel Sagard's *Le Grand Voyage au Pays des Hurons* (Lemeac, 1990), J.H. Cranston's *Étienne Brûlé: Immortal Scoundrel* (The Ryerson Press, 1969), Harold Innis's *The Fur Trade in Canada* (University of Toronto Press, 1977) and Olive Patricia Dickason's *Canada's First Nations* (Oxford University Press, 1992). Dickason's work, which is probably the most definitive work on First Nations history in Canada, was also used as a kind of final authority throughout.

Fur Trade Canoe Routes of Canada: Then and Now (University of Toronto Press, 1969) by Eric W. Morse gave valuable information on the old Indian trails between the Ottawa River and the Plains.

Three books on the Ojibwa, *The Ojibwa of Southern Ontario* (University of Toronto Press, 1990) by Peter S. Schmalz, *The Ojibwa of Western Canada: 1780 to 1870* (Minnesota Historical Society, 1994) and *Our Historic Boundary Waters: From Lake Superior to Lake of the Woods* (Adventure Publications, 1980) by Dr. Duane R. Lund, provided some of the historical information on the history of the Ojibwa in the 17th and 18th century contained in chapters ten and eleven. Basil Johnston's wonderful book *The Manitous: The Spiritual World of the Ojibway* (HarperCollins, 1996), was an excellent cultural resource. La Vérendrye's story was drawn largely from the copies of his dispatches back to Paris and New France, available in the Hudson's Bay Company archives at the Manitoba Provincial Library.

The quotes from Anthony Henday's journals on pages 222 and 223 were cited on pages 8 and 9 of *Blackfeet and Palefaces* (Golden Dog Press, 1995) by Eugene Y. Arima. *Blackfeet and Palefaces* was also a source for the story of Lagrasse and Leblanc in chapter sixteen. *The People,* (Fifth House Publishers, 1995) by Donald Ward also provided a useful guide to the Plains peoples. The Big Bear quotes in chapters fourteen and fifteen were cited in *Big Bear: The End of Freedom* (Greystone Books, 1984) by Hugh A. Dempsey. Dempsey's book, as well as *The Plains Cree: An Ethnographic*

History and Comparative Study (University of Regina, 1979) by David G. Mandelbaum, and Maggie Siggins's excellent work, *Riel: A Life of Revolution* (HarperCollins, 1994), provided background on the North-West Rebellion.

Finally, the mountain flying book referred to in chapter sixteen was *Mountain Flying* (Tab Books, 1991) by Doug Geeting and Steve Woerner.

INDEX